The Best
—— IS ——
YET TO COME

Sermons
Reflecting
the
Gift *of* Grace

WALT GERBER

To God, who gives us grace
without measure

TABLE OF CONTENTS

PREFACE

For those fortunate enough to sit in the pews or alongside the man on the chancel during Walt Gerber's twenty-eight years of ministry at Menlo Park Presbyterian Church (MPPC), in Menlo Park, California, this collection of sermons will do more than stir up nostalgia. The crises and names and dates may have changed from when the sermons were delivered, but the first thing that will strike you is the timelessness of Walt's words. Crises and names come and go, but the common struggles of human beings—and God's solutions to them—remain the same, "yesterday, today, and forever." You will find yourself inspired, renewed, convicted, exhorted, lovingly corrected, and moved, just as you were the first time you heard them. And, as always, you will be showered in God's grace.

These sermons were crafted by a man who started his ministry on the heels of a divorce, in an era where that was a likely disqualifier. He suffered from a constant struggle with anxiety, including panic attacks triggered by public speaking, and had his share of physical ailments. If you are encountering Walt Gerber's messages for the first time, prepare to throw your heart and hands open. Like the workers in the vineyard arriving at the eleventh hour, you too will receive a full measure.

In honor of Walt's long-standing and far-reaching impact on the many lives and ministries he helped shape, we have chosen a representative selection from his hundreds of sermons. Walt loved Jesus, prayer, people, and the Bible, and it shows in every sentence. In this book, you'll find his favorite references: "a hospital for sinners, not a house for saints"; "bloom where you're planted"; "contagious Christians." You'll find allusions to the wreath of rosebuds kept in the church, each bud representing an answered prayer. You'll find wisdom for daily living and loving, from our relationship with God to our relationship with family, to our place in church and kingdom.

These fifty sermons are not in chronological order, but rather are placed in a loose structure, covering foundational Christianity as it pertains to the Christian life and to the life of the church. But of course, there is so much overlap among these subjects that they really could be read in any order! For each sermon, we list the Scripture(s) treated and the date(s) delivered. We've also supplied a few questions for study and discussion after each one, if you want to dig further into each or use them in a small-group setting.

If this collection has made you eager to learn more from Walt, or if you knew him and would just feel comforted to hear his voice again, the family has made recordings of 625 sermons, spanning his entire time at MPPC, available at www.waltgerber.com.

Scott and Christina Dudley
Bellevue, Washington
2019

I asked Walt, early in my time here at MPPC, "Why have you never written a book, or done a conference?" He said, "I have no desire for people to know who I am, or know my name. If I'm lucky enough to make it to heaven, I'm going to sit in the corner, and whatever insignificant success or glory I've achieved, I'm going to throw at the feet of Jesus, who deserves all the praise."

Walt, in a nutshell.

Brent James, Lead Pastor
Peninsula Bible Fellowship
Bremerton, WA

Walter Woodworth Gerber was born January 24, 1937, in Glendale, California, to Walter Gerber and Mildred Robinson Gerber. He graduated from Occidental College, initially with a career in veterinary medicine in mind. That changed, however, in his senior year of college, when he felt called into ministry and went on to receive graduate degrees from Princeton Theological Seminary, San Francisco Theological Seminary, and the University of Southern California.

Before arriving at MPPC, Walt spent fifteen years in ministry in San Marino, Redondo Beach, and Malibu. He considered himself a beach bum through and through, but obediently responded to the call to take over as senior pastor of MPPC in 1974. Among his many legacies are his love for people, his passion for demonstrating God's grace, and his belief in the power of prayer. He had a way of speaking to people's hearts through his sermons like no one else. In addition, Walt excelled at developing, shepherding, and launching countless colleagues into their own lifetime of ministry. Many around the country are grateful and attribute who they are today to their time working under Walt's leadership. Finally, Walt's love for the holidays, especially Christmas, was contagious. His description of Christmas Eve being the "loveliest night of the year" lives on in the hearts of all who worshipped at MPPC during his twenty-eight years of service.

Favorite hobbies of his included cars and motorcycles, but time with family and friends was always most precious to Walt. Whether it was a shared meal or a vacation to favorite places like Balboa Island, Catalina Island, Lake Tahoe, or Oregon, creating memories was a priority and laughter a given.

Walt passed away on April 4, 2016. All who knew Walt loved him, but none more than his closest friends and family. He is survived and deeply missed by his loving wife of fifty years, Metta Shields Gerber; his children Dan Gerber, Tara Brees, Leslie Gerber, John Gerber, and Paul Gerber; and his grandchildren Tristan Gerber, Matthew and Benjamin Brees, Megan and John Luff, Rachel and Sara Gerber, and Emily and Peter Gerber.

We hope, through this collection of sermons, you too will continue to share in Walt's legacy of love, grace, and faith, which he embodied daily.

INTRODUCTION

by
Paul Gerber

One of my dad's favorite verses, which you will also find referenced in the first sermon of this collection, was Habakkuk 3:17–18:

Though the fig tree does not bud and there are no grapes on the vines, though the olive crop fails and the fields produce no food, though there are no sheep in the pen and no cattle in the stalls, yet I will rejoice in the Lord, I will be joyful in God my Savior.

Little did he know, retirement from Menlo Park Presbyterian Church would pose a similar challenge. He would have to choose to trust Jesus, even when the circumstances didn't play out as expected. He had such high hopes for lower stress, more family time, and more play time. He knew ministry wasn't ending, just the burden of expectations and the calendar full of obligations. In fact, in later years, he could hardly stand having any kind of appointment on his schedule at all. And the lead-up to the few—and I emphasize *few*—speaking engagements he did agree to . . . you might have thought he was carrying a cross with him, the agony was so great. But if you really kept track of his days, you would see that retirement only altered the *venue* of his ministry. He could not stop his relational pursuit of people and trying to fit Jesus into their story wherever he could.

The testing of his resolve did begin. It's not like he hadn't had extremely difficult things to deal with in life already, but there was almost a Job-like sequence to the final chapters of my dad's story. What it revealed was a depth of character and commitment I can only hope to imitate.

In Job, the devil comes to God and suggests that the only reason Job serves God so faithfully is that God has always been good to him. But, the devil prompts, "Stretch out your hand and strike everything he has, and he will surely curse you to your face. The LORD said to Satan, 'Very well, then, everything he has is in your power, but on the man himself do not lay a finger'" (Job 1:11–12). In my dad's mind, retirement stripped him of status. He didn't think anybody would really want to hear from him if he wasn't at the helm of MPPC anymore. He had a lot of insecurity, and found it challenging to be in church as just an attender. His ultimate dream of spending significant time on Catalina Island was indulged for a short time, only to be taken away and relegated back to dream status once again.

There followed deep family pain from broken relationships, straying paths, and great loss. In his marriage, there was a struggle about how to navigate totally different expectations for a post-career direction.

> *The LORD said to Satan, "Very well, then, he is in your hands; but you must spare his life."* (Job 2:6)

Then debilitating back pain struck, leading to two major surgeries. These were followed by a rare bleeding disorder that walked him so close to death, only to leave him with some real PTSD and all the medical and doctor follow-up stuff he truly detested. And finally, the physical and mental deterioration of vascular dementia slowly took his memory, his mobility, and his dignity.

But most painful of all, God allowed Satan to enter Walt's story through his deepest fear . . . abandonment.

One of the hardest things I have ever experienced was when my brother and I delivered my dad to Silverado Memory Care Facility against his will. Walt had great anger and couldn't understand why he had to go there. Of course, we did it out of love and necessity, but his dementia couldn't process that. In his mind, even his family had turned against him. I remember a few of us sitting in the library there with him. He was talking to a pastor friend, and—I'll leave out a few of his expletives here—he said, "Frank, this is terrible. I hate this place, my family betrayed me, I don't belong here . . . but *God is in charge.*"

This demented, wheelchair-bound, lonely, frail man would not lose his resolve that, in spite of his circumstances, God still knew the plans he had for Walt. Plans to prosper him and to give him a hope and a future. What he had preached for forty years was put to the test, and my dad chose obedience. I am 100% confident it made his heavenly Father so proud.

It occurred to me, in thinking about my dad since he's been gone, that I don't have a specific, tangible item to remember him with. He didn't pass along a watch, a pocket knife, or a special coin; he traveled pretty lightly on this earth and wasn't particularly sentimental. But I do thank Jesus for letting me see a reflection of him in my father, a gift that I get to take with me into eternity.

I know I'm not the only one who saw Jesus more clearly because of Walt Gerber. Through this collection of sermons, a few of the hundreds he gave, we hope your love for Jesus will deepen and become the rock on which you build your life.

THE KEY TO EVERYTHING

Proverbs 3:5–6
April 30–May 1, 1994

I recently read a book because the title intrigued me: *The Key to Everything*. Although I did not agree with the author's answer to the key to everything, I did create an answer of my own. I believe the "key to everything" for the Christian is to learn to trust God. If I'm asked the question at the end of my life, "What would you have done differently?", unless things change, I will have to say, "I would have trusted God more." Trust is something I'm still learning to do. I don't think I'm alone in this struggle.

Before proceeding, let me define what we mean by trusting God:

- Trust is taking God at his Word.
- Trust is believing God will fulfill his promises regarding our personal needs.
- Trust means we are not certain of the next step, but we are certain of God.

Our text is one verse, a verse I hope will help us on our journey toward learning to trust. First, the text commands us to trust God when it says, "Trust in the LORD with all your heart and lean not on your own understanding" (Prov. 3:5).

Why would God command us to trust him? One reason would be that God is trustworthy. God has never failed me throughout my life, even though at times things have happened that felt like he failed me. I imagine that's how some of you feel today—prayers haven't been answered; needs haven't been met. At times, we doubt whether God hears or cares. The good news is that God doesn't reject us for imperfect trust.

Heroes in the Bible had to struggle with doubt, a classic example being Abraham and Sarah. When told they would have a child in their old age, Sarah laughed at what seemed to be an impossibility. Nevertheless, in God's time, Isaac was born. God's promise was fulfilled. God is trustworthy even when our trust is imperfect.

A second reason trust is a command is because we are designed to function best when we link ourselves by trust to God's strength and wisdom. If I attempted to cope with my personal challenges and needs without trusting God's resources, life would be an unbearable burden.

It seems every Christian must make a choice about life: We can believe we're alone in the battle, and that it's up to us to solve problems by relying on our own understanding; or we can believe God wants to partner with us in the action, so that we never face any crisis alone.

There is an absolute correlation between our decision to trust and our finding the contentment and peace Jesus promises his followers. Without trusting God, stress, anxiety, panic, and chronic fatigue will be lifelong companions.

A second question is implied in our text: Why is trusting God so difficult?

Trusting is difficult for me because I realize that much of the time I'm relying on my own understanding about how God should solve my problems and meet my needs. What I call trust becomes nothing more than my attempt to manipulate God into fulfilling my wish list, into giving me what I want when I want it. Trusting God was never meant to be a source for instant gratification or for carte-blanche answers to prayers based upon our will rather than God's will.

When Paul was in a Roman prison, he wrote to the Philippians:

Now I want you to know, brothers and sisters, that what has happened to me has actually served to advance the gospel. As a result, it has become clear throughout the whole palace guard and to everyone else that I am in chains for Christ. (Phil. 1:12–13)

Paul's trust in God did not magically protect him from life's prisons. Trusting God is difficult because it is not a divine means for avoiding pain and problems, or for discovering a happy, carefree life.

Last week I visited with the bishop of the Evangelical Churches in the Ukraine. He told me of the suffering he endured under Communist oppression. At one point, he was brought to court and offered the ultimatum: Give up Christianity, or lose your children. He told the judge he couldn't deny his Lord. The judge threw him out of court as a fanatic, but miraculously did not take away his children.

Trusting God is difficult because it does not protect us from suffering.

As I approach the end of my twentieth year as your pastor, I have been writing some memories of what God has accomplished at Menlo Park Presbyterian Church. I'm amazed! God has worked miracles beyond anything I would have ever dared to ask, think, or dream. He has taken us through every kind of crisis: struggle, pain, down times. Yet God has been trustworthy. God has been free to do miracles in our midst, because from the beginning I knew this job would be over my head most of the time! So I threw caution to the wind and dared to recklessly trust my Heavenly Father. He has been very faithful.

Trusting God is difficult because our faith does not protect us from difficulties. Right now, most of us have areas where we are in over our heads, where we need resources far greater than our own—situations in which, without God's strength, we won't make it! This is true when it comes to parenting, running a business, or facing a medical or relational challenge. God never promised us a life without challenges. To live without this link of trust in an all-powerful, all-loving God is to live with stress, anxiety, and chronic misery. One thing is certain: When we look back on our lives, we will see that God has been trustworthy in every situation.

A final question to consider: If trusting God is a command, what does trusting look like? Our text says, "Trust in the LORD with all your heart and lean not on your own understanding; in all your ways submit to him, and he will make your paths straight" (Prov. 3:5–6).

Isaiah writes: "You will keep in perfect peace those whose minds are steadfast, because they trust in you" (Isa. 26:3). And, "In repentance and rest is your salvation, in quietness and trust is your strength . . . the LORD longs to be gracious to you" (Isa. 30:15, 18).

Let me draw a word picture of what trusting God might look like. I was sitting on a pier, looking at beautiful Lake Tahoe. Wind was cascading across the surface of the water. Boats moored on various buoys in front of me rose and fell with the wave action. Unlike the pier on which I was sitting, anchored to the rock below the water, these boats were impacted by every disturbance on the water's surface, going up and down with each wave pulling at their anchor ropes.

I thought as I watched this scene, "This is what trusting God looks like!" It's the confidence of knowing the Lord will do what he promised to do, giving us a stability and security nonbelievers know nothing about. As God's children, we are free from being at the mercy of ever-changing winds of circumstances. When a storm is raging, we know inside that we are God's children. He loves us. He is working out his plan for us that is best. We don't have to go up and down with happenings. We don't need to tug at the mooring ropes that tie us to reality.

Such a picture of trust is not unusual. We trust dozens of things and people every day:

- We trust the airplane pilot and the instruments when we fly.
- We trust those to whom we give our children in childcare.

- We trust professors who teach us.
- We trust chefs at a restaurant enough to eat food prepared in conditions we can't see.

Let me give you a second picture of trust. The last time we visited Disneyland, we rode Space Mountain. While on that wild ride, it occurred to me how much trust I place in the people who monitor the sequence of the cars and in those who had engineered the structure. I realized trusting God is like this ride on Space Mountain. We sit in the car of life and begin an adventure that sometimes thrusts us into total darkness. At times the car drops and turns corners. Our stomachs jump into our throats. But we can enjoy the ride because we trust the track is secure, we know our destination is certain, and above all, we know who is at the controls!

If God is allowing you to experience darkness right now, if life is tossing you around like a rag doll, let me close with two wonderful promises from the Bible. First from Peter the apostle:

> [T]hough now for a little while you may have had to suffer grief in all kinds of trials. These have come so that the proven genuineness of your faith—of greater worth than gold, which perishes even though refined by fire—may result in praise, glory and honor when Jesus Christ is revealed. (1 Pet. 1:6–7)

Then these famous words from Habakkuk the prophet:

> Though the fig tree does not bud
> and there are no grapes on the vines,
> though the olive crop fails
> and the fields produce no food,
> though there are no sheep in the pen
> and no cattle in the stalls,
> yet I will rejoice in the LORD,
> I will be joyful in God my Savior. (Hab. 3:17–18)

Questions for Study and Discussion:

1. Do you think of yourself as a trusting person? Are you more likely to feel God can be trusted in a tough situation, or to worry that he's not paying attention or doesn't care?

2. Think back to a difficult time in your life. Where was God in that situation, and did you feel trust or fear? In retrospect, can you see how he might have been at work?

WARNING! RELIGION MAY BE DANGEROUS TO YOUR SPIRITUAL HEALTH!

Romans 2:17–18, 25–29; 3:21–22
October 7–8, 1989

Last summer I did some fishing at Lake Tahoe. When casual conversation revealed to other fishermen that I was a minister, all had certain classic reactions. Some chose to keep me at a distance. Others wanted to talk about the evils of the institutional church or corrupt television preachers. Still others wanted to tell me about parents or grandparents who had been active in the church. All of them resisted my attempts to move conversation away from "religion" to *Jesus*.

This experience with fishermen seems to highlight the lesson in our text describing how "religion" can actually be dangerous to our spiritual health. I want to talk about some surprising hazards to knowing God that religion might be creating in your life.

A first possible hazard to our spiritual health is this: *Religion can become a substitute for a personal relationship with God.*

Our text says, "you call yourself a Jew; if you rely on the law and boast in God" (Rom. 2:17). "Jew" in our text we might equate with

"Presbyterian," "Catholic," or "New Age." Let me go back to my conversation with the fishermen. I asked them how things were between themselves and God, and they began to tell me about:

- their grandfather who was a Presbyterian minister; or
- how their parents took them to Sunday school when they were young, but why they don't currently need the church; or
- how they attend church, but God doesn't seem real or play any meaningful role in their daily activities.

As the conversation continues, I realize these people equate their relationship with God to membership in a religious group, or having relatives who belong to a religious group, but *personally* they don't know God, because they don't know Jesus!

I want to give a basic biblical truth to those who equate being Presbyterian, Catholic, or New Age with being a Christian: We don't know God in his fullness unless we know Jesus as Savior.

Millions belong to religious groups and yet, for practical purposes, live as total strangers to God, to his laws, to his love and friendship. How tragic—how like the dead religion Paul describes in our text. A first spiritual hazard religion can create to knowing God is people making "religion" a substitute for the life-changing relationship with God that is possible in Jesus.

A second hazard religion creates to knowing God is more dangerous: the belief that a good moral life earns for us the right to be intimate with God. *Moral behavior does not create a personal relationship with God.*

Our text says, "you rely upon the law and boast of your relation to God." Law, good works, and following tight rules are human attempts to be morally good enough to merit a relationship with a holy God, efforts that lead many to this deadly delusion: "I don't need grace and mercy from Jesus to establish a relationship with God. I'm good enough *without* Jesus to be on God's 'good person' list."

The problem with attempting to win God's favor by good works is that no one is good enough! Listen to the text:

For we have already made the charge that Jews and Gentiles alike are all under the power of sin.

As it is written:

"There is no one righteous, not even one;
there is no one who understands;
there is no one who seeks God.
All have turned away,
they have together become worthless;
there is no one who does good,
not even one." (Rom. 3:9–12)

A gentleman in our new-member class asked a practical question: "Why do I need Jesus?" His question is the first step in understanding an important truth: *Everyone*, no matter how moral, needs Jesus to achieve a saving relationship with God. Why? Because none of us are holy enough to be in relationship with God. The Bible says:

Therefore no one will be declared righteous in God's sight by the works of the law; rather, through the law we become conscious of our sin.

But now apart from the law the righteousness of God has been made known, to which the Law and the Prophets testify. This righteousness is given through faith in Jesus Christ to all who believe. (Rom. 3:20–22)

Here is the most important truth in this text: *Righteousness that leads to friendship with God does not mean moral perfection.* Rather, righteousness is simply our act of faith in reaching out to accept God's offer of friendship available in Jesus Christ.

I was having lunch with a friend recently, discussing how we wanted to deepen our relationship. We talked about barriers that made us hesitate to reach into each other's lives. I related how I viewed him as too busy and powerful for me to invade his time. I was shocked to hear that he felt intimidated by my position as pastor of this church. We discovered that real friendship is not rooted in our achievements or personal worth. Friendship is a gift we offer and receive. The only barriers to friendship would be pride that would make us attempt to earn it, or distrust, that would make us hesitate to accept such a treasure. That luncheon helped me understand what God means when he comes to us in Jesus and says: "I want to be your friend. I want to make you part of my forever family and use my resources to meet your needs. I don't have anything else on my agenda."

Intimacy with God cannot be earned; it can only be received as a free gift in faith. False religion would have us believe God's friendship must be earned, and for this reason such religion becomes a hazard to our spiritual health.

A third hazard created by religion to knowing God is that *religious ritual can become a substitute for a personal relationship with God.*

As Paul puts it, "a person is a Jew who is one inwardly; and circumcision is circumcision of the heart, by the Spirit, not by the written code" (Rom. 2:29). In Paul's day, the ritual of circumcision for the Jew was considered proof one was a member of God's inner circle. Today, many believe things are "okay" between themselves and God, because they

- were baptized as infants;
- attend worship regularly;
- take communion; or
- become inspired by good choir anthems and sermons.

Religious ritual means nothing unless worship is our personal response to the presence of Jesus in our lives. Friendship with God has nothing to do with external religious ritual. Only when we realize the bankruptcy of religious ritual to build friendship with the living God can we understand how faith in Jesus opens the door to intimacy with God.

So what's the bottom line? Here is the great news in today's message: *Christianity has not failed. God's kingdom is intact. Jesus remains the one hope for our world!*

Religion is the force that is failing; dead churches and movements propagating corrupt truth have betrayed many. How would we define dead religion? A dead religion is:

- one that no longer teaches that Jesus is the only way to find a relationship with God that changes lives; or
- one that rejects the Bible as the absolute authority for morality; or
- one that embraces every new fad of human behavior the Bible calls sin, and calls it righteousness.

Our text offers this truth to those who are in the bondage of equating dead religion with knowing God:

> *But now apart from the law the righteousness of God has been made known, to which the Law and the Prophets testify. This righteousness is given through faith in Jesus Christ to all who believe. There is no difference between Jew and Gentile, for all have sinned and fall short of the glory of God, and all are justified freely by his grace through the redemption that came by Christ Jesus.* (Rom. 3:21–24)

Let me illustrate, in closing, the difference between seeking to know God through religion and having a personal relationship with God through faith in Jesus.

Last spring some friends took us to a Neil Diamond concert. As we approached the gatekeeper to enter, he held out his hand for my ticket. I pointed to my friend and said, "It's okay to let me through. My friend has purchased a ticket for me." I did nothing to deserve attending that concert. My admission was bought and paid for by the love of a friend. When the time comes for me to enter heaven, and God asks why he should let me enter, I will point to Jesus and say, "My Friend bought me a ticket!"

Let me ask you the same question I asked my fishing buddies: What does Jesus mean to you?

- Are you one who is substituting religion for a life-changing relationship with God? Try Jesus!
- Are you trying to clean up your act, but know you are not making it? Try Jesus.
- For those who faithfully know and love Jesus and still know you are not perfect—keep on keeping on. We have a Savior!

This incredible truth is summed up in a familiar verse:

For God so loved the world (you and me), that he gave his only begotten Son, that whoever believes on him should not perish, but have everlasting life. (John 3:16)

Questions for Study and Discussion:

1. Which trappings of religion do you find most tempting to substitute for a living relationship with God? (Clue: If you're unsure how to answer this, which ones do you use as a yardstick to measure other people's sincerity of faith?)

2. How do you answer the question, when people ask you if you're "religious"? What do they mean by it? How can you redefine it for them and for yourself?

IF I SHOULD WAKE
BEFORE I DIE

1 Peter 1:3–7, 13
Easter, March 29–30, 1997

Sometime ago, I was in a Jacuzzi on top of a hotel roof, along with some slightly intoxicated people. They were playing a game based on the book *What If?* The game consisted of one person reading a question from the book, and everyone in the group proceeding to give their answers. When this particular question was asked, my ears perked up: "What if I knew I only had one year to live?"

One individual said, "I would party my head off." Another: "I would sell my house and go on a traveling, spending spree." Another: "I would eat and drink everything I could imagine, without worrying about gaining weight."

I wonder what your answer would be? I found it fascinating no one even mentioned life after death. Or God, heaven, or hell.

It was obvious for these people that everything they valued had to happen before death. Yet the fact of our mortality is very real. Spiritual hunger is real, even though we often mask it with preoccupation with all the temporary distractions our culture offers.

Recently, San Franciscans celebrated Herb Caen's eightieth birthday, and subsequently his death. Knowing it might be his last birthday, due to cancer, Herb was quoted as saying, "If I get to heaven it will be wonderful . . . but it won't be San Francisco." Mr. Caen's attitude toward life beyond the grave seems cavalier. Yet his remarks indicate a hunger for an existence after death, although he had no certainty about that life, nor could he conceive it would be better than life in San Francisco.

Spiritual hunger is real. *Time* magazine this week features on its cover a question: "Is There Life after Death?" Books on spirituality and near-death experiences are bestsellers. Two popular television shows, *Touched by an Angel* and *Road to Heaven*, focus on God, heaven, and angels. The tragic cult deaths last week were rooted in a perverted hunger for life beyond the confines of this world, a hunger fed by a sick leader.

Heaven isn't the only object of our spiritual curiosity. People are fascinated by hell, too. The *Chronicle* interviewed a cross section of people and discovered that the vast majority believe in hell. Many think hell is cold, while others think it's hot. Some say hell is here on Earth, but most think it isn't. Pretty much everyone has told someone to go to hell. This place of damnation has both captivated and terrified people for thousands of years.

What's my point? While spiritual hunger is real, few have found real certainty about life after death. Following the crash of TWA 800, my own heart was saddened by the interviews with relatives. Not one I heard expressed any certainty of where their loved ones were, or had hope of ever seeing them again. Death was the end!

Satisfying this hunger in our souls for life beyond the limits of our mortality is what Easter is all about.

Easter is the good news God has provided in Jesus, an opportunity for all his children to find eternal life in heaven. The problem is our indifference and skepticism, if not outright rejection, of this gift. Yet the reality of our mortality remains. Society continues to seek magical ways to conquer, defy, or deny death as seen in:

- fads of physical fitness, staying young forever, miracle diets, and beating disease; or

- a commercial featuring Melanie Griffith saying about a new cosmetic: "Don't accept aging . . . defy it!"

Because the death rate remains 100%, spiritual hunger persists. Many teenagers when asked do not expect to live out a full life span, and therefore live with the view of doing it all now, because there may be no tomorrow, and there is nothing after death. When asked why people take drugs, leave their families, or go into debt, their classic answer is, "The clock is ticking. If I am going to do it, I better do it now."

So what is this Easter good news . . . generally rejected by society? It's stated in the Bible:

> *Praise be to the God and Father of our Lord Jesus Christ! In his great mercy he has given us new birth into a living hope through the resurrection of Jesus Christ from the dead, and into an inheritance that can never perish, spoil or fade. This inheritance is kept in heaven for you.* (1 Pet. 1:3–4)

The Bible connects finding eternal life with being "born again," a term often misused or misunderstood. It's interesting that when Jesus talked to Nicodemus, one of the most religious leaders of his time, a man who believed in God, a good man, Jesus told him that if he wanted eternal life, he needed to be born again. The shocking news is that being religious, believing in God, and doing good things has nothing to do with finding a passport to heaven! According to Jesus, we find eternal life by accepting his diagnosis of our deepest need—namely, we need a completely new start, a new heart, a new birth. We find eternal life by agreeing with Jesus that we have sinned and cannot restore our relationship with God by any good works on our part. And we find eternal life by trusting that Jesus died for our sins on the cross, and that God raised him from the dead, conquering death.

Because Jesus lives, God can forgive our sins and will welcome us into heaven as a free gift! This gift of life we call amazing grace is one we can't earn or deserve. God loves us so much, he was willing to go as far as the cross, so we could be with him forever. This is the good news of Easter. But there's more! Easter hope is not only a treasure for the future; it's a powerful gift for *now*. The Bible says, "In all this you greatly rejoice, though now for a little while you may have had to suffer grief in all kinds of trials" (1 Pet. 1:6).

Many of us this Easter are perplexed and burdened by problems beyond our own strength:

- relationships, finances, jobs, health, children;
- we are concerned about our own country, as we seek to deal with complex moral, economic, and environmental challenges; and
- we are concerned about the world: Albania, the Middle East, Africa.

Christian hope provides believers with the certainty God has plans for our future, and that they are very good plans. History's final chapter is not gloom and doom but the triumph of good, truth, and righteousness. The message on the t-shirts Tony Campolo sells when he visits us captures the essence of our hope: "It's Friday . . . but Sunday is coming."

No matter how dark times and trials might be, a believer's future is assured. If God can conquer Good Friday through the resurrection of Jesus, he can conquer anything the forces of evil throw at us. Easter hope puts everything that drains us, frightens us, into a new perspective: We don't have to make heaven happen in this life. God has all eternity to make things fair, to heal hurts, and mend broken dreams. We don't have to join modern society in using the entertainment industry, sports world, physical fitness, the diet craze, or drugs to escape problems.

Jesus is our resurrected, triumphant King. We look forward to that day when every knee will bow, and every tongue will confess Jesus is Lord. When the kingdoms of this world will become the kingdom of our God and of his Christ. When sickness, death, tears, and all the brokenness in this world are gone forever, and righteousness and truth will reign.

This triumphal day is coming, as surely as Jesus is alive. That's why believers can rejoice in our times of trial. Evil will never have the last word. Nothing in this world can destroy God's long-term plans for us!

Let me close with a question: How can Easter hope become relevant for you? As a child, I always said my bedtime prayer, "Now I lay me down to sleep, I pray the Lord my soul to keep. And if I should die before I wake, I pray the Lord my soul to take." Reflecting on that prayer, I thought of turning the question around, asking, "What if we should wake before we die?"

Easter hope calls us to wake up to what's real, to live for what counts before we die and leave it all behind. Jesus speaks of "weeping and gnashing of teeth" after death. This refers to the regret people will feel when they realize they have devoted their affection, energy, and hopes on things time and death take away, while neglecting things that matter: their relationship with God and the gift of his grace, mercy, and forgiveness in Jesus our Savior.

Jesus offers the gift of eternal life to everyone here today, even if we feel we have blown it so badly that God could never love or forgive us. Even if we have done things we believe will forever keep us out of heaven.

I want you to know the very hands that were nailed to the cross to pay for your sins and mine are now open to receive you into God's forever family. You can become a Christian today, and Easter hope can become your hope. We become a Christian by saying to Jesus: "I accept you as my Savior. I can't save myself. I can't repair my broken relationship with God or atone for my own sins. I need you! I want to spend eternity with you and with those who trust you. Help me."

If you knew you had only one year to live, what would you do? The facts are we are mortal, and physical death is inevitable. If we knew we had only one year, or ten years to live, my prayer for all of us would be that our first priority would be to get things right between ourselves and God, by accepting Christ as our Savior. Death is inevitable; eternal life with God is a choice. Our decision to accept or reject God's gift determines where we will be, and with whom we will be, for all eternity.

As we go to prayer, if you lack certainty about the eternal future, if you want the free gift Jesus offers, even if you are filled with questions and doubts, just tell him you know you need him. Ask him to make himself real to you. His arms are open ready to receive you. There is no one he will cast out.

Lord, we celebrate the glorious news that you are no longer a humble carpenter, but a reigning King. Knowing you as Savior frees us from fearing God and living in dread of divine judgment we know we deserve. Lord, open every heart and mind here today to who you are, and to the grace you have provided through your cross and resurrection. You alone are God. We stand in awe at your power, wisdom, and above all, your love that created Easter, as we pray in the name of Jesus. Amen.

Questions for Study and Discussion:

1. If you only had one year to live, what would you do? How would your priorities change?

2. Are you experiencing a dark "Friday" in your life? What would "Sunday coming" mean to you? How do the promises of Jesus' resurrection impact your understanding of the situation?

Walt was legendary for his self-effacing, gracious spirit. Not long after completing seminary I was asked to be on the board of trustees at the same school. Walt had been a member of the board for many years. Many on the board commented they were not sure they had ever seen the pastor of such a large church with such a small ego. When Walt spoke about himself, it was inevitably a self-effacing comment about his battle with stress or worry or sense of inadequacy. When he spoke to others, it was inevitably to bolster them up and cheer them on.

When he spoke to the board he would invariably begin, "I'm probably the only one who feels this way." (He never was.) When he finished he'd say, "I've probably spoken too long." (He never had.) When he spoke of the church where he served, it was with a sense of wonder at what God was doing there, and a sense of joy that he got to be in the middle of it. To me came the joy of both serving together with him on the board, and after him at the church. The message most associated with Walt was his reminder that the church was not a museum for saints but a hospital for sinners. When he passed away it left the hospital a little sadder, but the heavenly museum of saints that much brighter.

John Ortberg
Senior Pastor, Menlo Church
Menlo Park, CA

HOUSE OF SAINTS OR HOSPITAL FOR SINNERS?

Luke 15:25–32
May 16, 1976

Almost every family or circle of friends has an individual labeled as a "problem." Problem people come in a variety of guises—those who drink too much, those who can't seem to stay married, those who are unable to hold a job, those who can't get along with the family, those whose moral lives violate our personal standards. Today our society is full of broken, oppressed, poor, sick, addicted, needy people. When Jesus talks about the elder brother, he talks about a spirit that is present in all of us to some degree—namely, a spirit that makes us feel superior to broken people. If we would be obedient to Christ, we must come to terms with such attitudes and seek divine help and forgiveness for bringing change.

What better drama of God's love can one find in Scripture, than this scene of the prodigal's return—dirt still clinging to his body, fresh from the pigsty—his morals totally corrupted—his track record as a son a pathetic failure. Look at the picture of the broken son in the arms of his loving Father. He is bruised but alive, broken but no longer lost. How masterfully Christ contrasts the love of the Father with the disdain of the elder brother. Standing at a distance, this poor fellow cannot understand why the whole household was throwing a party, just because his irresponsible brother has come home. Judgment and disgust fill his heart. Notice his attitude as he talks to his father—his pride, his self-righteousness, and his tragic disowning of his brother, whom he refers to as "this son of yours" (Luke 15:30). His anger and judgment cause him to miss the party and to lose relationship with both his brother and his father. He cuts himself off from the household.

In bold type, the "elder brother" is a call to responsibility! We are called to love and to accept "broken people," because we ourselves began as broken ones who needed a Savior. Untold damage has been done by congregations and individual Christians who claim to represent Christ, and yet exhibit a kind of exclusive, conditional love for "outsiders." How uncomfortable and accepted does a person feel around us—one who is hurt by sin, who is broken, whose moral life, whose total life experience does not conform to our mold of a Christian? Do we represent in their mind the elder brother or the father?

By negative example, the elder brother reveals this fantastic affirmation that God's love is inclusive, not exclusive, in nature. Struggling with the "elder brother" spirit still in me is heartrending. If I am honest, much of my love and time go to people who are lovable, who are my kind of people. It isn't easy for me to hear this call from Christ, telling me about my responsibility, if I take his name, to reach out to persons who are broken and offer them all the help, physically and spiritually, that they need.

To obey Christ in this means that, no matter what a person does, or what he or she stands for, I will accept and help that person, because as a matter of Christian principle I love him or her. What we learn from following Jesus about love, is that love is not something we feel, but love is something we are called to do. It is wonderful to feel a warmth and affection for people, but it is an adventure to obey Christ by loving in the sense of giving acceptance and help to one who, at first, we may not like—one who doesn't "deserve" it.

Love that is not expressed in action is not Christian love. You might have seen the poem entitled "Listen, Christian,"[1] in which the speaker talks of being hungry, only to have the Christian form "a humanities club" to discuss the problem. When the speaker is imprisoned, the Christian stays home to pray for him. When the speaker is naked, the Christian debates "the morality of my appearance." It goes on. When the speaker is sick, the Christian thanks God for the gift of health. When the speaker is homeless, the Christian sermonizes about "the spiritual shelter of the love of God." The Christian prays a lot—but *does* nothing, as if it never occurred to him that he could be part of God's answer to those prayers.

Jesus revealed how, on Judgment Day we see that those who are loved in God's sight are those who fed the hungry, clothed the naked, and visited the sick and the imprisoned. Christ's portrayal of the elder brother who was not able to love his own brother in his need challenges me to introspection and action. I want to go and take an inventory of what is really going on in my relationships with other people. No doubt I will discover Christ still has many changes to make in me before I can love broken people as he loves them.

A song from the '60s indicates a longing on the part of those outside the church to find ways to love their brother. Entitled "He Ain't Heavy, He's My Brother," the song is a message to us about carrying each other because "the road is long with many a winding turn." What would it take to recognize the bond with each other that we share in Christ? Because when we do, we will find that, in Christ, our brother isn't "heavy." In Christ, we are strong enough to bear each other's burdens and will actually find "the gladness of love for one another."

May that day come soon when our church and our lives exude the warmth and love in behavior telling the world that Christ came to save sinners—of whom, as Paul reminds us—we were "foremost." May the Spirit make our congregational life a healing hospital for sinners, not a gathering of "elder brothers."

Questions for Study and Discussion:

1. When in your life have you identified with the prodigal son in the story? When have you identified with the older brother? Who would you prefer not to have in the family of God, if it were up to you?

2. Where might God be calling you to "feed the hungry, clothe the naked, visit the sick and the imprisoned," but you've been holding back because you object to something about them? How can you overcome your biases, and reach out?

WHEN YOU'VE TOTALLY BLOWN IT

Luke 22:54–62
October 14–15, 2000

D o you have moments when memories of past sins haunt you? Times when you literally blew away your deepest convictions by irresponsible acts or decisions? Do you ever feel you have succumbed to sin so often that you have no hope of ever breaking free or being forgiven? Are you currently caught in some situation you know is wrong, but you can't or won't give it up?

If you identify with these questions, if you are a believer who can't stop sinning, if you feel guilty about the hypocrisy in your life, today's Scripture telling the story of Peter is for you. Peter is the disciple who denied Jesus, and yet became the rock upon which our Lord built his church. He is a man who loved Jesus and yet struggled with sin all of his life. Because he understood that God's grace goes deeper than our deepest sins, that God keeps no score of wrongs, that God's love is totally divorced from our performance, Peter was able to move from failure to new beginnings. To help us understand this incredible truth, let's study his story.

First, all Christians, like Peter, at times feel our lives are a huge disappointment to God. Peter loved Jesus, yet at a critical moment he denied him, saying, "I don't know him." Personally, I marvel at how often I've stood with Peter and by my behavior said, "I don't know him." Many of us cope with crushing guilt, because we know we are beat up, bedraggled disciples who can't give up sinning. My one confidence is that I know God loves me. Even when I'm fed up trying to be good enough, even when I know I'm not making the cut for meeting his standards of behavior, his unconditional love gives me the confidence that I can always go and throw myself on his mercy and hear him say to me over and over again, "Welcome home, son. I forgive you. Let's get up and do it again."

Paul the apostle had that same struggle with sin that you and I face. Listen to him:

> I have the desire to do what is good, but I cannot carry it out. For I do not do the good I want to do, but the evil I do not want to do—this I keep on doing. . . . What a wretched man I am! Who will rescue me from this body that is subject to death? Thanks be to God, who delivers me through Jesus Christ our Lord! (Rom. 7:18–19)

Most of us have said, by our behavior, what Peter said: "I don't know him." Many believers live under a cloud of guilt and fear, because of our constant sinning. We fear because we don't understand God's unconditional love. I say it over and over again: Christianity is all about grace, not about good behavior, or punishment if we blow it. Brennan Manning puts it this way:

> Often hobbling through our church doors on Sunday morning comes grace on crutches—sinners still unable to throw away their false supports and stand upright in the freedom of the children of God. Yet their mere presence in the Church on Sunday morning is a flickering candle representing a desire to maintain contact

with God. To douse that flame is to plunge them into a world of spiritual darkness.[2]

Grace means God is on our side through the cross of his Son. Therefore, we are victors, regardless of how well we have played the game. No matter how prayerful and moral we are, how religious we are, we will never be good enough to save ourselves. As Paul the apostle said, "I resolved to know nothing while I was with you except Jesus Christ and him crucified" (1 Cor. 2:2).

What Jesus did on the cross was sufficient. This is the good news of Christianity. Anything less is bad news, and a heresy that cheapens the sacrifice of Jesus. Scripture says:

> *The law was brought in so that the trespass might increase. But where sin increased, grace increased all the more, so that, just as sin reigned in death, so also grace might reign through righteousness to bring eternal life through Jesus Christ our Lord.* (Rom. 5:20–21)

Similarly, Augustine said that God works all things together for good in the life of the Christian, even our sins.

Recently I was driving home from southern California, along Highway 5. The speed limit is seventy miles per hour, and cars are always passing me doing at least eighty-five. On that particular day, I decided to step up the pace and keep up with everyone else. Suddenly I came upon a radar trap, where about ten Highway Patrol units were stopping speeders, those going the same speed I was traveling! I was equally guilty but experienced the grace of missing both the trap and the punishment. Thinking about what happened, I saw a parable of grace. Though my life is often a huge disappointment to my Lord—granted I am guilty of sin over and over again—my Lord still gives me the gift of his grace and unconditional love. That's why Christianity is good news.

You know the only sin that keeps us out of heaven? The sin of believing we don't need grace, that we don't need a Savior, that we can approach God with our own score card of righteousness. Forgiveness of our sin is a gift. Our relationship with Jesus is a gift—eternal life is a gift. The only labor in Christian living is that of praise and joyful thanksgiving for receiving God's unconditional love through faith. I like what Thomas Merton wrote: "Quit keeping score altogether and surrender yourself with all your sinfulness to God, who sees neither the score nor the scorekeeper but only his child redeemed by Christ."[3]

Peter learned a huge lesson that night when Jesus turned and looked at him, following his denial. Confronted by the intolerable truth of his inadequacy to be what his Lord called him to be, he was embraced by unconditional love, and it changed his life.

A second truth: while Jesus accepts us in our failure, he always points us to new beginnings.

In John's gospel, we find the touching story of the reunion of Jesus and Peter, after Jesus' resurrection. Rather than rebuke Peter for his failure, Jesus was concerned about one thing: "Peter, do you love me?" Peter was forgiven, restored, and became the rock of faith upon which the church is built.

Jesus came not to punish, but to offer forgiveness and restoration, encouragement and hope, a new game plan for our future. He offers this gift no matter how bleak our track record, how despicable our sin, how often we fall. Trusting Jesus as our Savior replaces our fear of God's wrath with unspeakable joy, and new hope of what we can become. Perfect love casts out fear!

Brennan Manning puts it so well in saying Jesus invites sinners, not the self-righteous, to his table. His kingdom is not an exclusive neighborhood, like airlines that have a class beyond first class for the super-rich, who because of personal resources can avoid the pain of air travel. It is far more like an AA meeting, where those present know they are sinners who cannot save themselves. "He comes for corporate executives, street people, superstars, farmers, hookers, addicts, IRS agents, AIDS victims, and used-car salesmen."[4]

This is the stunning good news of Christianity! Jesus comes to us today, as he did to Peter, offering new beginnings to believers who are caught up in a lifetime of bad choices. Because, as Thomas Merton stated it, "A saint is not someone who is good, but one who experiences the goodness of God."[5]

> *For it is by grace you have been saved, through faith—and this is not from yourselves, it is the gift of God—not by works, so that no one can boast.* (Eph. 2:8–9)

A footnote: how does grace lead to righteous living, and not license to sin? To ask this question implies a lack of understanding of the price paid for our forgiveness. Once we realize Jesus died to make possible the gift of grace, gratitude—a sense of deep indebtedness—fills our hearts. If we continue boldly to sin without regard to the cost of forgiveness, we don't understand the cross of Jesus, or the seriousness of sin.

Once Peter had been forgiven by Jesus, it would never be easy to hurt his Savior again—not because he feared his wrath, but because he loved him. Grace leads to holiness and obedience, motivated by our love and gratitude to Jesus. This truth led Peter to later write:

> *Therefore, since Christ suffered in his body, arm yourselves also with the same attitude . . . they do not live the rest of their earthly lives for evil human desires, but rather for the will of God.* (1 Pet. 4:1–2)

Paul the apostle wrote, "For sin shall not be your master, because you are not under law, but under grace" (Rom. 6:14).

Jesus hates sin, but he embraces sinners. He offers grace to all who know they need it and will reach out in faith to accept his gift.

I invite us to accept his gift of grace today, by repenting of sin, and asking him to allow us to enter a new week with a new beginning, new hope, free at last from the baggage of the past, and expectant of a better tomorrow. The most appropriate response to such incredibly good news is: *Praise the Lord!*

Questions for Study and Discussion:

1. Are you the kind of person who often feels guilty? Does it change your behavior toward God? How do you deal with guilt?

2. Can you think of a time when God's grace felt real to you, and you felt the burden of guilt lift? Did God then point you to a "new beginning"?

WHAT TO DO WHEN
YOU FEEL ANXIOUS

John 10:1–18
May 24, 1981

nxiety, like stress, is a common companion for many of us. Jesus made two strategic statements about his role in relationship with us that can help us cope with the enemy of anxiety. He said, "I am the gate for the sheep" and "I am the good shepherd" (John 10:7, 11).

Defining anxiety as a state of apprehension, uneasiness, or fear, due to some real or imagined danger, Jesus uses symbols of a gate and a shepherd to describe the resources he offers by which anxiety can be defeated.

A "gate for the sheep" is a beautiful analogy, describing our Lord's protective role over us. Even today, shepherds in Israel herd their flocks at night into either portable pen-type structures or into tiny box canyons. During the night hours, the shepherd sits or sleeps across the opening, acting literally as a human door, making it necessary for anything seeking to attack the sheep to pass first through the shepherd.

Since childhood, most of us have heard Jesus given the title of Good Shepherd and seen pictures of him holding little lambs in his arms. The title "Shepherd" is also associated with God in the Old Testament, most famously in Psalm 23, where David declares, "The Lord is my shepherd," and in Psalm 100:3:

> Know that the LORD IS GOD.
> It is he who made us, and we are his;
> we are his people, the sheep of his pasture.

Being a shepherd is a true profession in Jewish first-century culture. From early years, a shepherd is trained, until instinctively he comes to value his sheep more than his own life. King David, when a shepherd, speaks about fighting lions and bears, at the risk of his safety, to protect the sheep. Because sheep were raised for wool, not meat, in biblical times, the shepherd would have the same sheep for years, coming to know them individually, and giving each of them names, such as "Brown Ear" or "Broken Nose." Therefore, when people heard Jesus call himself the Good Shepherd and not a hireling, they heard him in this context of commitment to lay down his life for the sheep.

Once we decide to believe that Jesus is who he claims to be and begin to trust him as the Door and the Shepherd, we should begin to find release from anxiety. Note verse 9 of John 10: "I am the gate; whoever enters through me will be saved. He will come in and go out and find pasture." "In and out" is a Hebrew way of describing "anxiety-free" living, a lifestyle in which one is free to go anywhere at any time, because the country is at peace, law and order are in control. The psalmist claimed he was secure in his knowledge that God would keep him in his going out and in his coming in (Ps. 121:8). Once we actually believe Jesus is watching us like a shepherd, guarding us like a door, new courage takes over in our hearts, a new perspective helps us see daily struggles as challenges and adventures, not enemies. The writer of Hebrews beautifully articulates this security that is ours in Christ, a verse all of us should commit to memory:

"Never will I leave you; never will I forsake you." So we say with confidence, "The Lord is my helper, I will not be afraid. What can mere mortals do to me?" (Heb. 13:5–6)

If Jesus laid down his life to heal us spiritually, can't we trust him to meet every other need? Let me try to paint a word picture of our security in Christ that conquers anxiety. A shepherd loves his sheep, protects them, searches for them when lost, places healing medicine on them when sick or hurt. Being confident that Jesus is in charge of what happens to us, trusting that anything that touches us has first passed through his permissive hand of love, breeds a sense of security greater than any enemy or circumstance that causes us to feel anxious. All of us know how anxiety disappears immediately, once we possess resources greater than that which is causing us concern. Financial panic dissolves when sufficient money appears to pay the bills. Concern about our health is relieved when the biopsy returns negative.

Jesus offers himself as a promise that for anything and everything we confront in life, he is sufficient; therefore, we need not be anxious. Remember his very practical advice about anxiety:

Therefore I tell you, do not worry about your life, what you will eat or drink; or about your body, what you will wear. . . . [Y]our Heavenly Father knows that you need [these things]. . . . Therefore do not worry about tomorrow, for tomorrow will worry about itself. Each day has enough trouble of its own. (Matt. 6:25, 32, 34)

Let me ask a very practical question: If we trust Jesus to forgive our sins, to provide us with eternal life, to run interference for us when we face a Holy God, making it possible for us to be pronounced "not guilty";

if we stake all eternity upon this trust, why do we have such a difficult time trusting him as the Door of Protection and the Shepherd who guards our lives?

I've come to this conclusion about living: Life is going to be difficult. Our Lord was right when he said, "In the world you will have tribulation." There will always be reasons to be anxious if we want to be. But as Christians we have been called to overcome the world and the anxiety associated with it.

My jogging buddies and I decided the other morning that life is really a continuous parade of impossible situations and challenges that carry us from one crisis to another, forcing us to our knees. Our choice is to trust Jesus and be on top of things in spite of the crises—or to be consumed with anxiety. If we believe Jesus is who he claims to be, we have the resource of a sense of expectancy about his intervention—concerned, waiting, but not anxious—knowing a miracle is on the way. We don't have to push the "anxiety button" and chew ourselves up with worry every time we face a new crisis. The Bible tells us we were not designed by God to be sufficient in ourselves; we were designed to lean and depend upon God (2 Cor. 3:5). Impossible situations, in the hands of God, become adventures, knowing Jesus will break through to us again in an unexpected and totally adequate way. If we know our Shepherd will come with what we need, in times of crisis we don't have to be anxious. No human problem, in the hands of God, is impossible. The issue is, do we really believe this is true?

If you watch children, you see a parable of this dynamic in action. Isn't it amazing how many times children confront what they consider to be insurmountable situations with no apparent way out? Here is an inventory of impossible problems I counted in one day at our house:

- The world was coming to an end because a Little League shirt was in the wash on the day of the game.

- "I'm the only kid in the class without a digital watch."
- "My shoes are different from what all the other kids are wearing."
- "If I don't get this paper done, I won't pass."

Believe me, in their minds, these problems are gigantic, impossible. When they gain the maturity to put such problems into perspective, they will begin to understand how unnecessary churning anxiety really is, how nonproductive such consumption of energy can be. Yet you and I do the same thing when we fill ourselves with anxiety about things over which God is in perfect control!

Therefore, why not try this week to claim these promises of Jesus? Bring everything that is causing your stomach to churn and keeping you awake at night and lay it at the feet of Jesus. Pray for strength to trust him as the Gate and the Shepherd. Then start living just for today, confident a miracle is on the way, and that God is in control of tomorrow. Nothing is impossible with him. Perhaps Kierkegaard was right when he said, "Dealing with anxiety means having the courage to leap forward by faith into the confusion."

I'm discovering that exactly when you think the game is over, when there appears to be no solution, when you think you've had it, that is when our Shepherd appears with a solution beyond what we could possibly imagine or dream. Too many times in moments of crisis I have unnecessarily panicked, endured sleepless nights, churned—all because I refused to trust Jesus in being who he claims to be. After all my blood, sweat, and tears, Jesus always does come with a solution. During my forty-four years, he has batted 1.000! On the basis of these claims of Jesus in this text, I urge all of us to trust Jesus as the Gate and the Shepherd. Allow that confidence that emerges from such trust, to conquer our anxiety, and then let's get on with the business of living!

In closing, missionary and theologian E. Stanley Jones points out in *The Word Became Flesh* that, too often with anxiety, we deal with worries in triplicate: the worries of yesterday, the worries of today, and the worries of tomorrow. We thus

> *meet everything three times—yesterday, tomorrow, and today. So you are exhausted by over-attention to your problems. Meet them once—today—settle them, and then dismiss them and go on to the next thing. Anxiety is the advance interest you pay on tomorrow's troubles. And some people go bankrupt paying interest on troubles that never come.*[6]

Questions for Study and Discussion:

1. On a scale of 1 to 10, how would you rate yourself as a worrier? Do you worry all the time (10), or hardly ever (1)? In areas of your life where you don't worry, why don't you? In areas of your life where you do worry, what has been the result?

2. Can you think of a time in your life when you worried deeply about something? Did God feel present to you? Why or why not? Looking back, can you see a solution Jesus provided?

My dad had an uncanny ability to make you feel better about yourself and your life, even when things weren't going so well. I miss that about him the most . . . well, and that laugh of his. You'd start laughing just because he was laughing, never mind what the source was. Being with him just made you feel better.

Dad embodied three things for me that I will always remember him by:

1. *You can't love people too much. I think that throughout his life Dad was genuinely amazed that God really loved an Average Joe like him, faults and all. And so it was totally natural for him to want to share this love with other people. He did so eagerly and genuinely, knowing that underneath life's labels and titles, everyone else was an Average Joe or Jane like him in need of God's touch.*

2. *Life is frequently painful, frightening, and disappointing—for all of us. Dad was no stranger to suffering and anxiety, but these merely propelled him to reach out to others, to share in their pain. He encouraged others and was encouraged himself by connecting with people at their point of weakness and need, believing that life's afflictions were less fearsome when facing them together.*

3. *Looked at in a certain way, a lot of things in life are really funny. Dad's humor wasn't a polite, low-key affair, but an exuberant force of vitality that delighted in life's absurdities. It was the wild counterbalance to sorrow, giving light and hope to push back the darkness.*

Love, pain, laughter—together they made him real, just like the story from The Velveteen Rabbit *that he was so fond of quoting.*

He was real, and I think that's why people were so drawn to him.
He made us all feel better, no matter what life was throwing at us.
One of my favorite quotes from Dad: "The greatest blasphemy
is to make God boring."

Dan Gerber, son

Surviving
in the Wilderness

Exodus 2:11–22
January 19, 1986

This morning we begin a study of Moses, a leader of Israel whom God drove into the harsh environment of the Sinai desert for forty years, an experience that taught him obedience, faith, and submission to God's methods and timing. In the wilderness, his character was melted and molded into greatness, so that he could be used of God to liberate the Hebrews from Egypt. During 1986, most of us will go through our own wilderness experience. During such times, God's desire is to break and refine us, so we can be better used for his purposes in the world. Surviving in our wilderness depends upon advance preparation. Otherwise, our pain and fear will catch us by surprise and throw us into a spiritual tailspin. In fact, God wills that we do more than survive in these tough times. His plan for us is to "find the gold" in these experiences. That's what we want to talk about this morning!

First, what is a wilderness experience? A simple definition would be: "A wilderness experience is any happening that makes us feel far from God." Loss of a job, moral failure, trouble in our family, aging, the death of a loved one, physical or emotional illness, unrelieved stress at work;

such happenings can be "triggers," driving us into a wilderness of feeling separated from and forsaken by God. Traveling companions on such a journey include anger, doubt, grief, discouragement, depression, and temptation.

Given a definition, let's consider what drove Moses into his wilderness. Born a Jew, as an infant he was adopted into Pharaoh's household and was destined for high position in Egyptian government. One day, God stirred Moses' heart about the oppression of his people, a stirring that drove him to a critical decision: "Do I remain an Egyptian, or commit myself to liberate my Hebrew brothers and sisters?" Observing a Jew being beaten caused an outburst of rage that led Moses to kill an Egyptian. Word leaked to Pharaoh, and Moses became a fugitive. We plug into the story at this point, seeking lessons for ourselves from what happened to Moses, as he walked through the wilderness of Sinai.

Let me offer some observations about wilderness experiences. Most of our personal growth happens in tough times. Moses was in no way equipped to liberate God's people before his years in the desert. He was proud, stubborn, self-confident, and bent on doing God's business his own way, even to the point of committing murder. It took God forty years in the furnace of the Sinai to "break" Moses. Every wilderness we pass through seeks to teach us to surrender our pride, our plans, our spirit of "I can do it by myself," our refusal to trust God's timing and methods. Unfortunately, there is no painless way to learn these lessons of faith. Some lose jobs and financial security, so they can discover the adequacy of God as provider. Some walk the wilderness of grief, paralyzed by the death of a loved one or by divorce, unable to get on with living. People remain in that wilderness until they are driven into the arms of Jesus and discover his promise: "I will never leave you or forsake you." Some enter the wilderness of moral failure and exposure of sin. God's purpose is not to punish but to break them, leading them to confession and repentance.

Without such experiences, we continue to attempt to "pull the wool" over the eyes of God and other people. Many believers spend time in the wilderness of depression and fear about aging and death. Too many Christians claim they want Jesus to save their souls, but in reality seek to use Jesus only to extend and enrich their lives on Earth, with no thought of eternity. Once we believe our greatest treasure is to be with Jesus forever, we are free to fully live every moment of life God grants. Death is merely an event of going to be with Jesus—absent from the body, at home with the Lord (2 Cor. 5:8).

Obviously, the reasons we enter a wilderness are as varied as our names. For Moses, it was to break his pride, to teach him to trust God, to carve into his cranium that apart from God he could do nothing. The Sinai Desert tempered this great saint, transforming his pride into meekness, into unshakable trust in God's methods, even to the point of becoming willing to confront mighty Pharaoh with a shepherd's staff; even to the point of crossing a sea in the belief it would divide in half; even to the point of leading thousands into a barren desert without food or water, believing God would provide. Wilderness experiences have a way of knocking out our personal support systems, so we discover the adequacy of God for any burden or obstacles we cannot confront ourselves.

Here is good news about the wilderness: God meets us in tough times in surprising ways to deliver and sustain us. By a strike of providence, hot-tempered Moses struck out again at injustice by protecting some lady shepherds. As a result, he is invited to dinner, an invitation that led him to a wife and to the refuge of Jethro's home. When we are called to journey through a wilderness, we need friends, the touch of a loving hand, a family who can minister to us. Moses found resources to survive in his wilderness through the warmth of Jethro's household. Tough times drive us to depend on each other.

An interesting sidelight to this text is the Bedouin law of hospitality, still in effect today in the Middle East. Bedouins offer strangers help down to their last crust of bread because of this law: "Essentials of life were never to be denied any wilderness pilgrim, be he friend or enemy." Moses' healing and sustenance for his wilderness survival came through a family.

Entering 1986, every fiber of my being as pastor will be devoted to leading everyone in our church family to make friends, break into small supportive groups, share each other's lives, become accountable to one another, and be available for each other, so no one will walk through a wilderness alone. Our worship will model the importance of people ministering to people, rather than always centering on the professional up front. I pray God will continue to knock down our fear of sharing hurts and needs, of being vulnerable, in the mistaken belief we don't need anyone. In the wilderness we need each other!

Let me share my favorite verse from Ecclesiastes with you as a tool of preparation for wilderness experiences:

Two are better than one, because they have a good reward for their toil. For if they fall one will lift up his fellow. But woe to him who is alone when he falls. . . . [A] threefold cord is not quickly broken. (Eccl. 4:9–10, 12, ESV)

In summary, during 1986 many of us will be called upon to pass through wilderness experiences. Know in advance that this is a time for building, not destruction; a time of preparation, even though it is painful and costly. God is forging us for his purposes, seeking to make us whole and real and submissive to him. Months ago, I shared a story about the Skin Horse in *The Velveteen Rabbit* that perhaps summarizes God's intended effect of a wilderness experience upon our lives:

The Skin Horse had lived longer in the nursery than any of the others. He was so old that his brown coat was bald in patches and showed the seams underneath, and most of the hairs in his tail had been pulled out to string bead necklaces. He was wise, for he had seen a long succession of mechanical toys arrive to boast and swagger, and by-and-by break their main-springs and pass away, and he knew that they were only toys and would never turn into anything else. For nursery magic is very strange and wonderful, and only those playthings that are old and wise and experienced like the Skin Horse understand all about it.

"What is real?" asked the Rabbit one day, when they were lying side by side. . . . "Does it mean having things that buzz inside you and a stickout handle? . . . Does it hurt?"

"Sometimes," said the Skin Horse, for he was always truthful, "When you are real you don't mind being hurt."

"Does it happen all at once, like being wound up," he asked, "or bit by bit?"

"It doesn't happen all at once," said the Skin Horse. "You become. It takes a long time. That's why it doesn't often happen to people who break easily, or have sharp edges, or who have to be carefully kept. Generally, by the time you are real, most of your hair has been loved off, and your eyes drop out and you get loose in the joints and very shabby. But these things don't matter at all, because once you are real you can't be ugly except to people who don't understand."

"I suppose you are real?" said the Rabbit. And then he wished he had not said it, for he thought the Skin Horse might be sensitive. But the Skin Horse only smiled.

"Once you are real you can't become unreal again. It lasts for always."

The Rabbit sighed, he thought it would be a long time before this magic called Real happened to him. He longed to become real, to know what it felt like; and yet the idea of growing shabby and losing his eyes and whiskers was rather sad. He wished that he could become real without these uncomfortable things happening to him.[7]

But that's the point. We are like the rabbit. We want spiritual maturity, but we don't want to pay the price. Time in the wilderness that makes us shabby and pulls out our whiskers is not an experience we seek. Yet we cannot become all God has in mind for us to be without pain. Life is difficult. In the world we will have tribulation. But Jesus said, "take heart; I have overcome the world" (John 16:33). Moses found Jethro and the living God as forces that helped him survive the wilderness. I pray this year you will draw close to your Lord, and close to some friends in the church family, so you will be prepared for the growing times in store for you this year!

Questions for Study and Discussion:

1. What challenges do you anticipate in the coming year? Do you see any areas in your character where God may be wanting to work on you? (If you can't think of any, ask your family; they'll probably have plenty of suggestions.)

2. Who do you consider your close friends in the church family? Why? If you don't have any, what steps can you take to invest in some relationships?

Cultivating the Ability to Forget

Philippians 3:10–15
May 18, 1986

This morning I want us to think about a most vital dimension involved in loving another human being—namely, the ability to forget. Forgetting is an indispensable part of loving others as Jesus has loved us. Unfortunately, our brokenness as human beings leads us to remember things about each other that should be forgotten and to forget things that should be remembered. Jesus was right when he advised us, "No one who puts his hand to the plow and looks back is fit for service in the kingdom of God" (Luke 9:62).

Our text makes the same point: "Forgetting what is behind and straining toward what is ahead, I press on toward the goal to win the prize for which God has called me heavenward in Christ Jesus" (Phil. 3:13–14).

Isn't it fascinating how our memory computers can store infinite data about past mistakes, failures, and weaknesses of people who are precious to us? Then when our anger buttons are pushed, we spew out this memory data with deadly accuracy, an act which inflicts deep wounds on human hearts. One of the devil's great weapons against love relationships is our habit of bringing up a person's past and using it as a club of anger in the present, to nail a person with their past mistakes, to put them into an indefensible situation, leaving them no alternative but to strike back or withdraw. As the battle rages, open wounds are created that are difficult to heal. For the sake of our families, our friends, and our "church family," it is important we think about our Christian mandate to forget the past and reach to the future in all our relationships. Let's look at our text.

First, Paul suggests we forget what lies behind, using a verb tense indicating to forget is a choice we must make every day. The reason is obvious. Those we love can hurt and disappoint us daily. Our challenge is a decision: Are we going to continue digging up the past, allowing the putrification of yesterday to destroy still another day and carve wounds on those we love, or are we going to allow the Holy Spirit to help us bury the stuff of yesterday permanently and seek a new beginning, knowing, "today is the first day of the rest of our lives"? Jesus can provide us the unique ability to erase hurts and sins people we love have inflicted on us. To trust Jesus as Savior means we believe *he* forgives our sins, failures, and weaknesses, and takes them away, promising never to bring them up to us again. All of our skeletons, things of which we are ashamed that create heavy loads of guilt, our Lord buries forever, as far as the east is from the west. Consider how the psalmist beautifully describe God's compassion and gentleness in dealing with our past:

> *The* LORD *is compassionate and gracious, slow to anger and abounding in love. . . . [H]e does not treat us as our sins deserve, or repay us according to our iniquities . . . [A]s far as the east is from the west, so far has he removed our transgressions from us.* (Ps. 103:8, 10, 12)

His only request of us is that we be "kind and compassionate to one another, forgiving each other, just as in Christ God forgave you" (Eph. 4:32).

Today is Pentecost Sunday, celebrating the coming of the Holy Spirit and the birth of the church. Because the Spirit of Jesus is in us, forgiving and forgetting isn't wishful thinking—we can do it! Christians are a unique breed in a society unforgiving and merciless. As Jesus gives us an alternative to vengeance, we become lights of hope in a world torn by broken relationships. No wonder the first point in our text urges us to forget the past, as an act of Christian love and maturity.

Secondly, let's consider why forgetting is an act of love. Most of us know love relationships are too delicate to allow the past to pollute the present. A husband loses his way in a strange town, and the wife says, "Harry, you jerk, you always get us lost. Remember our vacation five years ago! We wandered around town for three hours, just because you were too proud to ask someone for directions!"

One of our children makes a mistake. Rather than deal with the one issue at hand, we unload all our memory data of their past mistakes, creating a load too heavy for anyone to carry. Every poor grade, every time they came in late from a date, every time they broke a promise. Verbally, they strike back at us because they feel like a failure and they can't handle the guilt. Jesus forgives and forgets our sins because he knows we can't handle the guilt load of yesterday and still be whole today. If I wasn't confident that Jesus buries my past, I couldn't survive in the present. Because Jesus forgets my past, I can forget it. That's what being loved by Jesus is all about! His presence in our lives is a constant encouragement.

Here is a painful question: Do people close to us feel we are a weight or encouragement? Does our relationship with our children, friends, members of our church family remind them of what they were in the past or of what they can become in the future? Do we throw salt on their "wounds" of the past in the name of love? Or in the name of love do we forget and bury their skeletons? No wonder Paul singles out forgetting as a key ingredient to Christian character when he says, "This one thing I do: I continually forget what lies behind, all the goofs and sins that life piles up, and I continually reach toward what lies ahead." Forgetting the past of those we love is more than a luxury on the sidelines of Christian living; it is front and center to our goal of learning to love each other as Jesus loves us.

Moving on, our text implies that forgetting the past is not enough, we must also reach for the future. Sometimes I wish I could painlessly drill holes in our heads and drain out all corrosive thoughts about yesterday that we bury in our memories. Our Lord is literally waiting to replace such memories with thoughts of expectancy, trust, and hope for the present and the future. Imagine the impact if we began to view those we love as Jesus perceives us, thinking of what they can become with our encouragement, rather than dumping upon them about what they were in the past! Everything about Christianity has to do with resurrection and new beginnings. Love means no matter how broken our past, how much we have hurt each other, there is still hope. God's Word is a help when it comes to forgetting the past and reaching to the future, because it teaches us we are all in process of becoming. "[I]f anyone is in Christ, the new creation has come: The old has gone, the new is here!" (2 Cor. 5:17).

Last week my wife gave love to someone our family cares about, love in the form of acceptance and encouragement to what this person can become, rather than focusing on the past. This is the letter she received:

> I wanted to thank you for risking getting involved in my hard day. . . . You said, "I am feeling your pain." I can't put into words why or how those words helped so much or exactly how they made me feel, but I can say "thank you.". . . I enjoy just being with you so much. To be honest I never hung around you in your kitchen so I could learn how to cook, I learned how to cook because I like hanging around you. And now I know and like to cook too—what a deal! I love you and how you are!

Unconditional, accepting love—love that doesn't throw up our past but focuses on what we can become in the future—is a force that changes people. Such attitudes also make people want to be around us. Imagine what it would feel like to receive a letter saying, "I like hanging around you because of how you support me and make me feel. And by the way, because you love me by forgetting my past, you have helped me change my future."

If my children . . . if my friends . . . if you, my church family, can feel that way about me, I will consider myself successful as a pastor who seeks to love.

What are you rehashing over and over again? What grudges, hurts, worries, and happenings are you allowing to corrode your soul? Our text urges us to make this decision: "I won't be addicted to and preoccupied with the putrid remains of yesterday any longer."

Let's all bow our heads. In this moment of silence, let's take these haunting memories poisoning our souls, and ask God to help us bury them forever. Imagine we are passing an offering plate. You are going to place that haunting memory into the plate. Give it to God. Ask him to take it away as far as the east is from the west. Know it will never come up again.

"Forgetting what is behind and straining toward what is ahead, I press on toward the goal to win the prize for which God has called me heavenward in Christ Jesus." Lord Jesus, that's our prayer for this morning. Amen.

Questions for Study and Discussion:

1. Do people close to us feel we are a weight or an encouragement? Does our relationship with our children, friends, and members of our church family remind them of what they were in the past or of what they can become in the future?

2. What do you most wish God and your loved ones would "forget" about you? What might God be calling you to forget today?

DEATH IS SWALLOWED UP IN VICTORY

1 Corinthians 15; 2 Timothy 1:10
Easter, March 26, 1978

A surprise happening is taking place throughout America. Treasures from King Tut's tomb are causing a mania to sweep every city where they are placed on exhibit. Tickets for viewing are sold out in advance, and then scalped for unbelievable resale prices. King Tut t-shirts, rings, and other objects are sold at a rate equal to the Star Wars craze.

Several years ago, I had the privilege of visiting the pyramids in Egypt and viewing these treasures at the Cairo Museum. Huge rooms are filled with foodstuffs, weapons, beds, and couches—a gold-studded chariot, a throne of gold, a solid gold sarcophagus that contained the mummy of the king. What pathos in viewing the very much dead Pharaoh, his treasures laid to rest with him—unused, aged, and slowly rotting away. King Tut symbolizes a culture totally preoccupied with death and dying. Pyramids, plundered lifeless shells, are all that remain of Egypt's futile attempt to make royalty live forever.

American culture finds itself lured by this same hunger for immortality. Another culture's effort to destroy death entices us. I am

71

mystified that thousands will pay, stand in line, and go to great inconvenience to view the rotting remains of a grave. Yet those same persons remain strangely indifferent, if not hostile, to the glorious message of Christ's empty tomb—to God's offer of immortality. What a contrast between the mummified remains of King Tut, and one visit to the empty tomb in Israel, where the words of the angel still ring: "Why do you look for the living among the dead? He is not here; he has risen!" (Luke 24:5–6).

God has given us Easter morning to feed our hunger for immortality. This is the Easter message: "Death [your death, the death of your loved ones] has been swallowed up in victory" (1 Cor. 15:54)! Paul the apostle wrote, "Christ Jesus . . . destroyed death and brought life and immortality to light through the gospel" (2 Tim. 1:10).

Today we would consider how Jesus Christ destroyed death.

First, the Bible claims that death is a real part of life. To affirm it is not to say God the Father frolics in our mortality—takes pleasure in human grief, disease, and loss. Death had its origin in the garden of Eden, when Adam and Eve rebelled against God's will—an act which was equated with choosing death over life. Everyone individually has inherited "fallout" from that original sin, and death is visible proof of that inheritance. We live near one of the world's great medical centers, dedicated to sustaining life. Yet, a few blocks west on Santa Cruz Avenue, is a graveyard—a reminder that science can sustain and prolong life but cannot prevent death. Every day in the newspaper, the obituary page reports names of our neighbors—one by one being snuffed away. Death is a pressing, vexing, grim reality.

A companion to the fact of death is the fear of dying. The Bible claims that sin has shackled us to a lifelong bondage to the fear of death (Heb. 2:15). Of all living things on earth, we alone are aware that one day we will surely die. Knowledge of our mortality creates its own tensions. Joints that grow increasingly tight, muscles that respond more slowly, skin that wrinkles, hair that turns grey, energy levels that decrease, all of these symptoms of our vulnerability haunt us during our lifetime.

A third dimension of death is the most painful. It has the ability to take those we love away from us. Fear about my personal end seems far less important than the possibility of losing a child, my wife, my parents. Separation from those we love is one awful potential death holds over us. Recently, our four-year-old son had surgery. Spending time in pediatrics brought us into confrontation with death among children. That experience burned into my consciousness that death is a painful, inescapable part of living.

Confronted by the fact of death, the fear of it, and the pain of grief that it brings, what does our gospel possess by way of answer to our need? Our Christian gospel booms out an answer: "Death has been swallowed up in victory!"

It is important we understand this promise. People still die—cemeteries have fresh graves. Paul the apostle described a conviction that permeated his whole being: "Jesus . . . destroyed death and brought life and immortality to light through the gospel."

Our Lord has done what no other person in history has been able to do. He fought and won a battle with mortality during his crucifixion and resurrection. He died for you and me—tasting death for us so that he might destroy Satan, who had the power of death over us (Heb. 2:9). Our Lord's cross, symbol of the church, is a constant reminder that our Heavenly Father knows all about death, not theoretically, but *personally*. Our Savior went into the pit of death, emerged victorious from the grave, and now lives to sustain us, when we or our loved ones stand at the entrance to that valley.

When I first started sailing, I remember my first trip to Catalina Island, off the coast of southern California. A minister friend and I had purchased a boat in partnership. Having no experience at sailing, fortunately for me, my partner knew what he was doing. On our way home, ten-foot waves, and a wind that forced our boat over to the gunnels, drove us with fury. I would have been terrified, except for the words of assurance from my partner. Having sailed for years in the Atlantic, he knew we were in no danger—he had been in this situation many times.

A hailing wind and a roller coaster ocean are not enemies to fear, but gifts to enjoy, if you are into sailing.

As human beings, when we are confronted by the terrifying storm of death and dying, our friend and Savior Jesus stands with us as One who has been there and back. By his resurrection, Jesus has transformed death into a journey with a known destination. Here are some of the greatest promises in the Bible:

> *Do not let your hearts be troubled. You believe in God; believe also in me. My Father's house has many rooms; if that were not so, would I have told you that I am going there to prepare a place for you? And if I go and prepare a place for you, I will come back and take you to be with me that you also may be where I am.* (John 14:1–3)

Paul the apostle gave similar assurance:

> *For we know that if the earthly tent we live in is destroyed, we have a building from God, an eternal house in heaven, not built by human hands.* (2 Cor. 5:1)

> *For to me, to live is Christ and to die is gain.* (Phil. 1:21)

Here is food for our instinctive sense that there must be a greater dimension to life than these brief threescore years and ten. Goethe rightly stated, "He is dead, who in this life has no hope for another."

Let us now consider this glorious message of Easter. "Death has been swallowed up in victory." To "swallow up" means to consume, to destroy completely. Paul the apostle says that our death is destroyed by our resurrection. Using the analogy of a seed, he says, "What you sow does not come to life unless it dies" (1 Cor. 15:36). Isn't it breathtaking when you think about it? A pathetic, weak, vulnerable body, dead, useless, buried—suddenly sprouts to a new life with God's resurrection power! We are raised like a wrinkled, decaying seed that puts out a root, then a stalk, and suddenly breaks through the ground in a glorious burst of new life. How foolish to say, "Because, I cannot understand the mystery of a seed producing life, I refuse to believe in a harvest!"

Peter Marshall tells a story which, in its own simplicity, is one of the best descriptions I have for our questions on the resurrection:

> *Two caterpillars were talking together as they crawled along the earth. One declared, "I imagine that heaven will be like an endless row of cabbages."*
>
> *His philosophical friend said, "You know, I believe that someday you and I will no longer have to crawl around on the ground, but we might even fly over that fence. What is more, we won't be puncturing cabbage leaves in order to eat, but we will someday be sipping dew and living on the honey of the flowers."*
>
> *His friend replied, "You poor demented creature. How foolish to be thinking about that which is supernatural. I am interested only in the here and now, in that which I can taste and feel. I am content with living among the cabbages."*
>
> *One day both of the caterpillars died and friends gathered around for the funeral service. After a long eulogy about their good lives, they were buried in a shroud—a chrysalis. A chrysalis breaks, and out of it emerges a moist lovely thing. Slowly it hoists into the fragrant air its delicate wings of beauty. As the wings dry, they gather strength and both of the butterflies become aware of their new world. Finally, they take off and they sail over the fence to sip the dew and to taste the succulent honey. The skeptical caterpillar, his eyes filled with amazement, said to his friend:*
>
> *"Oh, how blind I was, I couldn't even imagine in my wildest dreams that anything could be better than my world among the*

cabbages. Now it looks like nothing from there, compared to the beauty of our sailing here in the wind and enjoying life as butterflies. [8]

Today I affirm in the name of Jesus Christ, that we can share in the victory our Lord won over death and dying. When we confess Christ as Lord and Savior, he gives us eternal life. No words of Jesus assert more boldly his authority over death than those he speaks to Martha at the tomb of her brother, Lazarus. Addressing her grief, he says, "Your brother will rise again." She replies, "I know that he will rise again in the resurrection at the last day" (John 11:23–24). Then our Lord made this amazing claim:

"I am the resurrection and the life. The one who believes in me will live, even though they die; and whoever lives by believing in me will never die." (John 11:25–26)

To know Christ as Savior is to receive his life in us—a life that makes death simply an incident, not an accident, a doorway, not extinction. Death for the Christian is not imprisonment in a grave—it is breaking out of the chrysalis of mortality into the rich dimension of the eternal. For the Christian it is a commencement, a coronation, a consummation of all that life holds. This is the good news of Easter! Such hope centers in Jesus Christ—victory over death is not available, apart from knowing him as Lord and Savior.

My prayer today is that we Christians will find new cause for rejoicing that death has been swallowed up in victory. My hope is that those who hunger for forgiveness, wholeness, and a renewed relationship with God would in this service reach out in repentance and faith, allowing Christ to become your personal Savior and Lord.

Questions for Study and Discussion:

1. Which aspect of death has had the greatest impact on your life? Wanting to avoid it, fearing it, or losing others to it?

2. If you truly believed the Easter promise that "death has been swallowed up in victory," would this change in any way your outlook and behavior?

I adored being a pastor's kid. Ministry was dad's life focus, and as a result, this significantly affected our family life. There was sacrifice required from all of us for what ministry required, but there are no regrets, as this was God's plan for him.

Mom paid the highest price. Dad would be the first to acknowledge that God used her in a mighty way to partner with him in ministry behind the scenes. I appreciate fully that my parents created an unusually pressure-free environment for us to be normal kids. Dad embraced his own brokenness so openly that it enabled his family—those who worked with him, those he served, and me—the freedom to embrace my imperfections and insecurities, knowing that nothing could separate me from God's unconditional love or his.

Dad knew how to set the framework for church services beautifully. He scripted them from beginning to end in detail. As a father, he fulfilled an equally significant role in our family, by framing our days with devotions at breakfast and then connecting with us again at dinner with encouragement and often laughter. This ritual carried on even during vacations. I did not always appreciate this gift. One night I recall hurrying through my prayer at the end of devotions and having my privilege of watching TV removed. This seemed largely unfair, since brother John had fallen asleep and did not utter one word of a prayer at all and went unpunished!

From my earliest years, Dad set an example in the discipline of reading Scripture, belief in the power of prayer, and love and commitment to family. He was my spiritual leader. Little did I know that his struggles and wounds from anxiety, parenting, and divorce would be my own one day. As life beat me down, my hope remained steadfast because I saw how a broken ragamuffin like my dad never lost faith and could be used by God. My faith is strong because he pointed me to Jesus.

Leslie Gerber, daughter

Someone Is Watching over You

Mark 6:45–52
December 16, 1979

It was dark. Leaving Jesus behind, the disciples started sailing across the Sea of Galilee. From nowhere, the wind suddenly started roaring against them. Headway toward their destination was slow, forcing them to tack back and forth, beating against the waves created by the storm. Every swell sent a spray of water over the bow, soaking them to the skin. Holding the tiller, setting and resetting sails, meant that by the fourth watch those men were shivering, cold, and tired. Obviously, they wished Jesus had come with them, remembering his help in a previous storm, when with a word he calmed the waves. Now he seemed far away, out of reach.

Several weeks ago, a few of us set sail for San Francisco from Redwood City. As we left, hardly a breath of air was moving, forcing us to use the motor because the sea was like glass. After we reached Coyote Point, in a matter of minutes, a storm front moved in. A black layer of clouds descended. Winds up to twenty-five knots hit. Rain came so hard we couldn't see, and soon the boat was heeled over and we were flying! During those moments, I thought about this text—how the disciples must have felt in their tiny craft, fighting the storm. Water makes one feel very small, very dependent upon the Creator. There is a message in this text for us.

Note first that the disciples couldn't see Jesus, but he saw them! "And he saw that they were making headway painfully, for the wind was against them" (Mark 6:48, ESV). How fabulous to become aware that in our darkest hour, when we are tired, wrung out, cold, in "pain"—our Lord sees us, although we can't see him. He knows exactly what's happening. He feels the turbulence of world events around us. He identifies with the hungry, the homeless, the hated. He hears the rattling of nuclear sabers between nations, the wars and rumors of wars. He tastes the salt of his children's tears. Our Lord sees us.

Christmas reminds us that God is not removed. He has come to where we are, and he will remain with us forever. Jesus said, "I will not leave you desolate; I will come to you" (John 14:18, RSV).

A second truth emerges from the text: In spite of the wind, waves, and cold, the disciples never stopped plowing ahead. They refused to give up, heave to, and allow the storm to drive them where the winds were blowing. It was in the midst of their "tough obedience," beating against the storm, that Jesus came to them in a totally unexpected way. He came walking on water—right in the middle of their distress! Isn't it true that when we face times of testing, when we are experiencing tough obedience, when we are tempted to give up and go with the pressures, Jesus comes to us—often in the most unexpected ways. Ours is a faith that hangs on, anchored in the knowledge our Lord is watching and filled with expectancy that he will come to us in time.

Obviously, these are dark scary days, as the world erupts with hatred and violence. Christmas reminds us that God still has a plan. When people's hearts are failing them for fear of what is coming in the world, as Christ's disciples we are called to keep on living, planning for the future—refusing to give up. Why? Because our Lord is coming, as unexpectedly as he did to the disciples, walking right into the midst of these storms, not intimidated by the waves and winds of evil. Our future isn't dark, but glorious. This is true in our personal history and true in the cosmic sense, that the world—all creation—is moving to the glorious unfolding of God's perfect plan for his kingdom. As Jesus said, "the prince of this world . . . has no hold over me" (John 14:30).

There is a third vital truth in our text. When Jesus did arrive on the scene, he came fully in control, invested with authority: "Take heart—it is I. Have no fear." Jesus, with a word of command, calmed the wind and waves.

There is a beautiful story about Elisha in the book of 2 Kings. Syrian armies had surrounded Israel with an overwhelming military force. Humanly speaking, everything looked hopeless. Elisha's servant said, "Alas, my master! What shall we do?" Here was Elisha's answer:

> *"Don't be afraid. . . . Those who are with us are more than those who are with them." And Elisha prayed, and said, "Open his eyes, LORD, so that he may see" . . . and he saw the hills full of horses and chariots of fire all around Elisha.* (2 Kings 6:16–17)

May Christmas 1979 become a time when God opens our eyes, allowing us to see his invisible resources and power which encircle his world, setting limits to the forces of evil. We need to be reminded how great our God is, as our world groans in birth trauma toward the coming of the kingdom of righteousness.

Last summer, I witnessed an incident that illustrates how the resource of this text can teach us to use hard times for renewal of trust in God, rather than fall apart in fear. One joy in vacationing on Balboa Island is watching activity in the bay. The house we rent is near a bridge connecting the island to the mainland. Sometimes a skipper with too many cocktails for dinner will misjudge the height of the bridge—which varies with changing tides—and plow right into it. Inexperienced sailors will attempt to clear the bridge, miss by inches, and drive the mast right into it.

On this particular day, two ladies were learning to sail a small boat. A brisk wind had brought them downwind toward the bridge. Not knowing that turning around and going against the wind required different skills, they waited and turned away from the bridge at the last minute. Now the wind was blowing against them, requiring them to tack, a skill they lacked. When wind began to fill their sail, the boat would begin to tip, causing the ladies to feel they were going over, and so they would point directly into the wind, immediately placing them at the mercy of the current and the threat of going under the bridge. After thrashing around, not understanding how to use the wind to save themselves, both ladies grabbed paddles and started toward shore. They had no idea someone was watching. By this time we were hysterical, but then we decided to help. Literally we had to swim out to those two, climb into the boat, and demonstrate basic sailing skills, assuring them the boat would not go over, if it tipped. In fact, the boat had to tip to make headway against the wind. In a short time, they were able to tack back and forth, using the wind to take them away from danger and transforming their trauma into an enjoyable afternoon of sailing.

What a lesson for us who face modern wind and storms, sailing in small boats of human strength and resources. Like the two women, in tough times we focus on going under the bridge, or tipping over, wearing ourselves out in fruitless activity fighting the wind. When we're just about ready to throw in the towel and paddle to shore, we forget Jesus is watching us, and he knows when to come and climb aboard.

Christmas is God's annual reminder that "Someone is watching over us," and he will come at the right time, transforming the very forces which threaten and frighten us to our advantage—because he is Master and Lord of the storm.

Speaking to this issue, Malcolm Muggeridge in his book *Conversion* urges us to look beyond the wreckage we see around us, the failed political institutions, the dashed earthly hopes, because

> *when every possibility of help from earthly sources has been sought and is not forthcoming, when every recourse this world offers, moral as well as material, has been expended to no effect; and in*

the deepening darkness every glimmer of light has finally flickered out--it is then that Christ's hand reaches out . . . his light shines brightest. . . . So, finding in everything only deception and nothingness, the soul is constrained to have recourse to God himself and to rest content with him.[9]

We are called to hang on when the storm is raging—so teaches Jesus Christ!

Questions for Study and Discussion:

1. Do you ever feel like God isn't paying attention to the "wind and waves" in your life? Like the two women learning to sail, what "fruitless activities" do you turn to, in your crises?

2. Walt tells us that before we see Jesus, he sees us. How can knowing this change how we view the storm and how we respond to it?

Your Incredible Potential as a Christian

Ephesians 3:14–21
September 21, 1980

Today, we consider our incredible potential as Christians, described by Paul praying for the Ephesians,

> *that out of his glorious riches, [God] may strengthen you with power through his Spirit in your inner being . . . that you may be filled to the measure of all the fullness of God.* (Eph. 3:16, 19)

We need to understand what it means to be strengthened in our inner person, to be filled with the fullness of God, because finding such power is the secret to success as a Christian. If suddenly you could tap into God's power and make it operative in your experience, what would be different? Recent sermons have reflected my conviction that God is going to use our church family in mighty ways during the '80s. For that miracle to happen, each of us must come to new maturity in Christ, able to appropriate this power God has provided to accomplish ministry. Isaiah

uses an eagle to illustrate the dynamic effect of supernatural power flowing through a Christian:

> *[T]hose who hope in the* LORD *will renew their strength. They
> will soar on wings like eagles; they will run and not grow weary,
> they will walk and not be faint.* (Isa. 40:31)

After talking with someone who observed eagles in southern Florida,
and then reading about these birds, I understand why Isaiah would
choose an eagle to illustrate God's power operating in the life of a
believer. Eagles soar for hours in sustained flight without moving
their wings. Such ability is the result of a long process of learning.
Eagles stay in the nest up to eighty-five days after hatching from an
egg. They need advanced maturity before attempting their first flight.
Once an eagle reaches the point where it is time to leave the nest, the
first flight is obviously scary, until the young bird discovers a force
observers cannot see. Eagles soar without flapping their wings, because
by instinct they learn to use the lifting power of thermals, spiral-like
winds that lift a bird to great heights. By simply opening their wings,
which sometimes are up to eight feet in span, eagles can catch these
spiraling currents of air and float effortlessly. Without thermals, eagles
would exert so much energy that they could not find sufficient food to
survive. These few facts prove helpful in understanding what it means
for us to be strengthened in our inner person and to be filled with the
fullness of God.

Tasks confronting us in the '80s seem awesome. I was looking at a
picture of a starving child on our brochure for the mission conference
this October, and it broke my heart. I think of the hostages, of the
wars and rumors of wars, of hate and violence and immorality. I seem
personally so helpless to do anything for needs such as these. The good
news for Christians who are awed by the task before us is that God has
not called us to take personal responsibility for the whole work of his
kingdom, only for that part for which he has equipped and empowered

us—a fact that doesn't dry my tears about human suffering, but frees me to concentrate on the ministries I am called to perform.

I want us to study the eagle as symbolic of the mechanism by which we tap into God's fullness and power to accomplish our individual ministries.

For example, imagine the impact, after you have lived your Christian experience like a hummingbird, flitting from one task to another, your wings whirring in endless activity, finally feeling exhausted and burnt out. Contrast those feelings with discovering that you are not a hummingbird, but rather an eagle. And God has not asked to you to flap your wings, but rather to stretch them out in faith and ride the thermals of his power. Suddenly you begin to soar, allowing the winds of the Holy Spirit to lift you to new heights and perspectives of effectiveness. Heights you could never achieve when you created your own lift by flapping wings of human potential alone.

Let me zero in on what the fullness of God and being strengthened in our inner person can mean in our daily experience. Listen to Paul continue his prayer for the Ephesians:

> *Now to him who is able to do immeasurably more than all we ask or imagine, according to his power that is at work within us, to him be glory.* (Eph. 3:20–21)

Let's define what "abundantly" means. "Abundantly" describes a lifestyle of faithfulness, not sensationalism. Many of us are put into chains because we see nothing sensational or exciting or useful to God about our daily routine, and we have no hope for things ever being different. So we leave "calls to serve Christ in the '80s" to those who are sensational in our eyes, those to whom we believe God has given all the gifts and opportunities.

An abundant life in God's sight need not be a sensational life. Few of Christ's twelve disciples ever did anything sensational enough to be written down and remembered. Paul prays that our inner person might be lifted to new heights—heights from which we begin to see our non-sensational daily routine as a vital part of God's eternal purposes. Then we can return on Monday morning to the "grind," armed with a sense of purpose and calling, soaring with God's power, rather than falling exhausted. Every Christian needs to know that what we do every day are tasks done unto God (Col. 3:17), with reverberations that touch eternity. God's kingdom will be built by all of us doing our small jobs faithfully. Common, ordinary Christians make up God's army in the world. The battle against evil will be won by ordinary Christians. People claim Abraham Lincoln once said, "God must really love common people, because he made so many of them."

I believe the battle against evil forces engulfing our world will be won in the nuts-and-bolts, meat-and-potatoes happenings of everyday experiences, rather than in sensational moments. A friend describing his experience in World War II said the big test of courage was being faithful in the endless, boring routine of waiting, rather than in the great battles, which happened only infrequently and were quickly over. You and I will feel the impact of being filled with God's fullness, as we begin to appropriate the power already in us and walk into the classroom, the office, the kitchen, soaring above what society calls routine, seeing it as God sees it—ministry that will help change the world. Life lived in this context bulges with joy and meaning.

How does one plug into this inner power about which Paul prays? Our text claims it begins with a personal relationship with Jesus, "that Christ may dwell in your hearts through faith. . . being rooted and established in love" (Eph. 3:17). One cannot soar on the power of God's thermals without first stretching our wings of faith, reaching out and claiming, "I need a Savior, and I claim Jesus. I believe he was the Son of God, that he died for my sins, that he rose so that he could give me eternal life."

Soaring like an eagle must begin with knowing Jesus as Savior, experiencing that miracle of being born again, beginning anew, then growing in our faith to where we know Jesus can be trusted, that his promises are sound. Then we are ready to graduate from the nest of infancy in Christ and begin soaring to maturity.

A second step in appropriating this power is to remember it takes an eagle up to eighty-six days to venture out of the nest. Learning to use God's thermals in daily living takes time, learning, sacrifice, waiting. I believe our congregation has as much food on the table for Christian growth as any place in the country.

Note your bulletin today, "fat" with opportunities for growth, including classes by which you can learn the Scriptures, a must if you want to soar for Christ. You cannot be effective as a Christian without regular study of the Bible. We have classes to help you discover your spiritual gifts, classes and small groups to help you understand and express Christian love, to knock down walls in your life and build bridges with people. Tonight you can study the Holy Spirit.

Think for a moment. You studied for years to learn your vocation. You work fanatically to learn tennis and other sports. You spend hours planning for your future and make great sacrifice to assure security tomorrow. Some of us spend hours every day to stay in physical condition. Parents go to classes to learn about having babies. Where does Jesus and our life of discipleship fit in, if he is the focal point of our lives?

One cannot learn to soar for Christ by osmosis, any more than you can get your body in physical condition or learn a vocation without sacrifice and discipline. Here is the call I extend to you in these critical days: Make time to grow to maturity in Christ. If you are not in the Scriptures and in prayer daily, you will never develop the hunger to grow, to reach out of the nest into the heights of greatness for God.

A final word: The toughest call of the Christian is to remain faithful in the non-glorious "walk" routines of daily living to which God has called us. Isaiah describes Christian growth as a process. We begin flying in sensationalism, graduate to running, and reach the ultimate when we can walk through the mundane happenings of every day and not faint. Soaring like an eagle through the ordinary walks of life is where we reach our incredible potential as disciples of Jesus Christ, one who came and lived, worked and related as a carpenter and servant, not a superstar. Yet, one day, the world will bow at his feet.

Questions for Study and Discussion:

1. How often do you read the Bible? Do you have a system or plan for study? If Scripture-reading is part of your life routine, what impact has it had on your Christian walk?

2. Where in your life do you "flit like a hummingbird," doing things under your own power, rather than soaring on God's thermals? Where are you tempted to act like a superstar, rather than submitting your daily life to walking with God?

WHEN JESUS DEALS WITH IMMORALITY

John 8:1–11; 1 Corinthians 3:16–17
September 16, 1979

Attending a seminar at UCLA, I heard a renegade church leader speak on morality. His statement about the morals people choose was rooted in their view of God. This man had rejected the idea of a personal God, and instead insisted that any authority outside the person himself was idolatry. Therefore, rather than teaching people to turn to God for their security, we should be teaching them how to survive *this* world.

His words are symptomatic of why a moral blackout dominates society. If people believe no personal God exists—it's logical to reject divine law governing human behavior—as well as divine judgment for breaking the law. People begin to call good evil, and evil good. Such attitudes are reminiscent of the period of Judges in the Old Testament, when people made their own rules and did as they pleased. Consequences of such liberation from God's order always remain the same: Families disintegrate, sexuality becomes an object of worship, people become enslaved to their own passions—ultimately a nation is destroyed. As Peter wrote in his second letter, "They promise them freedom, while they themselves are slaves of depravity—for 'people are slaves to whatever has mastered him'" (2 Pet. 2:19).

Abraham Lincoln's words seem prophetic when he claimed that if America is ever conquered, it will not happen by enemies invading across the sea, but by moral corruption within.

While on Balboa Island this summer, one favorite moment was to stop at the donut shop—after a jog. If that sounds incongruous, it is. While there, it was pathetic to listen to a group gathering each day, made up (for the most part) of men in their fifties and sixties, who had bailed out of their marriages, behaving as less than gentlemen toward women walking by. These were financially successful men, seeking to divide behavior between their professional and personal lives. Such dualism is impossible, but it is indicative how desperately our society needs what Jesus has to teach about moral law.

A woman is brought to Jesus, accused of adultery. According to Old Testament law, her punishment was death. Religious leaders are creating a test case. If Jesus fails to uphold the death penalty, they find grounds to seek his death, for violating Mosaic law. Here is our Lord's response.

First, Jesus deals with judgmental attitudes of the self-righteous accusers. Notice he refuses to answer the question, "Should this woman be stoned?" Instead, he bends down, writes on the sand with his finger. Some guess he wrote the Ten Commandments. Whatever did appear in the sand changed the emotional focus of that crowd of accusers from judgment against the woman to awareness of sin hidden in each of their own hearts. Jesus helped them see how all judgment belongs only with God. Rising from his knees, he quietly said, "Let any one of you who is without sin be the first to throw a stone at her." Then, beginning with the eldest, who possessed the greatest collection of sordid memories, the executioners went away. Turning to the woman, Jesus then asks, "Where are [your accusers]? . . . [N]either do I condemn you. . . . Go now and leave your life of sin" (John 8:2–11).

Here is one of the greatest of Christian truths: Before we can grasp Christ's teaching about morality, our focus must change from preoccupation with throwing stones of accusation at others to grasping our own need for forgiveness. Our church family, each of us as individuals, must leap over this habit of judging and accusing others. Then we can help each other in times of moral failure. Because people expect to be judged, particularly by the church family, they hesitate to seek help during times of moral temptation and failure.

Once judgment has been cast aside, we are ready to hear what Jesus says about moral law. He affirms the existence of right and wrong by refusing to whitewash the woman's behavior. His statement "Go now and leave your life of sin" declares that adultery is sin. Sin deserves death. What's new in this drama happens when Jesus unveils grace that overcomes death. This woman is guilty—caught in the act. Her accusers are there, ready to execute her. At great risk to himself, our Lord intercedes in her behalf. Grace means that, although guilty, God doesn't deal with us as our sins deserve. Keep in mind: The sole reason our Heavenly Father can allow us to go free is because his Son Jesus died in our place. Grace happens because Jesus the Lamb of God took upon himself the death our sins deserve. Grace can only be understood if we stand with this woman—fully aware of our guilt—aware of the awesome reality of divine judgment—and our personal helplessness to do anything. Only when it registers in our heads that we are delivered from guilt and death, does the gift of grace create a "love reaction" toward him who saved us from such a predicament. Jesus knelt to write a second time in the sand. Some conjecture he wrote, "By my stripes you are healed," upholding God's justice that the wages of our sin is death, while offering God's grace to us at infinite cost to himself. This drama of law confronting grace is one of the most beautiful in the Bible.

Consider one more dimension of grace. Jesus dispersed her accusers and said, "Neither do I condemn you. Go now and leave your life of sin." Suppose he had said, "Go now and leave your life of sin, and then I will forgive you." Suppose God's forgiveness is contingent upon our never sinning again, once he's let us off the hook. Suppose the woman was brought to Jesus again, with the same problem. Would he have let the crowd stone her? How you answer that question determines your understanding of grace. According to the New Testament laws of love, Christ would have forgiven her—again and again and again! Her motivation for becoming obedient, after receiving grace, is not fear of punishment, but growing love for this One who keeps giving forgiveness, at such pain to himself. Gradually that kind of love gets into where we feel things and make decisions. Here is how Paul describes this dynamic in 2 Corinthians:

> *For Christ's love compels us, because we are convinced that one died for all; and therefore all died. And he died for all, that those who live might live no longer for themselves but for him who died for them and was raised again.* (2 Cor. 5:14–15)

John puts it this way in his epistle, "My little children, I write this to you so that you will not sin. But if anyone does sin, we have an advocate with the Father—Jesus Christ, the Righteous One. He is the atoning sacrifice for our sins" (1 John 2:1–2).

Today Christ calls his people to live holy lives in an unholy environment. What a struggle that call becomes, as we are bombarded on all sides to be unholy. The battle becomes more fierce, as we resist this idea of being holy, separate, different. Israel was like us. God called them to separate themselves from a world hostile to his will. Their response was to go full steam in becoming like the nations around them, borrowing their gods and customs. History proves the fatal consequence of such behavior. German theologian Helmut Thielicke had this to say about his German people, who tried to exclude God and his laws, prior to World War II:

> *The tragedy for our German nation was that it proceeded with fanatical energy to solve economic, social and political problems, and simply ignored the fact first and foremost it needed a Redeemer.*[10]

According to Thielicke, the nation closed its eyes to the existence of both God and the devil. Ignoring the commandments of the former, they were therefore led about by the latter. He concludes, "We no longer knew God, and therefore we lost the real proportions of life and were stricken with blindness."[11]

John begins his gospel claiming that Christ's light has come to penetrate the world's darkness, but people loved darkness better than light "because their deeds were evil." My prayer today is that God may enable us to take new inventory of our personal lives—open up closets previously closed to our Lord's light—confess and get washed from that which breaks his heart—give ourselves new determination to being holy, different, separate—so that we might, through our lives, become Christ's light still shining in the moral darkness enveloping our society.

Questions for Study and Discussion:

1. Which kind of immorality in our culture or in others' behavior upsets you the most? Where are you most inclined to find yourself judging or being hard on others? Where are you most inclined to judge or be hard on yourself?

2. Have you ever experienced a "love reaction" in response to God's grace to you? How did it change your attitude or behavior?

When two members of Menlo Park Presbyterian Church's search committee, John Jenks and Stu Adams, flew down to meet Walt and have dinner with him in Malibu, they might have expected to find an ambitious young man, eager to "move up" from a small beach-town church of six hundred to a 1,500-member congregation in the heart of the business and education world. Instead, over dinner, Walt shared his feelings of inadequacy: "The more I thought about it, the more convinced I became that I couldn't assume the leadership and the pulpit of a large church in a community of so many very intelligent people, including Stanford faculty and very successful business people. I'm too young, thirty-seven years old, with very limited church leadership experience."

Out of obedience, however, he accepted the job, only to find that—yikes!—everything he feared was true! After six months in Menlo Park, Walt even thought of returning to his previous role in Malibu, since the position was still open, only to realize that his very feelings of inadequacy were central to his call. For his entire tenure at Menlo Park, those feelings would never leave him, but they forced him to dependency on God and not his own talents.

John Jenks
(summarized by Metta Gerber)

TRUST ME WITH YOUR NOTHINGNESS

John 6:16–21, 36
September 9, 1979

Today, I want us to think together about a truth difficult for a group of superachievers (like most of us) to grasp. Here it is: Human resources *alone* are not sufficient to do God's work. Becoming aware of our inadequacy is a prerequisite to our being mightily used of God.

This truth runs counter to almost every grain of our being. From year one we have been conditioned to reject in ourselves and in others what is inadequate, incompetent, or broken. If we want a job done, we look for "proven winners." Now our text hits us with this whopper: When God builds his church team, he uses revolutionary criteria. Listen to Paul describe the early disciples:

> *For consider your calling, brother: not many of you were wise according to worldly standards, not many were powerful, not many were of noble birth. But . . . God chose what is weak in the world to shame the strong, God chose what is low and despised in the world, even things that are not, to bring to nothing things*

that are, so that no human being might boast in the presence of God. (1 Cor. 1:26–29, ESV)

It's really true: "God's ways are not our ways." For example, Jesus warned how difficult it is for rich people to enter his kingdom. Education, wealth, talent, success, fame—these are qualities treasured by the world's system, but they never rate first with God. Obviously, God doesn't reject human talent. As our heavenly parent, he gave us minds and other gifts to cultivate and use. Christians need feel no guilt for being competent or successful. However, our text stresses that our talents cannot replace our dependence upon God. Such insight helps us pray, "Father, *in spite of* my abilities and achievements, when it comes to building your kingdom, doing something that lasts forever, I don't have it. I need you, working in me and doing through me what I can never do by myself. *Help me!*"

Making peace with these facts opens the door to our story.

The scene is a crowd of hungry people sitting on a hillside—miles from the nearest supermarket. Seeing an opportunity to teach disciples new dimensions of trust, Jesus asks Philip, "How are we going to feed these people? Dig into your pockets for some money, and go buy bread for them."

Our Lord was pushing his disciples into a position where their own resources became totally inadequate. Philip blurts out, "Jesus, two hundred days' wages wouldn't be enough to buy this crowd even a little. Come on now—be reasonable. You can't be serious."—a typical faithless reaction to a divine possibility.

Jesus wanted Philip to share the thrill of being part of a miracle—of being up to his earlobes in a ministry beyond his personal potential. Lacking faith, he misses his chance. Digging into the pockets of his own resources—of course he came up short.

Andrew did better. Hearing his Lord's suggestion, he began to look around at what was available before he said, "It can't be done!" Finding one sack lunch from a small boy that contained five little cupcake-size barley loaves and two fish, he brought it to Jesus saying, "Lord, this is all we've got. Not much, when you look at five thousand people. Anyway, here it is. You take it. See what you can do with it."

Now Jesus is in a position to operate. The rest is history.

Asking the crowd to sit down, he took the sack lunch, blessed it, and started distributing food. I can't explain scientifically what happened that day, beyond the fact that Jesus multiplied one sack lunch until five thousand people had a sit-down dinner! What's more, twelve baskets or "doggie bags" of leftovers were collected! That's God at work. That's what happens when we dare to put what we have into our Lord's hands.

All of us know Jesus didn't come to give five thousand hungry people a meal. His purpose was much bigger. He wanted to demonstrate to the crowd how he was the Bread of Life by which they could find eternal life. He sought to teach his disciples a vital principle about God's method of operation in the world, how our Heavenly Father takes inadequate human resources and accomplishes divine objectives through us his children. I found a motto that epitomizes this adventure of placing our inadequate resources into God's hands: "We the unwilling, led by the unqualified, have been doing the unbelievable so long, with so little, we now attempt the impossible with nothing."

What a truth by which to live! Most of us fear inadequacy so much, we will do most anything to avoid situations where we might fail. Yet Jesus says that's a habit we must break, if we want to be part of God's action in the world. He urges us to be like the "bread" in our story—our own sense of adequacy broken—before we can be used to feed others. But once we put our "zero" into God's hands, he parallels our strength with his own, and our potential for ministry is multiplied one hundred or even ten thousand times. Listen to a promise back in Leviticus:

And you shall chase your enemies, and they shall fall before you by the sword. Five of you shall chase a hundred, and a hundred of you shall chase ten thousand, and your enemies shall fall before you by the sword. (Lev. 26:7–8)

Confronting the impossible will always be a part of life. Knowing we can put ourselves into Christ's hands at such moments is power. Faith means we need not respond to impossible situations saying, "Lord, do you know what you are asking? How can I feed five thousand? I don't have what it takes to do my job, raise my children, overcome my grief, make it in school, give 10 percent of my income to your work, face life as a single, resist the temptations buffeting me, get involved with that person or ministry that is way over my head."

Those excuses don't hold water for Christians. One hook upon which I'm hanging my faith has everything to do with Christ's invitation: "Trust me with your nothingness. Your little is enough, when I'm in it."

This is the year I pray God will help every person in this church family to begin to function with this indomitable faith. When we are weak, we are strong.

Here is another treasure from the story: Jesus speaks to our fear of inadequate resources, such as food and clothing. Most of us have jittery thoughts about tomorrow. What if we became incapacitated, no longer able to earn an income? Such fears reflect the belief our future rests upon our health, our ability to provide for ourselves. Jesus says that isn't true! Our income, our future security is a gift from our Heavenly Father. God's ability to provide for us is not contingent upon our continued health or potential for employment. He can provide for us out of nothing. What a thrill to watch our heavenly parent come through, when we don't have the slightest human chance of making it without him. Jesus was teaching this truth, when he said:

> *I tell you, do not worry about your life, what you will eat or drink; or about your body, what you will wear. . . . If . . . God clothes the grass of the field . . . will he not much more clothe you, O you of little faith? . . . Therefore do not worry about tomorrow.*
> (Matt. 6:25, 30, 34, NIV1984)

Jesus acted out this truth by feeding five thousand with nothing. God is committed to provide for us his children, supernaturally, if he must. This is a promise: God will take care of you. It's been proven valid for thousands of years. Jesus breathes on nothing and makes it something. He makes the impossible possible!

Here's the bottom line, when we think about Jesus feeding the five thousand: Where are you facing the impossible this morning? Where are you looking for resources? Are you like Philip, using human limitations as excuses for not trusting God? Or are you Andrew, facing a tall mountain, looking first at your own resources, trusting your Heavenly Father to make up the difference, and then starting to climb? I know hundreds of examples where God has broken into the human predicament and accomplished far more than what can be explained by human power alone. Many sect groups thrive on one premise—they teach that God works miracles. Let me say, the Christian church believes and expects our God to meet us at the doorway of the impossible, take our hand, and climb with us. Franklin D. Roosevelt won public admiration by making people aware of his great head and powerful shoulders, rather than his paralyzed legs. Faith in Jesus seeks to turn self-pity, fear, and excuses for action, into self-respect, belief in the total adequacy of our God for any situation, and reckless boldness to try anything, face everything, because we know if God is for us, no one can be against us.

Today, I challenge you. Be an Andrew. There is no thrill greater than confronting what appears to be the impossible, holding in one hand our personal resources, inadequate as they may seem, and holding the hand of Christ with the other—and feeling in your soul that divine surge saying: "With Christ by my side, I can overcome the world!"

Questions for Study and Discussion:

1. Where are you facing an impossible situation in your life? Do you tend to respond more like Philip, or like Andrew? What would it look like to give God that situation?

2. Has God ever used your small offering to do greater things? What do you have to offer him today, and how can you, like the boy in the story, make that offering available for God's use?

Do People Really Change?

Jeremiah 1:5, 18:1–5
February 19, 1989

A new member said something that sticks in my memory: "One of the most encouraging parts of Christianity for me is the good news that Jesus Christ really does enable people to change."

Suppose God came and made you a proposal, "I will make any changes in your life that you desire!" Most of us would take him up on his offer. Some would ask for physical changes:

- to be taller or shorter, or for their feet to be smaller;
- to be more beautiful or handsome;
- to have healing from emotional and physical illness;
- to be younger—or if you were like my son, fifteen years old and wanting to drive, to be a few years older.

Others might ask to be married; to be more socially assertive and acceptable, to have more friends and feel better about themselves; or to find a different job or make more money.

I'm amazed at how many people, when their guards are down, would readily seek God to change things they believe are robbing them of life at its best. Our text today speaks of God being the Potter and our lives being clay. God told Jeremiah, "Go down to the potter's house, and there I will give you my message" (Jer. 18:2).

In seventh-century Israel, the potter's house was central to the community because he made containers in which to store grain to help survive the winter and to store water to survive drought. Pottery enabled people to cease being nomads, following the food and water supply; thus, they could remain in one place to make civilization happen.

Jeremiah went to the potter and watched him work on his wheel. Taking a lump of clay, the potter exerted pressure, until a useful vessel emerged out of a formless mass. That day, one lump of clay wasn't taking shape as the potter planned, so he took the clay, rolled it back into a ball, and started all over again.

Watching this scenario, suddenly Jeremiah saw a parable of how God can take the nation of Israel, or a human life that is defective, and remold it into something good. Questions immediately emerge:

- What kind of changes can we expect God to make in our lives?
- Does this story offer hope to get rid of things we don't like about ourselves?

Let's study the text to see if there are any answers.

First, *God has a plan for us—a plan structured before we were born.* God said to Jeremiah: "Before I formed you in the womb I knew you, before you were born I set you apart" (Jer. 1:5). None of us are accidents! When things happen to us that make us believe we are victims of chance and fate, or that there could not possibly be any plan for ultimate good operating in our lives, it's encouraging to be reminded that our Heavenly Father does have a plan for us; our lives are not a mistake.

Eugene Peterson, in his book *Run with the Horses*, asked a question that pushed some buttons inside me. Do you remember as a child, ever being the last one chosen for a team, while two captains argued about who would be stuck with you, the *liability*? Not so with God! No one can replace us. Before we were good for anything, God decided we would be good for his purposes on Earth.

Romans 8 affirms God's plan for us to become like Jesus. What's fascinating is that the many things we seek to change about ourselves—things we believe are robbing us of life at its best—God could be using to mold us into the image of Jesus! Unfortunately, many of us don't trust God enough to believe he has a plan operating in our behalf, or to make peace with those hard things God allows to remain in our lives to fulfill his plan for us.

Most of us still want our way, rather than God's way. We compare ourselves with others, saying to God, "What's the big idea? Why do I have to hurt so much in order to fulfill your plan? My neighbor is also a Christian, and you aren't asking him to put up with the same things I have to endure! Why do my children cause such pain, and those of others are such a blessing? Why is my body so stricken with disease, and others never have a sick day in their lives?"

Paul wrote to the church at Rome: "Shall what is formed say to the one who formed it, 'Why did you make me like this?'" (Rom. 9:20). Our challenge is, do we trust God enough to trust his plan, even if it seems unfair, unjust? Even if it hurts? Do we want to be molded into the image of Jesus, even if it means not receiving changes on our wish list?

Remember this challenging verse? "Trust in the LORD with all your heart, and lean not on your own understanding. In all your ways acknowledge Him, and He shall direct your paths" (Prov. 3:5, NKJV).

Jeremiah learned a second lesson at the potter's house: Not only does God have a plan for our lives, but *God's plan for us is to become givers rather than takers.*

Consider the text again: "Before I formed you in the womb I knew you; before you were born I set you apart; I appointed you as a prophet to the nations." The word "prophet" can mean "one who gives." Jeremiah was called to use his life as one who gives. Jesus also came as one who gives. When we begin to bear his image, we will become givers.

What is God doing in our world today? He is busy saving, rescuing, enlightening, caring, forgiving, encouraging, healing, restoring, spreading love. A spiritual war is in progress between evil that seeks to tear down, and God who seeks to build up. God is for life and against death; for love and against hate; for hope and against despair. God calls us to use our lives during the week, to be lovers and givers in the name of Jesus.

At some point, it will finally dawn on us that God doesn't exist to fix things on demand that we believe will make us happier. God's agenda is to mold us into givers who will care for his hurting world.

Last spring, I was watching a couple of sparrow parents raise their young. Day after day they would busily look for food, returning to feed their noisy, hungry youngsters, who always had their mouths open to receive. Theoretically, birds could stay in that nest and never fly, if their parents continued to feed them. However, their destiny was to fly, not to remain trapped in their nests of comfort, living as parasites on their parents.

Finally, the day came when those sparrows began to push their young out of the nest. This process must have been terrifying and confusing to the young birds. It seemed cruel to be forced to leave the warmth and protection of their nest, take a leap off the roof, flap wings, search for their own food, avoid neighborhood cats, assume responsibility. However, sparrows are not destined to stay in a protected nest—they are destined to fly in the wild!

God is preparing us for that day when we leave the protected nest of being dominated by self, when we become like Jesus and begin to live to give.

Giving is what we Christians do best. Giving is designed right into our hearts. Why not? Life and everything else we possess have been given to us. To bear the image of Jesus is to be a giver.

Jeremiah learned a third lesson: *God seeks to change things in us that distort his unique plan for us to become like Jesus.* I don't think this means

God will make us grow six inches taller at age forty, or make us blond and beautiful, however. Our text reads, "the vessel he was making of clay was spoiled in the potter's hand" (Jer. 18:4, ESV). Jeremiah then saw the potter take the spoiled vessel and "[rework] it into another vessel, *as it seemed good to the potter to do*" (emphasis mine).

God does change things in us that are blocking the fulfillment of his plan for us. For example, I have observed that God allows people to change jobs that free them for ministry. Monday's *San Francisco Chronicle* told of people who are changing jobs, leaving high salaries and high stress, and moving to jobs of service with a fraction of the salary because they "want something where they feel they are touching another person's life." I have also seen God change habits that inhibit our Christian witness, to allow us to be healed of emotional and physical disorders that impede our lives as givers, and heal us of pain in relationships that so consume us that we have nothing left to give.

God will grant our request for changes that help us become more like Jesus. He will not grant requests for change that cater to our selfish limited desire for happiness in this world. He has something far bigger in mind for us.

So, the answer to the question, "Do people really change?" is *yes*. If God does the changing, and if those changes fit into God's plan for us. Our challenge is to trust God enough to surrender ourselves to his plan, rather than demand he conform to *our* plan. One of the biggest lessons in life is to understand that God is the Potter and we are the clay. So often we spend our lives attempting to be the potter and making God the clay, demanding that he perform for us on demand, to meet our needs, make us happy, fulfill our requests.

Paul said: "For to me, to live is Christ" (Phil. 1:21). What does that mean? It means we live to give. It means we follow our Lord's model to wash our neighbor's feet, rather than clawing our way to the top of the pack at any cost.

Last week we laid to rest one special member of our church family. I am always fascinated with what we remember about a person when they leave us. When we thought of Elvira, we thought of what she gave to her husband, children, and seven grandchildren; we thought of how she spent her life serving others, shopping for shut-ins, reading for the blind, caring for two ladies who were stroke victims, encouraging them, taking them to lunch; and then her endless tasks of serving Jesus in this church for thirty-eight years. It occurred to me again that Jesus was right when he said, "It is more blessed to give than to receive" (Acts 20:35).

What are people going to say about you when you are gone? In Arlington Cemetery, there are thousands of graves with simply the name, date of birth–date of death. That dash represents a life. What are you doing with yours? The only way to invest that dash with eternal significance is to use it to give and send treasures ahead to heaven. I challenge you to stop seeking to use God to fulfill self, and allow him to mold you into Christ's image as a giver; and then to search for that one spot in the world you touch during the week, where Jesus wants to use you to make a difference.

Let me close with my version of that popular Serenity Prayer, which I am sure you have heard:

> *Lord, grant me the serenity to accept the things in myself you do not wish to change; courage to allow you to change things that need to be changed to make me more like Jesus; and wisdom to know the difference.*

Christian maturity happens when we reach that place of surrender where we can say in faith, "Only to be what he wants me to be, every moment of every day."

Questions for Study and Discussion:

1. If you could be "zapped" and change something about yourself, what would you choose? Why? How do you imagine your life would change? Have you ever asked God why he chose to let that remain part of your story?

2. Can you think of ways in which something difficult in your life has helped you become a giver—that have made you become, even in a small way, more like Jesus?

WHEN YOU FEEL OVERSTRESSED

John 8:13–20
May 17, 1981

Recently our family was reading the Bible together on the subject of controlling anger. As I was reading, my son began heaping extra sugar on his cereal. When I suggested he didn't need so much sugar, he pushed away his cereal, claiming he didn't want anymore. Before I knew it, my angry words were raining down like a monsoon. Attempting to continue reading about controlling anger, I felt like a hypocrite. My children either were too kind or too intimidated to laugh at me, but as far as family worship, we lost it for that day. Thinking over my lack of patience, it occurred to me how often those I love receive only the dregs left over, after everyone else has had a piece of me. Stress and pressure can drain us, until there is no emotional reserve left. I share this scenario not as a personal defeat, but as part of a victory I am experiencing, in learning to cope with pressure and balance my priorities. Like most of us, my job involves tremendous stress. Twentieth-century American life can exert so much pressure that the joy of living is choked out of us.

Here is a list of questions I find helpful in identifying whether you need help in coping with stress:

1. Do you usually plan more for your day than you're actually able to accomplish?

2. Do you ever go to bed worrying about unfinished tasks?

3. Do you ever feel tired, just thinking about everything you have to do?

4. Do you sometimes feel that you're meeting everyone's needs except your own?

5. Have you ever wanted to just "drop out of the human race" for a week?

6. Do you sometimes lose your temper for little or no reason?

Jesus offers practical help in coping with stress, if we are his disciple. Studying his ministry, we learn Jesus never succumbed to stress and pressure, although he was constantly buffeted in his daily routine. Today we study a little-known "I am" claim of Jesus in John 8:18: "I am one who testifies for myself; my other witness is the Father, who sent me."

Pharisees are questioning our Lord's authority, credentials, and personhood, seeking to discredit him among the people. Such stress was common in his ministry. He was daily crushed by crowds, plagued by demands to come here or go there, attacked by temptation, and having his methods and motives challenged. In this debate with the Pharisees, Jesus reveals his secret for coping with pressure.

He knew who he was; he had found himself. His identity was secure in the knowledge that his Father loved him, that a divine plan was operating in his life. Jesus had roots. Listen to him answer his critics from the base of a secure ego in verse 14, "Even if I testify on my own behalf, my testimony is valid, for I know where I came from and where I am going." Once we know who we are—deep inside where we feel things—pressure from the outside does not shake us up.

Because no human parents are perfect, no one grows up with a totally secure self-identity, a fact which causes great pain and confusion. Seminars and charisma-filled leaders make millions, taking people on journeys of self-discovery, in search of selfhood. Until we know who we are, where we have come from, and why we are here, we are victims to groups, people, mates, friends, and bosses, who squeeze and pressure us to conform to their molds—molds in which we know we don't fit.

Jesus claims that if we follow him, he will give us a new identity. Here is what Jesus says about who we are: We are children of God, infinitely loved by our Heavenly Father. Once we are reborn into his forever family, a divine plan becomes operative, in which we find a unique place where God wants us to serve him, build his kingdom, and grow into that person he wants us to be for all eternity. Basically, we are called to a life of self-giving love.

John gives a summary statement of this new identity, "How great is the love the Father has lavished on us, that we should be called children of God! And that is what we are!" (1 John 3:1, NIV1984). Can you find a better answer anywhere to the question, "Who am I?"

Once we have this security of identity tucked deep inside us, we have an internal pressure to push against any external pressure exerted by circumstances. If we make the decision to allow God to write our price tag of self-worth, using criteria that will matter one hundred years from now, we are free from seeking our worth from the ever-changing criteria of our culture. If Jesus had been a people-pleaser, rather than a God-pleaser, he could not have been the world's Savior! People-pleasers are in slavery!

Can you imagine the freedom, when you no longer feel intimidated by the reward-and-punishment syndrome of ratings given by others? When you are no longer judging your worth as a person by physical attractiveness, your IQ, the institution in which you were educated, the neighborhood in which you live, the color of your skin, the number of figures in your checking account, whether or not you live in an apartment or on an estate, work in the trades or teach with a PhD? Jesus says you are God's child, and that the primary purpose of your life is to love, where you live. Your worth as a person is related to how much you open yourself to be a channel of Christ's love.

Here is the bottom line of truth in this text: Once we choose Jesus as Savior, we can be free from forces which intimidate us with pressure and stress, if we allow God, rather than people, to write our price tag of self-worth. This truth is working for me in my task as pastor. Once I am free from ministering to please people, being enslaved to a million opinions, I am truly free to lead, to serve, and to care for this congregation because my ego is not on the line. Jesus lived his whole life with one agenda—to please his Father; and this is how his Father evaluated his Son's life: "This is my Son, whom I love; with him I am well pleased" (Matt. 3:17).

Our hunger for recognition and approval from other people drives us toward the success syndrome. It's not the result of their intimidating personalities—it's our problem, because we hunger more for people's approval than for God's approval. Such addiction is slavery. Once we know who we are and where we are going, we can relax and enjoy living and enjoy people. We can accept failures and lapses in others and ourselves. We can take time to play and get away from pressure, as Jesus modeled in his "getaways" to the mountains. In Christ there is forgiveness and always the gift of another day, so we are not blown apart by mistakes.

Let me close by describing a current blessing I am enjoying from using the insights of this text. I know God put me on this earth to do more than work. I am called to enjoy family, friendships, and life itself, in relationships of love. Sometimes I forget what I know and slip back into my workaholic syndrome. Today I seek again to keep my priorities straight.

Several years ago, I shared this letter, written by a monk, that best describes a weapon I am using to wage war on stress and pressure, to find a balance between work and time for living and loving. If you recall, he writes about what he would do differently, if he had his live to live over again. How he would let himself make more mistakes, be sillier, take fewer things seriously. And he would take the time to enjoy the scenery, saying:

> *I would climb more mountains, swim more rivers, and watch more sunsets.*
>
> *I would do more walking and looking. . . .*
>
> *I would have more actual troubles, and fewer imaginary ones.*

Even though he'd always been "one of those people who never go anywhere without a thermometer, a hot-water bottle, a gargle, a raincoat, aspirin, and a parachute," he thinks another shot at life would find him traveling lighter. In short, writes the monk,

> *If I had my life to live over I would start barefooted earlier in the spring and stay that way later in the fall.*
>
> *I'd pick more daisies.[12]*

I pray these insights from our text might provide you with new resources to win the battle against stress and pressure.

Questions for Study and Discussion:

1. How would you answer the questions Walt posed in this sermon? What are the sources of pressure in your life, where you feel you most need to keep up and keep spinning?

2. What identity does the Bible claim for you? How would it change things, in the places you work so hard and feel the most pressure, to ask, "Do I do this to please people, or to please God?"

Genuine vs. Phony Faith

Matthew 16:1–4, 13–18, 24–27
February 16–17, 1991

E vents of the last few weeks are forcing us to think about God and ask questions:

- Does God really hear and respond to my prayers?
- Will my prayers cause God to change his mind, alter my circumstances, bring an end to the war, recession, drought, personal pain?

Many Christians do not believe God is personally involved in their lives. Such persons are constantly seeking further proof that faith in Jesus puts them into contact with God's power.

Let me ask some questions:

- Is your faith in Jesus giving you inner peace and stability in these turbulent times?
- Or, is your faith in Jesus a "roller coaster"—up when your prayers are being answered, and down when he seems deaf to your requests?

Jesus contrasts genuine versus phony faith. First, genuine Christian faith remains stable no matter what answers God gives to our prayers. In contrast, phony faith demands that God give constant proof of his love by responding positively to our personal agendas.

In our text, religious leaders came to Jesus demanding, "What sign do you give of your claim to be the Messiah?" Jesus answered, "An evil and adulterous generation seeks for a sign, but no sign shall be given to it except the sign of Jonah" (Matt. 16:4, ESV). These guys were not seeking reasons to follow Jesus—they were looking for reasons to reject his authority over their lives.

Jesus gave only the sign of the prophet Jonah, which he described earlier in Matthew's gospel: "For as Jonah was three days and three nights in the belly of the whale, so will the Son of Man be three days and three nights in the heart of the earth" (Matt. 12:40).

The sign of Jonah could mean two things:

- As Jonah's message was God's last word of warning before destroying Nineveh, so Jesus is God's last word by which people can escape divine judgment.
- As Jonah was miraculously delivered from death in the belly of a fish, so Jesus will be resurrected from the dead. This resurrection will be God's proof he is his Son, capable of forgiving sin and giving eternal life.

Jesus gives no further evidence today to motivate us to trust him than those signs already given in his earthly ministry, cross, and resurrection. Genuine Christian faith demands nothing more, and trusts God's love no matter what answers he gives to our prayers.

I received a rose last week with a letter describing how, after years of waiting, this person had not received any positive responses from God in her area of need. Nevertheless, she returned the rose with this mature spiritual insight: "God may or may not choose to answer my prayers in the ways I wanted, but that's okay. He loves me and I love him, and that's all that matters. He will not withhold one good thing from me. My heart is full!"

This is genuine faith. Trusting God:

- when we didn't get the job;
- when the person we prayed for didn't survive;
- when answers to our prayers gave us nothing we felt we needed;
- when reality seems to contradict God's love. The drought gets worse. The recession deepens. Our personal needs become more painful.

If this is genuine faith, how do we get it? Let's go on with the text. Using Peter as his model, Jesus gives us another contrast between genuine versus phony faith: genuine faith begins with a personal confession that Jesus is the Christ, our Savior—God in the flesh! But phony faith affirms Jesus as one teacher among many, to be followed or rejected according to our personal preference.

For years Peter followed Jesus. Now, Jesus asks him a question: "[W]hat about you? Who do you say that I am?" Peter confesses, "You are the Christ, the Son of the living God" (Matt. 16:15–16, NIV1984).

Genuine faith is personal confession that Jesus is the Christ, God in the flesh. Genuine faith takes time to mature. For Peter it took three years of watching and listening to Jesus before he was able to make his confession.

Our Lord responded to Peter, "Blessed are you, Simon son of Jonah, for this was not revealed to you by man, but by my Father in heaven" (v. 17, NIV1984).

Genuine Christian faith comes into being when the Holy Spirit opens our minds to understand Jesus is God in the flesh, coming to save us from our sins. Usually it takes time to absorb enough evidence to make our confession of faith.

Last Monday night we received 140 new members into our church family. Several of those people have been attending our church over a period of ten, twenty, or even thirty-eight years. Listening to the teachings of Jesus, observing Christians, going through difficult times in their own lives. Finally, that special moment came when they could confess Jesus is the Christ, the Son of God, "My savior."

To those seeking evidence in order to believe he is the Christ, Jesus offers:

- his life and teachings;
- his sacrifice on the cross;
- his resurrection, gift of forgiveness and eternal life; and
- his church and our life together.

If these "signs" are not enough, nothing else will create genuine faith within the hearts of those who seek a Savior.

Jesus draws a final contrast between genuine versus phony faith:

- Genuine Christian faith is costly at first followed by a reward.
- Phony faith is cheap at first, but in the end, it costs a person everything.

After informing his disciples that his ministry would end on the cross, Jesus gave them this promise: "If anyone would come after me, he must deny himself and take up his cross and follow me. For whoever wants to save his life will lose it, but whoever loses his life, will find it" (vv. 24–25, NIV1984).

Rather than a magic umbrella of protection, Jesus promises a cross to those who follow him. What is a cross? Consider these examples within our own church family:

- One fellow was told he was jeopardizing his career by this "Jesus stuff," making others uncomfortable by his changed behavior.

- Another lost the support of her non-Christian family.

Sometimes a cross is willingness to stick to our commitments, even when there are few rewards for hanging on. Other times, a cross can be a decision to remain holy in an unholy world. Still other times, a cross can be the decision just to "show up" and remain responsible, even though every fiber of your being wants to take a vacation from being responsible.

I have concluded that people often discover genuine Christian faith through a "cross" of brokenness, a period when all support systems but Jesus are ripped away. Only when other support systems are gone do we realize Jesus is enough.

Sometimes we can be very stubborn in letting go of lesser things. Sometimes God uses extreme measures to loosen our grip on things we cannot keep, so we are free to grasp those things we can never lose. These extreme measures Jesus calls a cross.

Our text raises the issue of genuine versus phony faith. Genuine faith is commitment to Jesus Christ, regardless of the rewards we receive in this life. I firmly believe it's worth any cost to belong to Jesus, the King of Kings, Head of every nation on Earth—the one before whom every person in history will bow in submission—the ultimate judge of every human being. My greatest treasure is to be assured Jesus will say on Judgment Day, "You belong to me!"

If Jesus is the Son of God, all time and eternity hang in the balance to the answer you give to this question: "Who do you say that I am?"

Genuine faith confesses: You are the Christ, the Son of God—and I commit myself to you, trusting your love for time and eternity—no matter what the cost!

Questions for Study and Discussion:

1. If you were asked, "Who is Jesus?" how would you respond? Has your answer changed over time?

2. What characteristics did Walt assign to genuine versus phony faith? Where would you say your faith is genuine, and where do you need more growth and maturity?

"He changed my life" is a phrase that thousands of us have said about Walt and will say for years to come.

My first real conversation with Walt happened six years after I started attending Menlo Park Presbyterian Church. I had joined the staff, for one year only, as the interim college-group director, giving it just the one year because I was determined to be a college professor. Somehow that one-year thing never seemed to register with Walt; he basically just ignored it.

Nor was I ever supposed to preach during my one year, but there was a last-minute need for a preacher and Walt scheduled me. It was the end of August, when church attendance is low, and I think he figured I couldn't do much damage.

After I preached the first service, he took me into the sacristy and said, "You're going to be a great pastor."

I thought, "You mean, professor, Walt . . . but thanks anyway."

He gave me three suggestions for improvement, put his hand on my shoulder, and said, "God's going to use you."

As he left, I thought, "I'll follow him anywhere." Ninety seconds, and he changed my life. I went into that room a professor and—poof!—came out a pastor.

It wasn't what he said. It was how he said it. Like he believed in me. Like he saw things in me that I didn't see in myself. There is a verb for what I experienced. I was "Walted." If you've ever been Walted, you know the way Walt could deeply encourage you and make you feel at ease. You know the way he made you believe that, with Jesus, the best was still to come. The way he made you know that God is in a good mood.

He was a walking battery, ready to charge anyone up who needed it.

But the best thing Walt did for me and for thousands of us was always point us to Jesus. With Walt, it was all about Jesus.

Sometimes I'd call or visit him for advice. I'd present some problem I was dealing with in my new church and he'd say, "Yes, that's hard. Well, this is where you'll learn to hang on to Jesus."

Then I'd present another issue, and he'd say, "Yes, that's hard."

"Yes," I'd think. "I know it is, Walt, that's why I'm asking you about it!"

"Well," he'd say after a while, "you'll learn to hang on to Jesus."

"Yes, yes, yes," I'd think, "but give me a practical answer."

I finally realized that that was his answer. Not only his answer, but his strategic plan, his long-term vision, quarterly goals, milestones, and all his measurables . . . Jesus.

Scott Dudley
Senior Pastor, Bellevue Presbyterian Church
Bellevue, WA

THE BARNABAS TOUCH

Acts 15:36–41; Philippians 2:1–5
May 19–20, 1990

Today we study a lesser-known hero of the New Testament named Barnabas. His name means "son of encouragement," a name reflecting a lifestyle of love and caring. Barnabas sold property and brought the profit to be used for the poor (Acts 4:36–37). Shortly after Paul's conversion, when all Christians in Jerusalem still fearfully considered Paul a persecutor of the church, Barnabas stuck his neck out and vouched that Paul was really a Christian. Paul and Barnabas became close friends.

One day, a young Christian named John Mark was invited to join these two men on a missionary journey. Persecution was intense. Young Mark became frightened and ran home. Later, Mark wanted to try again. Paul didn't want to risk a second failure with a guy who had broken under pressure. Young Mark was devastated to hear his hero say, "You had your chance and blew it. Possibly you'll minister again, but not on my team!"

But just when Mark felt his worst, Barnabas came saying, "Hey, Mark, *enough*! I still believe in you! Everybody is entitled to a mistake. To prove Jesus hasn't given up on you, I'm leaving Paul. You and I will be the new team!" (Acts 15:36–41).

Every one of us need this "Barnabas touch." Therefore, let me high-light two biblical truths from our story.

First, every Christian needs a Barnabas. Why? Because, like John Mark, we all make big mistakes; we all encounter difficulties. God doesn't want us to go through tough times without a Christian friend by our side. Some of you, because of the size of this church, have felt abandoned in periods of personal pain. You reached out for someone, and no one was there. My prayer is that God will help our church family do an even better job caring for each other. We all need the Barnabas Touch. As the Bible says:

> *Two are better than one. . . . If either of them falls down, one can help the other up. But pity anyone who falls and has no one to help them up.* (Eccl. 4:9–10)

James Baker is a Christian and also Secretary of State. Asked about the most important lesson he learned in Washington, he answered:

> *I have learned that temporal power is fleeting. . . . The people who wouldn't return my phone calls before I came to Washington are not going to return them after I leave. . . . Too often independence, self-reliance, are said to be the path to success. But the truth of the matter is, we do need one another if we are going to make it through this life in our private and our public capacities.*[13]

Needing each other—that's a very Christian kind of need. James Baker speaks of his Christian friends as partners, people with whom he shares life's journey. Jesus relied on friends like Peter, James, John, Lazarus, Mary, and Martha.

The story of Barnabas warns us: Don't get so caught up in the fast lane of life that you trade the cultivation of Christian friendships for material goals. Tough times will come—moments of failure, temptation, despair, grief. Jesus created the church because he doesn't want us to face these times alone.

This week there have been some tough moments for me. Happily, an investment I made in friendship paid off with a card on my desk this morning, which reads:

For the times I've needed the blessing of kindness,

For the times I've needed the blessing of understanding,

For the times I've needed reassurance,

For all the times I've needed a friend like you. . . . Thank you.

This verse was added from Philemon 1:7: "Your love has given me great joy and encouragement."

When we give the Barnabas touch to another person, that same love comes back to minister to us! That's the law of friendships. Give and it will be given to you.

Be aware, real friends who are there when you need them, who are sensitive when you're hurting . . . friends like that don't just happen. They must be cultivated. You share meals, movies, and other social events. You invest time, being willing to be vulnerable, pledging confidentiality.

If you don't have a Barnabas—if you are not in a support group—I hope this sermon will motivate you to take every action necessary to fill this void. I can't think of any better wisdom to help you emotionally, physically, and spiritually.

Now to the second truth in our story: "Every Christian is called to be a Barnabas." It's risky business to get involved with people and their problems, to join a group. However, once we receive the "Barnabas touch," like an involuntary reaction we feel compelled to reach out and touch others.

I want to share a chapter in my life, unfamiliar to most of you, that might explain why I preach so much love and grace, and why I'm so eager for everyone in our church to have Christian friends and join a support group.

Years ago I was a struggling youth pastor, seeking to relocate. At that point in my life, for a whole bunch of reasons, I was a broken guy needing lots of encouragement, needing a friend who believed in me. I interviewed at several churches and was flatly rejected. No one wanted a wounded bird on their staff. By God's grace I met Paul Cox, a pastor in Redondo Beach, a man who knew about giving grace and new beginnings without judgment. A few weeks later, I was given a job.

Two sidebars: Shortly after my interview with Paul Cox, I had made the decision that if Redondo said no, I would leave the ministry. That, and I had met a young woman on my first Sunday in Redondo Beach. One year later, Metta and I were married. Twenty-four years and four children later, I still thank God for sending a Barnabas named Paul Cox to give a John Mark named Walt a second chance at ministry and a new beginning with life itself.

My whole ministry since that experience has centered on encouraging people to cultivate friendships and to be available for others in tough times, as Paul Cox was available for me.

Being a Barnabas means we are willing to come alongside people who are struggling. Usually such persons are those with whom we have invested time, who trust us. Ralph Waldo Emerson wrote:

> *We take care of our health, we lay up money, we make our roof tight, and our clothing sufficient, but who provides wisely that he shall not be wanting in the best property of all—friends?*[14]

There are so many ways to give the "Barnabas touch." I mentioned to a prayer group how occasionally I allow critical letters to get to me. The next day I received a beautiful note: "Walt, you are doing a great job. If you get any more critical letters, send them to me. Let me be your complaint department!"

I can't describe the healing impact of that kind of love and encouragement. That's the Barnabas touch. Such a gift would not have happened, if that person had not taken time to write a letter, to reach out and touch. It takes time to be a Barnabas, to reach out to those in pain.

Last week, our church family lost a good friend, Francis Johnson. Francis was a Barnabas of the first magnitude. I remember shortly after I arrived, he said to me, "Walt, I don't want to be one of those old fogies, criticizing everything you attempt to do that's new. If Menlo Park Presbyterian Church is going to grow, it has to change. I want to support you in preparing for the future, rather than be an anchor holding you in the past."

Francis kept his word. Consistently for the last sixteen years, this man gave me the Barnabas touch in many beautiful ways. I will miss him, but his model will continue to inspire me to do a better job reaching out to others.

One of my many dreams for this church family is that God fills us with support and encouragement for each other, gifts Jesus equips us to share, if we open ourselves to his Spirit.

The bottom line our text teaches:

- Don't walk through tough times alone! And
- Take time to cultivate friendships! Join a support group.

When you invest in friendships while the sun is shining, friends will be there in times of crisis.

Giving people the Barnabas touch works. Listen to an obscure text in 2 Timothy. Paul in prison, deserted by his friends and very discouraged, writes, "Get Mark and bring him with you, because he is helpful to me in my ministry" (2 Tim. 4:11).

Mark had grown up. Now he gives Paul the "Barnabas touch."

A gift I wish for all of you: Friendship is the comfort, the inexpressible comfort of feeling safe with a person having neither to weigh thoughts nor measure words, but pouring them all right out just as they are, chaff and grain together, certain that a faithful friendly hand will take and sift them, keep what is worth keeping and with a breath of kindness blow the rest away. A friend is one who knows all about you and loves you just the same. A friend is one who walks in when the whole world has walked out.

Perhaps this verse summarizes it all: "Carry each other's burdens, and in this way you will fulfill the law of Christ" (Gal. 6:2).

Questions for Study and Discussion:

1. Where in your life have you experienced the "Barnabas touch" from someone? Where in your life have you been a Barnabas to another? Would the people you encounter consider you more a Barnabas, or a critic and naysayer?

2. Friendships require nurturing. Where might God be calling you this week to encourage and invest?

There Is a Place for You

1 Corinthians 1:26–29, 12:12–27

May 7, 1989

In 1980, Mr. Jaime Escalante came to Garfield High School in East Los Angeles with a dream that barrio kids could learn and break free from their trap of mediocrity in our society. Against incredible opposition from his colleagues, who said it couldn't be done, Mr. Escalante taught his students advanced math, to the level where they were able to take the Advanced Placement Test for Calculus. These students gave up summer vacations, arriving early at school and staying late, because they caught a vision that they could do something they hadn't done before. With enough faith, blood, sweat, and tears, they could win victory over mediocrity. And they did!

In 1982, eighteen students from Garfield High School passed the Advanced Placement Test for Calculus, much to the surprise of the Educational Testing Service.

In 1983, thirty-one students passed this placement test.

In 1984, sixty-three students passed.

In 1985, seventy-seven students passed.

In 1986, seventy-eight students passed.

In 1987, eighty-seven students passed.

This truth relates to us, in that many of us are "barrio Christians," totally conditioned and intimidated into spiritual mediocrity by our surrounding culture. We have been reduced to thinking the purpose of Christianity is to make us personally successful. I believe God wants to change us. He wants us to take our eyes off ourselves and focus on others. He wants to give us a vision:

- that we can do more for Christ than we think we can;

- that we can do more than we ever dared attempt to do before; and

- that we can do more than a skeptical world watching us thinks we can or will do.

Recently I was talking with a gentleman who lives part of the year at Palm Springs, and the other part in a lakefront house at Tahoe. He described how he and his wife had been planning this kind of retirement for years. Most of us would feel God had richly blessed us if we had such an existence. I asked him if he was happy. His response didn't surprise me: "I'm so bored. I wish I had something significant to do with my life. Golf isn't enough!"

Beginning last January, this pulpit began challenging us to invest ourselves in some kind of ministry to others. God designed us to do more with this treasure called life than spend it on ourselves. The most happy people I know are not the wealthy and powerful who spend life on themselves, but those who have found the secret of giving themselves away for the sake of others. In this perspective, let's study our text.

First, *every Christian has a unique ministry to perform within the body of Christ.* Our text reads, "The body is a unit, though it is made up of many parts; and though all its parts are many, they form one body. So it is with Christ" (1 Cor. 12:12, NIV1984).

When Jesus physically left this world, he did not leave a club to exist in his memory. He commissioned a group of disciples to continue his work of caring for people. Christians are the flesh and blood "body" of Jesus, still at work in the world today. Testimonies in this service reveal the joy that happens inside of us when we step beyond ourselves, our own agendas, and become involved with someone else's need.

If God would grant you one wish, what would be your request? I wonder how many would ask for the equivalent of a house at Tahoe and Palm Springs, security for retirement, and other toys our culture associates with success? Haven't we heard enough evidence that a life built around self brings only misery? Wouldn't it make sense to at least begin listening to people who are finding joy and fulfillment by investing themselves in others? You and I were designed to live by a creed greater than the modem cliché: "He who has the most toys wins!"

In stark contrast, Jesus taught, "whoever wants to save their life will lose it, but whoever loses his life for me will find it" (Matt. 16:25).

If you want to find life at its highest and best, find your niche of ministry! A second truth in our text: *Accomplishing our ministry does not depend upon our competence, but upon the inner working of God's Holy Spirit.*

Two opposing attitudes cause many to fail in attempts at ministry. One group says to God, "Look, Lord, I feel it's time for me to share my talents and power with you. If you and I combine our resources, we can make things happen. Let's be partners!" But no one, no matter how powerful, educated, or successful, is competent to do ministry for Christ—until God energizes us with his Holy Spirit. You and I have nothing to offer God—except availability!

The second attitude is the other side of the coin. We come to God asking, "How can I do anything for you? I'm not qualified to represent you in the world. I don't have any skills for ministry!"

I believe the real reason we fail to find our niche for ministry has to do with pride and selfishness. Either we seek a ministry that glorifies our personal power and resources rather than God, or we are so afraid of appearing foolish that we won't risk doing anything for others. We are afraid to fail. Or we are so busy doing our own thing that we don't have time to seek God's purpose for us. Either way, *self* is the barrier to our being used of God.

Bjorn Borg was the leading tennis player in the '70s. He was a legend in his early twenties, possessing wealth and fame unequaled in the world of tennis. In the '80s, his life went into steep decline, and he dropped out of sight. Many rumors suggest he has attempted suicide. What happened to a man who seemingly had everything for which to live? Those who know him say, "Borg could not adjust to living outside the spotlight. When his skills declined and public interest turned to new heroes, Borg couldn't cope. His whole life was tennis, and he could find no meaning for his life apart from tennis."

This is a description of one who lives for self. How tragic! How common. Overcoming self and allowing God, through his Holy Spirit, to fill us with his power and love is the means by which we do ministry. Such a decision will provide us with a lifestyle of riches that neither Borg nor the gentleman with homes at Tahoe and Palm Springs know anything about—inner peace, joy, and a deep awareness that our lives are counting for God. Secular society rates us on the basis of physical appearance, athletic ability, net worth, measurable intelligence, pleasing personality. God measures our worth by our willingness to make ourselves his instruments of love in a hurting world.

Suppose we took this text seriously. At a dinner party, someone asks us, "What do you do?" Our answer no longer would be a dissertation about our accomplishments and positions of power. Instead, we might say something like this: "I'm trying to do what Christ wants done for people in my world of financial planning/construction/medicine/in my home as a parent/in my classroom as a student/in my work among people who are retired and still have lots to give." Or, "I'm a lawyer by profession, but I'm really caught up in serving people in the inner city."

I think that if these responses were said often enough, and acted upon, they would be revolutionary in telling the Bay Area that Christ is alive and well. Imagine beginning each day with this prayer: "Lord, today give me your eyes, so I can see the hurt and need around me. Give me your power so you can meet these needs through me. Give me a heart ready to pursue your agenda, rather than my own."

Let me summarize:

- God has a unique niche of ministry for each of us;
- we cannot accomplish this ministry by pumping up our own egos, but by daring to make ourselves available to the Spirit of God so our life focus can be on the needs of others.

I was reading about the Japanese concept of purchasing property in the United States. Rather than evaluating the profit potential of a piece of property over the next three to five years, the Japanese evaluate its worth over a lifetime. Therefore, they're ready to take greater risks and pay higher costs for properties than most Americans.

I pray we might begin to measure the value of our lives using God's criteria of eternity, rather than by the short-term goals of what our secular culture calls "success."

What about you? We have heard from a few people today who have dared to step out, to get beyond themselves. Why not begin by taking a step outside yourself this week?

- Find one person in the office, classroom, or neighborhood who needs you.
- Become involved in a community or foreign ministry in which you actually invest yourself in people.
- Teach children in our church school for the summer months, giving our regular teachers a break.
- If you have the gift of making money, I remind you that the caring ministry of MPPC rests upon our willingness to share. If our church is going to give over three million dollars this year, it means all of us have to step outside of ourselves.

As we enter this World Outreach Week, I challenge you to start a journey outside of yourself. A secular world watches a church like ours. Most are skeptical that we will do anything more than attempt to use

Jesus to advance our own success and wealth. Why not surprise the spectators? For you who are in such pain today, the thought of caring for others seems impossible. Let me suggest that the greatest therapy for hearts that are breaking and bodies that are hurting is to get involved with someone who needs you!

And when you find your ministry, please write and tell me about it.

Questions for Study and Discussion:

1. When told that you have a ministry in Christ, what is your reaction? Do you feel energized or inadequate? In what ways have you subsided into a "barrio Christian" mentality?

2. As you think where you spend most of your time and energies, where might God be leading you to a ministry opportunity? Who might he want you to reach out to, or where might he be asking you to invest?

God's Answer for Chronic Fatigue

Deuteronomy 5:12–15; Isaiah 58:13–14
May 23–24, 1992

L ast week we discussed these biblical mandates from Philippians 4:4–6 for coping with stress:

- "Rejoice in the Lord always," no matter what's going on in your life;
- Have no anxiety about anything; and
- Pray about everything, filled with expectation because we know God will respond.

I believe obeying these divine guidelines can make our lives become a fulfillment of this promise from Jesus: "I have come that [you] might have life, and have it to the full" (John 10:10).

Today I want to talk about another gift God gives us to relieve our stress: the gift of rest, of taking time to *live*. Time is life! Bob Welsh, in his book, *There Is More to Life Than Having It All,* tells how Robert

Simon, a CBS news correspondent, was taken captive by Iraqi forces during the Persian Gulf War. After being freed, Simon told reporters that, during his imprisonment, he realized everything he had ever done or seen throughout the world as a correspondent meant far less to him than his *relationships*.

Why do we start thinking about how we are investing our lives only when we are in danger of losing them? Why do our day-to-day schedules often reflect just the opposite of what we say is important to us? It seems we have pushed the fast-forward button on our lives, and we desperately need to hit the "pause" and "play" buttons. Today I want to discuss how God offers us help in trading "fast-forward" for "pause" and "play," by studying one of his Ten Commandments: "Observe the Sabbath day by keeping it holy" (Deut. 5:12).

A first truth to note in this commandment: *Setting aside one day each week for rest is not religious ritual; it's a precious divine gift.*

When God commanded us, "Observe the Sabbath day by keeping it holy," he was reminding us he didn't create human beings to run on "fast-forward" seven days a week. Disobeying his commandment causes us to think, "I'm so busy doing what I have to do, I can't find time to do things I want to do. I'm existing, but I'm not living, and I can't break free."

In Thornton Wilder's play *Our Town*, the character Emily, who died in her thirties in a tragic death, is given a chance to go back and witness the day she turned twelve. In doing so, she realizes all the nuances of life she had never seen. She says:

> *It goes so fast. We don't have time to look at one another. . . . Good-bye world, good-bye to clocks ticking and Mama's sunflowers and food and coffee. And new-ironed dresses and hot baths and sleeping and waking up. Do any human beings ever realize life while they are living it—every minute?*[15]

In America the idea of a Sabbath, taking one day in seven for rest and enjoyment, has been dead for decades. As a result, our schedules have raced out of control. We can shop twenty-four hours a day. With phones in our cars, we can capitalize on commute time that used to be set aside for thinking, reflection, prayer. What's more critical, we are even training our children to be like us, filling every minute of their days with activities, leaving little time for "doing nothing," for being children, for having a family life. One survey indicated that only 30 percent of families share dinner together.

Knowing the addictive nature of hyperactivity, God *commanded* us to take one day a week to rest, to enjoy, to push the "pause" and "play" buttons. God took a day off himself, after he created the world. The Bible says:

> *Remember the Sabbath by keeping it holy. . . . For in six days the Lord made the heavens and the earth, the sea, and all that is in them, but he rested on the seventh day. Therefore the Lord blessed the Sabbath day and made it holy.* (Exod. 20:8, 11–12)

This gift of resting one day a week was part of creation, given *before* Moses received the Ten Commandments!

For you who worship on Saturday and wonder if you are violating the Sabbath, please understand this command to honor the Sabbath day is a principle, not a specific day. As a pastor, I never take Sunday off—I take Friday! For the Jews, it was Saturday. The principle we are called to obey is to take one day a week for recovery after expenditure, for refreshment after exhaustion, for relaxation after stress.

God created life to be lived in rhythm, like the rise and fall of the tides, light and darkness, spring and winter. Even our heart alternates between beating and resting. There are times when we have to allow ourselves to just *be,* rather than *do.*

When the Jews were delivered from bondage in Egypt, they observed Saturday as a time to remember their four hundred years of slavery, in which they never had a day off. Listen to our text:

> *Remember that you were slaves in Egypt and that the* LORD *your God brought you out of there with a mighty hand and an out-stretched arm. Therefore the* LORD *your God has commanded you to observe the Sabbath day.* (Deut. 5:15)

How strange that many of us are willing to fall back into the role of slaves to schedules, disobeying God about observing a day of rest! No wonder many are in bondage to stress, pressure, hypertension, worka-holism. No wonder many suffer regret for decisions in allocating this non-renewable resource called "time."

A first truth in this text affirms: *Setting aside one day a week for rest is not a luxury but a necessity—a gift from God we neglect at our peril.* And the second truth in this commandment is immediately apparent: *Obeying this commandment requires discipline.* Our text says:

> *If you keep your feet from breaking the Sabbath and from doing as you please on my holy day, if you call the Sabbath a delight and the* LORD'S *holy day honorable, and if you honor it by not going your own way, and not doing as you please or speaking idle words, then you will find your joy in the* LORD. (Isa. 58:13–14)

Discipline is required to take a day of rest, because most of us are addicted to activity. We can't stop! We don't know what to do with a "day off" that isn't crammed full of things to do! Note the text tells us *not* to do as *we* please on our day of rest. In our culture, this means to stop the hyperactiv-ity to which we are addicted . . . and take time to rest and to live.

Remember porches? When I was a child, almost every house had a porch. Our neighbors would sit on their porches in the evening and watch the world go by. On the porch, people would read the paper and catch up on what had happened that day with the family. The porch was a place to think. Now television has replaced the front porch, and with that change we have lost sunsets, conversations, and relationships. If you doubt the role television plays, think of the publicity of Johnny Carson retiring, a man people claimed was sort of a "savior" for them, taking them through times of need—and all of that help came through an electronic box!

Discipline is required to reclaim our day of rest and the relationships we have lost. Too often our day off is filled with frantic hyperactivity, doing things we think have to be done instead of doing things we want to do.

Let me list some symptoms that might indicate we are not exercising the discipline necessary to observe a Sabbath day:

- We become so tired that rest doesn't transfuse us with new energy.
- We go on a break and can't get our mind off work, returning with no sense of refreshment, only dread of facing the tasks of another week.
- We daydream of breaking free and walking away.
- Or, our bodies begin to revolt in ill health.

Refusing God's gift of a day of rest can cause our souls and bodies to cough, sputter, and eventually break down. Last week in staff meeting, we were told about a minister who couldn't say no to anything. He never took time off and always pushed his energy level to the limit. A friend told him, "You are going to take a rest one way or another. Take time off, or you will take it on your back or in the grave." That minister died at age fifty-three!

Disobeying this command can literally kill us emotionally, spiritually, and physically! I repeat: God didn't plan for us to limp through life chronically tired, enslaved to work, missing relationships and the pleasure of simply taking time to live. Observing the Sabbath becomes a source of joy, a delight. However, to obey this command requires the strictest spiritual discipline.

As we close, let me suggest how to enjoy a Sabbath day. I believe a day of rest should include:

- time for fun, doing things we *want* to do, as we break our addiction to schedules;

- time to rediscover the art of conversation, of simply enjoying family and friends;

- time to take naps, go for walks, go out for brunch;

- time for reflection, an "accounting module" in which we evaluate our relationships, marriage, job; and

- a time when we break the rhythm of work and think about *why* we are working.

To summarize the wisdom in this commandment: Be reminded that setting aside a day of rest for rest is not a luxury but a necessity; it is a gift that requires discipline to enjoy; and, it is a day that needs to be planned, so that rest and renewal can happen.

One writer says:

> *What is life about? It is not about writing great books, amassing great wealth, achieving great power. It is about loving and being loved. It is about enjoying your food and sitting in the sun, rather than rushing through lunch and hurrying back to the office. It is about savoring the beauty of moments that don't last...the sunsets, the leaves turning color, the rare moments of true human communication. It is about savoring them, rather than missing out on them because we are so busy and they will not hold still until we get around to them.*[16]

As we approach summertime, I invite you—I give you *permission* in the name of Jesus Christ—to consider this commandment and take time for rest. Do it regularly, one day a week.

Questions for Study and Discussion:

1. How disciplined are you about keeping a day of rest in your week? What gets in the way? What are the results?

2. How might God be calling you to break your addiction to "hyper-activity"? What small step could you take to carve out Sabbath in your life?

WHY DO BAD THINGS HAPPEN TO GOOD PEOPLE?

2 Corinthians 12:7–10
October 30–31, 1999

All of us at some time will lock horns with the issue of a loving God and a suffering world—earthquakes, nuclear accidents, hurricanes, disease, broken relationships, violence, injustice.

Probing deeper, throughout the whole Bible suffering is part of the biography of God's people. Job, being the best example, was a righteous man whom God allowed to be buffeted by satanic tragedy. Sooner or later, all of us will be sitting where Job sat—on the ashes of human loss and inexplicable pain. When we have been knocked helpless by the unexpected or felt the numbness of a senseless loss, what do we do? How do we cope?

Let's learn from the apostle Paul, as he found spiritual resources to persevere in tough times. When we suffer, Jesus doesn't give us an explanation, he gives us his presence. Our Lord did not say, "I have explained the world"; he said, "I have overcome the world."

Paul the apostle had what he called a thorn in his flesh, "a messenger of Satan":

> *Three times I pleaded with the Lord to take it away from me. But he said to me, "My grace is sufficient for you, for my power is made perfect in weakness."* (2 Cor. 12:8–9)

Jesus didn't give Paul an explanation for why he had the thorn. He simply responded that his grace and power were sufficient. Obviously, this was not the answer Paul expected or desired, but his faith was so strong that he embraced this marvelous mystery of our faith—namely, that weakness is strength, when we hold the hand of Jesus in the midst of our pain.

I was so impressed by the faith of the Baptist pastor in Texas, following the shooting in his congregation. When asked by Larry King, "How does your faith sustain you in a time like this?" he said, "We know beyond a shadow of a doubt where our loved ones are, with whom they are, and that's enough."[17] Rather than seeking to explain the tragedy, knowing these victims were in the presence of Jesus was enough.

When in crisis, our feelings make us think we need an explanation. Actually, what we need are resources to get through the crisis. Two weeks ago, Renee Bondi was with us. Doug Ferguson, our associate pastor, asked her, "How did you survive becoming a quadriplegic, months before your wedding, and then living as a wife and mother?" Remember her answer? "Jesus Christ!" That answer makes no sense if Jesus is a stranger. It makes total sense if we know him as our Savior and best friend. Not an explanation, but a presence.

When Jesus sought to comfort his disciples the night before his death, he comforted them by promising that he would see them again, and that their sorrow would be turned into joy. Jesus meets us in our sorrow. Isaiah tells us, "Surely he took up our pain and bore our suffering" (Isa. 53:4). Jesus himself promises, "Never will I leave you; never will I forsake you" (Heb. 13:5).

Last weekend we were blessed by Brennan Manning, our speaker for the Family of God conference. He told of his years in the depths of alcoholism, a broken-down drunk—even though a priest. During those dark times, one friend would fly down once a month, sit on the curb with him in his alcoholic state, and assure him, "Brennan, it's going to be okay. You are going to be all right." He said Jesus enfleshed himself in that friend, enabling him to grasp the grace to find his way to recovery. Not an explanation, but a presence—that's a first resource Jesus gives us to cope with pain.

A second resource for coping with suffering: if we can't change the situation, through faith, we can change our attitude. "Therefore I will boast all the more gladly about my weaknesses, so that Christ's power may rest on me" (2 Cor. 12:9b).

Here is a guy with a huge thorn in his flesh. When Jesus answered "no" to his begging for healing and relief, Paul did something only one who holds tightly to Jesus can do. He changed his attitude from begging for relief to boasting about what his Lord was going to do with his weakness.

Going back to our conference speaker Brennan Manning, what impressed us was not his eloquence, but his humility and willingness to boast about how God had taken him from the brokenness of the gutter of alcoholism to a pulpit ministry that disarms the hardest skeptic. What's more, he was quick to say God loved him just as much when he sat in the gutter, as he did when he was preaching the good news to us. That's how faith can change our attitude toward thorns that cause so much pain.

Chuck Swindoll writes:

> *The longer I live, the more I realize the impact of attitude on life. . . . It will make or break a company, a church, a home. The remarkable thing is we have a choice every day regarding the attitude we will embrace for that day . . . I am convinced that life is 10% what happens to us and 90% how we react to it. And so it is with you. We are in charge of our attitudes.*[18]

Awful things happen to Christians, many of which will never be changed in this life. But one dimension of suffering that can always be changed by trusting Jesus is our attitude. Keep in mind, our attitude matters to God and impacts what watching people think of our Savior, as they watch believers in crisis.

The TV show *48 Hours* featured a family that had been struck by a hit-and-run truck driver seventeen years earlier. In that accident, their baby boy had been burned over 88 percent of his body. Recently, the driver had been found and brought to trial. After years of suffering, the whole family appeared in the courtroom to confront the driver. The boy, at seventeen, is grossly disfigured, but his attitude is beautiful. He is a Christian. When asked if he held resentment against the driver, he said, "No, I have forgiven him. I just want him to know the incredible suffering he caused, when he left without looking back." His attitude of forgiveness, acceptance, and looking for the blessing in his pain prevented him from being eaten alive by bitterness and hatred. Trusting Jesus can transform our attitude when we confront suffering.

A third truth to consider: suffering can be a stepping-stone to ministry. Once we trust Jesus enough to change our attitude, every painful event in our lives can be put to use. Listen again to Paul's faith in the midst of another page of suffering in his life: "I want you to know, brothers and sisters, that what has happened to me has actually served to advance the gospel" (Phil. 1:12). How can he think this?

> *[W]e know that in all things God works for the good of those who love him. . . . For I am convinced that neither death nor life, neither angels nor demons, neither the present nor the future, nor any powers, neither height nor depth, nor anything else in all creation, will be able to separate us from the love of God that is in Christ Jesus our Lord.* (Rom. 8:28, 38–39)

One elder who has been in the twelve-step program reminded us that most of the leaders in twelve-step recovery come from the ranks of those who found healing in the group. Any thorn which we are called upon to endure is never wasted in God's economy. Suffering can enlarge our view of God and expand our faith and usefulness, or it can fill us with self-pity, poisoning our hearts with bitterness.

In my experience, every tragedy, pain, suffering, grief, disappointment, and loss I have been called upon to bear, is a central ingredient to any usefulness I have had in ministry. It's true—weakness is strength. God's resources become operative the moment we confess our helplessness. I'd like to read the following poem entitled, "The Blessing of Unanswered Prayers":

I asked God for strength, that I might achieve; I was made weak, that I might learn humbly to obey.

I asked for health, that I might do greater things; I was given infirmity, that I might do better things.

I asked for riches, that I might be happy; I was given poverty, that I might be wise.

I asked for power, that I might have the praise of men. I was given weakness, that I might feel the need for God.

I asked for things that I might enjoy life, and I was given life, that I might enjoy all things.

I got nothing that I asked for . . . but everything I had hoped for.

I am among all men, most richly blessed.[19]

So what about you today? What is your thorn? What is your attitude toward its presence in your life? Be reminded that God loves you. Nothing in your life right now is a denial of his love. Know that your doubting, anger with God, despairing that He hears or cares—all of those feelings are okay. Our Lord doesn't rebuke you, He cries with you. You belong to him; you are his child.

I invite you to take your thorns to God in prayer and lay them at his feet. Tell him all that you feel about your illness, your wayward child, your loneliness, your painful marriage, your endless struggle with finances, your feeling your life is a grave disappointment to God and to those you love, your constant regression into sin. Our thorns are as different as our names. Remember the promise of God through Joel the prophet: "I will repay you for the years the locust have eaten" (Joel 2:25). And the words of Habakkuk:

> *Though the fig tree does not bud and there are no grapes on the vines, though the olive crop fails and the fields produce no food, and though there are no sheep in the pen and no cattle in the stalls, yet I will rejoice in the LORD, I will be joyful in God my Savior.* (Hab. 3:17–18)

Bring your thorn to God, along with all the pain and bitterness connected with bearing it. Let him love you. Let him hold you in the palm of his hand. Let him restore and establish your joy and fill you with his strength. Remember: when we are weak, we are strong.

Questions for Study and Discussion:

1. What thorns in your life has God chosen not to remove? How did you respond? If you never received an explanation, have you ever experienced a "presence"?

2. How might it change our attitudes while suffering, to believe what Brennan Manning declared, that God loved him just as much when he sat in the gutter, as he did when he was preaching the good news?

When I met my dad, I was seven years old. This would be my third foster home. Initially, I did not want a new home. When we knocked on the door, Walt answered and welcomed us. A very warm and inviting welcome indeed! After a tour of the house and time spent with the family, I thought this wouldn't be so bad after all. While official adoption would take place much later, from day one my dad and I had a special connection. No question he was my hero and always my biggest advocate.

I adored him and followed him everywhere, telling him everything about my day. "Such big stories!" he would say, as he turned and walked down the hall. I had to chase after him, saying, "I'm not near done with my big stories!"

I loved it when he would pick me up from school on his motorcycle and take me for wild rides down the Pacific Coast Highway. When we got home, he would tell me the speed we reached and asked if I was scared. "No, I loved it!" I said, and we laughed together.

Tara Brees, daughter

Prayer Transforms Merely Existing into Living

Luke 11:1–13, 18:1–8
March 21, 1982

I yearn, for the sake of all of us, that God might bring a revolutionary change in our prayer habits! For my own life and ministry, prayer is a tremendous, incredible, life-changing resource—a power that makes the difference between just existing and really living. Without prayer, I wouldn't be making it as a pastor, husband, father, or friend. Handling those countless impossible situations crossing my path daily would quickly become an impossible obstacle. Because this is true for me, I ask myself, "Why do most Christians take so little time for prayer?" One survey indicates the average Christian spends three minutes a day in prayer. Only one percent of Christian couples pray together. If reward is one motivator for behavior change, let me affirm you can't imagine the impact for good that daily prayer will provide for you. Last week our guest mentioned that the great saint George Mueller logged fifty thousand specific answers to prayers! I'm not surprised.

Recently Dr. Munger[20] took a group of staff and church leaders for an all-day prayer retreat. You might ask the question: "How could anyone spend a whole day in prayer?" I doubt you would think it strange if an individual spent a whole day fishing, shopping, or golfing. My point is, we need a clearer understanding of the meaning, purpose, and potential power prayer provides for those who would give it a central place in their priorities. God asks us to pray about everything—when we feel overburdened or frightened, and as a source of divine wisdom when we face decisions and don't know which way to go. Personally, my reservoir of answered prayer is astonishing.

God has responded miraculously to my specific needs and requests when I didn't conceive of any possible human solution. I'm convinced of God's closeness and availability in our daily experience, a closeness we appropriate through prayer.

In the hope that you might discover this potential for yourself, I want to share two parables of Jesus revealing what God is like—information that hopefully will explode some of our misconceptions and stimulate us to pray.

In our first story, Luke says of Jesus, "he told his disciples a parable to show them that they should always pray and not give up" (Luke 18:1).

Read the newspapers, and it's easy to lose heart! Consider your own impossible challenges on any given day, and it's easy to lose heart. I'm convinced, if we seek to live whole Christian lives in these broken times, we must tap into this divine energy source called prayer. God wants to hear from us and promises that when we ask for a fish, he will not give us a scorpion. When we ask for bread, he will not give us a stone. Jesus says we need not lose heart, even when faced with over-bearing burdens and situations, because with God *nothing* is impossible. God doesn't run out on us when the pressure is on, nor does he shout down to us when we cry out, "Hey, I'm busy now; you handle it yourself." Jesus says we are not bothering God when we pray. He is not too busy. A first truth about prayer is that it is a resource against losing heart, because it is an act of faith, claiming we believe God is available, that he does love and care about us and will share his unlimited, divine resources in response to our prayers.

A second truth about prayer Jesus unveils in these stories concerns God's nature. Many of us have misconceptions about God's character. Jesus says God is not a reluctant neighbor who must be persuaded and threatened, in order to help us in time of need. God is not a reluctant judge who must be badgered into responding to our cries for help. Perhaps one reason we neglect prayer is rooted in our personal misunderstanding of God's character.

Jesus says God is a Father who makes himself totally available to us. He never sleeps. He listens when we speak. His arm need not be twisted in order to respond to our needs.

Jesus reveals prayer is not our attempt to overcome God's reluctance to help us, or to awaken him to awareness of our need. Prayer is not an act of confessing to a vindictive judge, to win him over to our point of view. God already is on our side, our Friend whose heart is already open to us, whose ultimate desire is to share life's struggles with us. I believe one reason we avoid prayer is that we don't understand or believe God's attitude toward us. The psalmist wrote:

My help comes from the LORD, the Maker of heaven and earth. He will not let your foot slip—he who watches over you will not slumber; indeed, he who watches over Israel will neither slumber nor sleep. (Ps. 121:2–4)

Do you believe God is a Father who hears you? Do you believe he is totally available and responds when you pray? If so, apart from prayer, how do you expect to claim these promises of Scripture:

Cast your cares on the LORD, and he will sustain you; he will never let the righteous be shaken. (Ps. 55:22)

When I am afraid, I put my trust in you. In God whose word I praise—in God I trust and am not afraid. What can mere mortals do to me? (Ps. 56:3–4)

Prayer is the act of "casting our burden" and "putting our trust."

These two parables provide a third truth about prayer. Jesus teaches that we are to be *persistent* in praying. Both stories indicate persistence is a vital ingredient to effective prayer, a fact which raises questions: Is God hard of hearing, that we must repeat ourselves? Does he need to be convinced and persuaded, before he will respond to our requests?

I believe there are several answers to such concerns.

Dr. Lloyd Ogilvie suggests that the purpose of prayer is not to open God's ears, or his heart, or to change his will. Persistency in prayer builds *our faith,* so that our ears, hearts, and wills become conformed to God's purposes. Persistent prayer is an exercise of discipline, helping us grow away from wanting and demanding things from God, to where we can say to God, "Father, it's no longer important what I want in this situation. I know you love me and I trust you. What do *you* want? I trust you that your ways and methods are higher and wiser than mine. I am your servant."

Persistent prayer also helps us when God says "no" to our prayer requests. Waiting provides opportunity for growth until we reach that perspective of accepting a "no" as God's ultimate "yes," even if it's a "yes" we will understand only in eternity. Think about it: If God provided instantaneous, unqualified responses to all our prayers, soon we would view him as simply a source for immediate gratification, a God who exists to serve us, rather than one we worship and serve.

Note what Jesus says about God's answers to our prayers: "For everyone who asks receives; the one who seeks finds; and to the one who knocks, the door will be opened" (Luke 11:10). Jesus was not specific. He did not say what we would receive when we ask, what we will find when we seek, or what door will be opened when we knock. God will answer our prayers, but not necessarily in the way or at the time we ask or expect. Only mature faith can trust all of God's answers to prayer. Most of us still come as a child, demanding what we want from a parent, with closed minds that a parent in greater wisdom will often say "no" to one thing so that we can have a greater benefit.

A third dimension for understanding persistent prayer is that such regularity provides us with an opportunity to experience God's highest purpose for prayer, namely to find relationship with himself. Listen to Jesus:

If you then, though you are evil, know how to give good gifts to your children, how much more will the Father in heaven give the Holy Spirit to those who ask him! (Luke 11:13)

Here is a profound teaching about prayer: The highest purpose of prayer is not to receive answers for our requests. The highest purpose of prayer is to enjoy friendship, relationship, and conversation with God—a gift made possible by the Holy Spirit, a gift so precious that it makes all other reasons for prayer dull by comparison. I wonder how many of us actually enjoy and look forward to being in God's presence, to relating with him as we do with a friend? It was this dimension of prayer Jesus modeled during his ministry, when he often spent all night in prayer with his Father.

I close with this exhortation: Pray! Pray constantly. Pray expectantly. Pray fervently, in faith, knowing God is listening and is more anxious to answer than you are to pray. Pray for our missionaries, for our nation, our president, and leaders. Pray for peace, for an end to the insane nuclear arms race. Pray for yourself, your family. Pray for our church family, for our staff, officers, church, schoolteachers. Pray for our church family unity, and vision for what ministry God wants us to accomplish.

I have shared before how a group of people meet on Monday morning to pray for the requests you turn in. Every Saturday evening, a group of us meet to pray for Sunday morning. There is an adult class that teaches people how to pray. Join a prayer group. Everything this church accomplishes is the result of prayer. If you need miracles in your personal life, pray. God answers prayer! When answers come, give him all the glory. As the poet Tennyson wrote, "More things are wrought by prayer than this world dreams of."

The difference between a Christian who prays and one who doesn't is the difference between a person who *lives* at the edge of adventure, and one who merely *exists*, surrounded by insurmountable mountains.

Questions for Study and Discussion:

1. Describe your prayer habits. How frequently do you pray? How long? Do you follow a routine? Have you ever experienced an answer to prayer? If yes, how did you respond?

2. How would it affect your prayer life to know that God was already on your side, or to understand that he might be using prayer to make changes in *you*?

WHEN YOU HAVE WAITED
FOR GOD LONG ENOUGH

Hebrews 10:35–11:1; Psalm 40:1–5
January 25–26, 1992

Have you ever reached the point where you feel you have waited long enough for God to meet a certain need in your life? Waiting upon God—trusting his timing and methods—is the greatest challenge I face as a Christian. It seems that no matter how hard I pray, God asks me to wait for almost everything I really want—for everything I feel I desperately need—and such waiting really tests my faith!

Most of you are waiting upon God today for something:

- Some are waiting for employment and relief of that unbearable burden of financial stress.
- Some are waiting for emotional or physical healing—and the pain goes on while God seems deaf to your prayers.
- Others are waiting for healing in your marriage.
- You might be waiting for God to clarify the future of your children.
- Right now, *all* of us are *waiting for rain.*

Happily, the Bible reminds us God cares about us, that he is trustworthy, and that ultimately our waiting will be rewarded. Let's search for the wisdom in our text about learning to wait upon the Lord.

First, waiting on God is a major ingredient of our Christian faith: "Now faith is being sure of what we hope for and certain of what we do not see" (Heb. 11:1, NIV1984). Faith is unshakable trust in God's methods and timing, even when circumstances all deny the logic of such trust. Faith is trusting God even when waiting is causing us agonizing pain and we can't understand God's lack of response. Faith is certainty God loves us, even though right now it's so dark we can't see his plan.

Why is waiting an ingredient of faith? If we had instant responses to our prayers, faith would be unnecessary. We would become pampered children who use God, rather than worship him. God is God, and he refuses to become a servant to our whims and wishes.

Our text reminds us how God's favorite people throughout history have been asked to wait for things they desperately wanted—and many of them died waiting! That's faith. Chapter 11 of Hebrews closes by saying, "These were all commended for their faith, yet none of them received what had been promised" (v. 39).

Think of Abraham and Sarah. God promised them in their old age that they would have a son. Twenty years later, Isaac was born! Think of Mary and Martha's agony when their brother Lazarus was sick unto death. Jesus heard about their crisis and still remained where he was for three more days. By the time he did arrive, his friend Lazarus was dead, and the two sisters were furious. They felt betrayed by Jesus' delay, and obviously wanted to say to him, "If you really cared about us, how could you have waited so long that you allowed your friend Lazarus to die?"

I think of the pain in our church family today—the things so many of us are waiting for—and God's agonizing delay in responding to those needs. A delay we don't understand, a delay that's testing our faith to the breaking point.

Let me summarize this first truth in our text:

- Throughout the ages, God has asked his children to wait.
- Without waiting, faith would be unnecessary.
- And, all waiting is rooted in God's love and is part of his perfect plan for us.

A second truth in our text is that waiting in faith will be rewarded:

> *So do not throw away your confidence; it will be richly rewarded. You need to persevere so that when you have done the will of God, you will receive what he has promised. . . . "my righteous one will live by faith."* (Heb. 10:35–36, 38)

James also writes, "You have heard of Job's perseverance and have seen what the Lord finally brought about. The Lord is full of compassion and mercy" (James 5:11).

Several years ago, I was speaking on the subject of waiting and reminded us of this basic truth: God may seem slow, but he is never late.

There is reward in waiting. One of God's rewards for waiting is to develop in us the priceless treasure of Christian character. Think about it in your own life: What has kept you close to the Lord and built your faith? What has forced you to lean on God in blind trust because you didn't have any place else to go? Isn't it usually the pain of waiting for God to respond to your deepest cries for help?

The psalmist says: "I waited patiently for the Lord; he turned to me and heard my cry. He lifted me out of the slimy pit, out of the mud and mire; he set my feet on a rock. . . . Blessed is the one who trusts in the Lord" (Ps. 40:1–2, 4).

Here is an important insight I have discovered about waiting. God is waiting for us:

- to allow the trauma of waiting for answers to our prayers to drive us to himself;
- to discover that he alone can make our lives complete;
- to get our focus off of what we want and feel we desperately need; and
- to believe God's goodness and love is all we need to cope while waiting.

God is enough. Such knowledge enables us to postpone immediate gratification of our desires and builds in us that priceless treasure of Christian character.

Stephen Covey, in his book *Seven Habits of Effective People,* affirms that the true character of a person can only be seen in the long measure of things, in our long-term relationships—in marriage, with children, with colleagues on the job, with friends. Mature human character never appears as a blip on the screen, but is grown slowly over the long haul, after years of waiting and self-discipline.

I'm convinced that if God is asking us to wait for something, he has a reward in mind—the reward of developing our character, to make us more like Jesus himself. Please don't misunderstand. God is concerned about our needs, our heartaches and longings. What I hope the Holy Spirit will help us see is that there are spiritual treasures even more precious than God responding to our "want and wish list."

So our text gives a basic message today: If we are waiting on the Lord, remember that he is trustworthy. Remember that he knows our deepest desires and most desperate needs, and in his own time and way he will come to us. While we wait, if we understand good things are happening inside of us where our character is being molded for all eternity, we will learn to wait without feeling angry, hopeless, anxious, abandoned, or defeated. We will trust God's love, timing, and methods.

Remember, we are waiting upon a God who is all-powerful, with whom nothing is impossible! Our lives are his project, which he has promised to bring to perfect completion.

The Bible tells us God is "able to do immeasurably more than all we ask or imagine" (Eph. 3:20); and that "all things work together for good to them that love God, to them who are the called according to his purpose" (Rom. 8:28, KJV).

One final P.S.: Don't stop living while you wait! Don't think your life will begin when you get married, or have enough money, or find the ultimate job. Or when you are healed of your emotional or physical pain. Or when the lives of your children finally get straightened out. Live today. Paul the apostle went on living while waiting for God in his prison cell. He witnessed to his guards and continued building the church of Jesus. In the same way, while you are waiting:

- Get your focus off your own needs and get involved in the needs of others.

- Believe your life is fulfilled by Jesus alone and not in anything you can achieve, buy, or convince God to give you.

- Remember God is trustworthy. He will never come with too little, too late.

- Believe the process of waiting is filled with the purpose of carving the very character of Jesus into your soul.

Believe with the psalmist when he said, "*I am still confident of this: I will see the goodness of the LORD in the land of the living. Wait for the LORD; be strong and take heart and wait for the LORD*" (Ps. 27:13–14, NIV1984).

Hang in there—waiting isn't wasted time.

Questions for Study and Discussion:

1. Where in your life are you waiting? You've wished and prayed, and God doesn't seem to have moved? How has the waiting affected your attitude toward God?

2. Have you ever waited and then, finally, seen God act? Looking back, might there have been reasons for your wait? What did you learn from it, if anything?

A LOVE BIGGER THAN
OUR SECRETS

John 4:7–26
October 16–17, 1999

oday, I want us to think about secrets—about the dark side of our lives we sometimes hide from everyone but God—habits, deviant behavior, addictions, deeds in the past we can't forget. Psychologists tell us that only hidden things can hurt us. And Jesus said, "whatever is hidden is meant to be disclosed, and whatever is concealed is meant to be brought out into the open" (Mark 4:22). Secrets force us to live with fear of exposure—guilt, a feeling of hypocrisy—coupled with a sense we are trapped and can't break free.

Christianity is good news because Jesus promised that if we confess our secrets to him, he will not only forgive us but empower us to change, to start over again and live transformed lives.

No story in Scripture better illustrates that God's love is bigger than our secrets than this dialogue between Jesus and the woman of Samaria, a woman with three strikes against her. She is a moral outcast, a hybrid Jew, and a victim in a male-dominated culture. That's why she said, "How is it that you, a Jew, ask a drink of me, a woman of Samaria?"

First, some history: An ancient feud existed between Jews and Samaritans since 720 BC, when the northern kingdom of Israel was invaded by the Assyrians. Jews intermarried with these invaders, creating a hybrid offspring called Samaritans. For centuries, a racial barrier existed between "pure" Jews and "hybrid" Jews. In this drama, our Lord demonstrated how God's love climbs over every kind of racial, moral, or gender barrier. Let's watch Jesus build a friendship that sets this woman free from her secrets, enabling her to become a transformed person.

First Jesus makes an incredible offer: "If you knew the gift of God and who it is that asks you for a drink, you would have asked him and he would have given you living water" (John 4:10).

Every human heart has a thirst Jesus claims he can satisfy: a thirst for acceptance, forgiveness, hope; a thirst to leave the past behind and start over again; and a thirst for life beyond our mortality. Many seek to satisfy their thirsts with various libations of this world, by accumulating or upscaling their status, power, or consumerism; or by sexual addictions, substance abuse, or workaholism.

Jesus tells the woman in our drama and all of us that nothing in this world can satisfy our soul's thirst, apart from a relationship with him.

At first, this woman sarcastically interprets our Lord's offer of living water as a flowing spring—a magical gift freeing her from having to carry water containers to the well. How tempting it is to "use" Jesus as a solution for our needs: to heal our financial needs; to heal the pain in our bodies or stress in our souls; or to heal relationships or feelings of inadequacy that plague us. Because of this temptation, living water is often "sold" by preachers who claim, "Come to Jesus and you will find a miracle cure for every burden life inflicts upon you!"

As a second truth, Jesus reveals this woman's incredible need. Rather than giving her a "time-saving device" for transporting water, Jesus desires to give her the far greater gift of putting her in touch with her spiritual need. He tells her:

> *Everyone who drinks this water will be thirsty again, but who-ever drinks the water I give them will never thirst. Indeed, the water I give them will become in them a spring of water welling up to eternal life.* (John 4:13)

Jesus then opens the door for her to see her need, by saying: "Go call your husband." She meekly responds, "I have no husband." Tenderly he exposes the fact she has had five husbands, plus her current "live-in." *Wham-o!* All of her pain and guilt come to the surface. Pain and guilt from a past littered with sin, failure, rejection, and unfulfilled dreams.

Using this story as a catalyst, it would be good for us to check out our motivation for seeking Jesus:

- Are we here today to "commune" with Jesus, to more perfectly conform our lives to his will? To refocus from self, to care about serving others?
- Or, are we here today to "consume" our Lord's blessings, loving him for what he does for us? Attending worship to have our tastes and needs met, to be more successful, to have problems solved?

Consumer or communer? That's the question raised in this story. Do we want a relationship with Jesus as Lord of our lives, or do we merely desire his blessings?

In exposing the woman's secrets, Jesus is not seeking to humiliate her. He wants to help her understand she isn't hopelessly caught in her past and present circumstances. His offer of living water, in the gift of forgiveness, freedom, and new beginnings, can bring her total healing. As he makes contact with her deepest need, notice how the conversation suddenly jumps from well-water to the question: "Where is the best place to worship God?"

One demonic dimension of the human heart is that we attempt to hide our deepest spiritual needs in the form of denial. Denial is a powerful roadblock to healing of our inner secrets, and it's often expressed in the common attraction to what I call generic spirituality. This is the belief that resources for fixing my needs lie within me. If I can just tap into my inner energy, adopt positive mental attitudes, I'll be fine. Only when we make contact with the depth of our spiritual need, after self-help methods of generic spirituality prove deficient, does the living water Jesus offers become relevant. The psalmist illustrates one who has made contact with his spiritual need:

> My guilt has overwhelmed me, like a burden too heavy to bear. . . . I groan in anguish of heart. . . . For I am about to fall, and my pain is ever with me. I confess my iniquity; I am troubled by my sin. . . . Come quickly to help me, my Lord and my Savior. (Ps. 38:4, 8, 17–18, 22)

Awareness of our need is the catalyst leading us to believe Jesus alone holds the cure for what's wrong with us.

Thirdly, Jesus offers an incredible cure. Because the woman in the story was a Samaritan, she was excluded from her only hope for forgiveness—animal sacrifice at the temple in Jerusalem, a place out of bounds to a Samaritan. Tenderly, Jesus shares the good news that God isn't found in a place, but in a person, the Messiah. What's more, God is not an angry deity ready to "zap" her for her sins, but a Father who knows all about her and loves her just the same. This God can be worshipped anywhere, without a special temple. The woman responds by saying, "'I know that Messiah' (called Christ) 'is coming.'" And then Jesus reveals God's incredible cure for the thirst in her soul—*himself*. "I, the one speaking to you—I am he" (John 4:25–26).

I have said so often, "Christianity is not a religion, but a relationship." This woman had her religion, but it was deficient. Jesus is the Lamb of God, God in the flesh, who does what animal sacrifice could never do. He takes away the sins of the world. When Jesus offers "living water," he is offering us himself! When Jesus claims to be the Messiah, this woman is brought to a place of decision—a crossroads of belief.

John Bunyan, author of *Pilgrim's Progress*, was haunted in his early Christian experience by feeling he had committed the unpardonable sin, that he was too gross for even God to cleanse. When he read this story of the woman of Samaria, however, he connected it with the promise of Jesus given in John 6:37, "whoever comes to me I will never drive away." John Bunyan found healing then, finally believing Jesus could forgive even him.

I know there are those who sit in worship today with shame, guilt, or fear haunting their souls. You hear about the forgiveness Jesus offers but still believe that your personal sin is far too great for even Jesus to forgive. These feelings of shame fill my own heart far more frequently that I would care to admit.

Let me say it again: There is no person here today whom Jesus cannot and will not forgive, no matter what litters your track record. To drink of the living water Jesus offers requires that we believe what he is saying is true. We allow him to walk with us through the pain of truth-telling, exposing our secrets, opening every closet filled with skeletons of sin, every habit, addiction, every wrong relationship, all our greed, pride, immorality, and selfishness. Once these skeletons are exposed, Jesus forgives us, releases us, and sets us free. The cross of Jesus covers all sin. The only sin God can't forgive is our refusal to accept his incredible cure, because we don't believe we need it, or because we feel our sin is too great for him to forgive.

Jesus came here with authority to forgive sins and to pronounce us righteous in the sight of God. His atoning death, his spilled blood, cancels all sin.

I'm always amazed how current biblical stories can be. I am interested in subjects on magazine covers, used to attract readers: miracle diets to keep one young and healthy; new information about how to be sexy and attractive; scandal stories; articles about money—how to get it, how to multiply it, and how to spend it. None of these libations offered by our secular culture will permanently satisfy the thirst of the human heart. Yet the mystery remains. Most people reject the gift of our Lord's living water, a fact best illustrated in that now-famous statement of Jesse Ventura: "Religion is a sham, a crutch for weaklings."

The good news Jesus has for those of us today who are in touch with our needs, and who believe he holds the cure, is that, like the woman in our story, we can be forgiven, healed, and given a new beginning. We don't know all the details, but the woman did drink of living water that day, and it transformed her life. So dramatic was the impact of her encounter with Jesus that she went back to the townspeople who had abused and rejected her and invited them to come and drink of this living water themselves. I wish I could have been there to hear her say, "Jesus knows all my secrets, and I'm no longer ashamed. I'm forgiven! I'm free! I'm whole!"

Before we go home, let me ask, "How about you?" He brought you to church to make you an incredible offer of living water to heal your incredible need—sin. And he offers an incredible cure, by trusting him as your Lord and Savior.

What's your response? Would you allow Jesus to quench the thirst in your soul? If you feel a need to confess secrets to a safe person, Charlie Campbell will be in our healing service today to be personally available for you. You can drink of this water in the quietness of your own heart right now. We can be free from our secrets and leave church with a brand-new beginning.

Questions for Study and Discussion:

1. Where do you turn most frequently for comfort and relief, or just to escape thinking about something that troubles you? How long does the comfort last? Does it have any cost for you?

2. What truth would you tell Jesus now, in order to taste the living water he offers? What skeleton do you keep in the closet that you can hand over to him in prayer? Have you ever confessed this sin to another person, to hear the reassuring words "You are forgiven"?

My relationship with Walt started with, and can be measured by, moments in chairs.

I was thirty-eight when Peninsula Covenant Church in Redwood City, California, called me to become its lead pastor. Soon after I called Walt, who had recently retired from his long and successful tenure at Menlo Park Presbyterian Church. He gladly welcomed me into his home, and we sat in chairs in his front room.

After some introductory conversation I said, "Walt, I have some questions. May I ask you a few things?" He welcomed my questions. "How did you do strategic planning?" I asked. My pen was ready and my journal was open, but his answer wasn't at all what I expected.

"Strategic planning? We just prayed and asked Jesus where he wanted to take the church!" Every pastoral category I threw his way—weekly schedule breakdown, sermon planning, staff development, staff hires—it all was answered with the same: "We just prayed."

One time the chairs were at a local restaurant. I had called an impromptu meeting based on what I thought was an emergency. He dropped what he was doing and met with me. "I think it's over, Walt!" was my opening line. I honestly forget the specific issue I was having, but some Peninsula Covenant Church members were upset with me and threatened to leave the church if I didn't do such and such. After I laid out the whole situation, Walt, who was between bites of sourdough bread dipped in olive oil, looked at me and said, "That's it? Are you kidding me?" He then laughed and said, "Gary, you think that will do you in? Show them the exit door and thank God!" He then proceeded to share with me from his wealth of wisdom about church dynamics and how I will never please everyone.

And the chair relationship continued. . . . There were memorable conversations in chairs on Catalina Island, in chairs at

Starbucks, in chairs in my office, and in chairs in my home. For a good part of a decade, when I was in the pulpit, Walt would sit in the pew and cheer me on through his countenance and after the service go out of his way to encourage me.

He was Yoda; I was Luke Skywalker. He always would speak of grace, of his love for people, of his utter disbelief that God would use someone like him. And he would joke and laugh—his sense of humor abounded.

I am compelled to exhort us all to the lessons I learned from Walt: love people, live authentically, side on the side of extravagant grace, laugh often, believe that God is a good, good Heavenly Father, and by all means, leave room in your life for an open chair! There is a generation of men and women behind us all who would benefit from the relational investment we make in their lives.

Gary Gaddini, Lead Pastor
Peninsula Covenant Church
Redwood City, CA

LEARNING TO LISTEN
TO EACH OTHER

Matthew 13:13–14; Ecclesiastes 5:1–2
October 16, 1983

Helen Keller was asked, "If you could have either hearing or sight, which would you prefer?" Her answer? Hearing.

I believe the ability to hear, to really listen to another person is fast becoming a lost art in human relationships. An elder gave me an article from *Forbes* magazine, claiming that the main task of a consultant in solving problems is to listen to employees, because managers will not take the time to listen. Another elder suggested that a current thrust in selling is to listen to clients' needs and sell to meet those needs, rather than seek to sell a product they may not need. Our kind of world is making hearing more difficult. Noise levels in our daily environment cause a loss of physical hearing. Stress levels, preoccupation with self, and sin can cause a hearing loss in our hearts. Although our church possesses preachers, teachers, evangelists, prayer warriors, and mission troopers—all desperately needed ministries—we also need listeners. How long has it been since someone complimented you for being a good listener?

One great act of love is to give another person our undivided attention. Because of our noisy, stress-filled environment, we have developed skill in hearing without listening, becoming selective to what and to whom we listen. As we become serious about loving each other as Jesus loves us, it's important we study what Scripture says about learning to listen as an act of love.

First, Scripture links our ability to listen to each other with our willingness to listen to God. In Ecclesiastes we read this wisdom: "Guard your steps when you go to the house of God. To draw near to *listen* is better than to offer the sacrifice of fools" (Eccl. 5:1, ESV, emphasis added).

Elijah learned that the ears of our hearts easily become unable to hear the still, small voice of the Lord above the noise of earthquake, wind, and fire. God is a gentleman and will not burst into our daily conversation uninvited. Consider Revelation 3:20 (NIV1984): "Here I am! I stand at the door and knock. If anyone hears my voice and opens the door, I will come in to him and eat with him, and he with me."

God speaks to us when we read Scripture, when we have personal prayer, and during worship and class study. He speaks to us through other people in small groups and in the handiwork of creation. If we choose to avoid places and times where God speaks—if we stay so busy in pursuing things of this life that we are never quiet enough to hear his still, small voice—it shouldn't surprise us if suddenly he seems far away.

Here is a vital point about listening: When we choose to allow God's voice to be drowned out by our daily schedule, soon the voices of people with needs for whom God is holding us responsible will also be lost in the roar of activity. Losing the ability to hear the voice of our Heavenly Father allows the preoccupation with the idols of this world to set the "select knob" of our hearts' ears toward those who meet our needs rather than listening to those who need us.

Here is the bottom line of what I hope we will learn about listening today: *Being heard is so close to being loved that the two acts are indistinguishable.* To listen to someone is to love them as Jesus loves us. James offers this wisdom about listening: "My dear brothers and sisters, take note of this: Everyone should be quick to listen, slow to speak and slow to become angry" (James 1:19).

A second lesson about listening is to realize that giving our undivided attention to a person is a choice with a high price tag. Setting priorities about whom we will listen to is costly for a number of reasons. To make time for one person means we say "no" to another. Often we feel conflict over giving time to a person we believe can serve us. I find making such decisions is tough. Listening with undivided attention requires the hard work of concentration and shutting out personal interests and pressures. People know if we are being honest listeners. My wife knows when I am hearing her, and when I am just standing there. So do my children. When I'm preoccupied, when my body is there but I'm somewhere else, my wife will ask the simple question: "Where are you?" At that point I know I've had it! Most of us have had our small children seek our attention by manually turning our face and putting it next to theirs saying, "Listen to me. I want to talk to you."

Giving undivided attention is hard work from a mechanical viewpoint. There are some 600,000 words available in English, with an educated adult using approximately two thousand. For the most-used five hundred words, a standard dictionary lists 14,000 different definitions. Add the nonverbal dimensions of communication; considering that eighty percent of what we communicate is nonverbal, we begin to understand the cost of choosing to listen to our neighbor. The challenge emerges again. To whom are we choosing to listen—to those God has called us to serve, or to those who can serve us? Loving each other as Jesus loves us is always hard work!

A third lesson in learning to listen has to do with suspending our expectations and judgments. So often our communication with God centers in our efforts to convince him to do our will, rather than listening to his will for us. Unfortunately, we adopt the same behavior with each other. We tend to listen to one another with evaluation and expectations, a habit which makes us unable to hear.

A family of three, mom, dad, and son, sat down in a restaurant and began to order dinner. "And what will you have?" asked the waitress. Six-year-old Johnny replied, "I'll have a hamburger, French fries, and a coke." His mother said, "He will have a Salisbury steak and mixed vegetables." "Do you want ketchup and mustard on that hamburger?" the waitress asked Johnny. Johnny turned to his mother in astonishment and said, "Mom, she thinks I'm real!"

Suspending our tendency to judge another person while we listen to them, ceasing to make people accept what we think is best for them as did this mother for her son's diet, communicates to our neighbor, "I think you are real. You are worth my time and full attention." Keep in mind, being heard is so close to being loved that it is almost impossible to distinguish between these two acts. Listening without judgment shows respect for the other person's freedom to perceive, to feel, to value, to hold opinions different from our own. In the midst of such an atmosphere of respect and freedom, people who feel heard will take the risk of sharing deeper feelings, bringing them out into the open and dealing with them in the gentle environment of another person who cares. Listening is healing. God does not ask us to have answers, judgments, or magic cures for people's needs, only a heart that will enter their heart and listen. Remember that when our Lord was on the Mount of Transfiguration with Moses and Elijah, God interrupted Peter's plans and told him, "This is my Son, whom I love. . . . Listen to him!" (Matt. 17:5).

During our Lord's ministry, he demonstrated incredible skill in listening to children, to a man filled with demons, to a woman from Samaria with a shady background, to blind Bartimaeus, whom everyone passed on the street. His kind of listening love won the world. His was a human-divine feeling, caring, touching, listening love. In our busy, noisy world, if we are serious about loving our neighbor through listening, we will have a similar impact for healing people, as did Jesus.

May God open the ears of our hearts that we might begin to hear him, and to hear each other . . . and understand this is one of the most important ministries of Christian love.

Questions for Study and Discussion:

1. Have you ever experienced feeling truly "heard"? Who are the people you go to, when you need a listening ear? Does anyone come to you?

2. What makes it difficult to listen to some of the people in your life? What might be some of the things they are trying to express, behind their words? How can you be a more loving listener to those people?

God, I'll Do It, But Not Yet

James 4:13–17; Romans 13:11–14
January 14, 1979

When I was in college, many of my friends had a habit that drove me crazy. Blessed with nerves like steel, they could wait until the night before it was due, and then go to work on a term paper that had taken me weeks to complete. On the day before a final, they would cram like mad, after I had been burning the midnight oil for days. Most unnerving of all, my procrastinating friends were able to pull top grades!

Most of my life, I have pushed myself to do everything today. Part of me longs for the tranquility of being able to put things off! Certainly, in some respects, procrastination is a virtue. However, early in this New Year, it is important we consider biblical teaching about procrastination in relationship to following Jesus Christ. If you are serious about reaching new mountaintops in Christian maturity during 1979, those goals must be consciously set and strategized. Tracing through Scripture, we will discover why procrastination is dangerous.

A first obvious reason procrastination is no option for the Christian is that the Bible commands against it. Paul wrote to the Ephesians,

"Be very careful, then, how you live—not as unwise men, but as wise, making the most of every opportunity, because the days are evil (Eph. 5:15–16). Similarly, Jesus taught, "As long as it is day, we must do the works of him who sent me. Night is coming, when no one can work" (John 9:4).

And Augustine, the great saint of the early church, tells how he often prayed before he became a Christian, "Lord, give me chastity, but not yet!" Not until he was convicted by this Romans 13 passage did he change.

So goes the "theme song" of many of us: "Lord, I'm available, but not yet. I'll give, crucify self, become involved in your church's ministry to the world, but not yet. I'll break that habit, become the husband or wife, father or mother you want me to be, but not yet."

Where has God been knocking on certain doors in your life? Has your response been, "Okay, okay, I hear you, but not yet!"?

Jesus met a man who wanted to become his disciple. When Jesus said, "Come and follow me," the man responded: "Teacher, I'll follow you wherever you go . . . but let me first go bury my father" (Luke 9:59). He meant, "My father is old—let me stay with him till he dies, then I'll come and follow you." Certainly his excuse for delay seemed reasonable. However, Jesus wouldn't accept it! Jesus told him, "Let the dead bury their dead—you come and follow me!" (v. 60).

Our Lord consistently taught that "now" is the acceptable time, "now is the day to do what you intend to do for me." Jesus knew a basic fact about human nature: All of us prioritize what's really important to us. Not until we make spiritual progress a priority will we witness major change in our Christian experience. God takes time seriously. Time is a nonrenewable natural resource. Once an hour passes, it can never be recovered. Where we invest our time is witness of what's really a priority in our hearts.

The year 1979 can be one when we allow God to accomplish remarkable miracles in and through us. People in this sanctuary can give specific dates when God acted in 1978 to change their lives:

- "The day I stopped being enslaved to alcohol or smoking."
- "The day I decided temper or depression were destroying me, and sought God's help in changing my reactions to frustration."
- "The day I decided to trust, rather than worry."
- "The day I took seriously becoming a spiritual leader in my family."
- "The day I made myself available to visit in convalescent hospitals."
- "The day I accepted Jesus as my Savior, and passed from death to life."

No wonder God commands against procrastination! To postpone his plans for our continuing maturity is to rob ourselves of a miracle. Senator Harold Hughes of Iowa gave his testimony at a mayor's prayer lunch in Iowa. He quoted the famous G. K. Chesterton phrase, "Christianity has never been tried. It has not been tried and found wanting—it has never been tried," then talked about the miracle of his own life. He had been an alcoholic and caused pain and suffering to his parents, his wife, and children. He saw the ruin he had made of his life and prepared to kill himself. Then, for the first time in many years, he prayed, "God help me, I cannot do it alone." He did not tell anyone about his prayer at the time; he had told so many lies to his wife and children that no one would have believed him. But he has not had a drink since that day nineteen years ago. The senator stated that it was a daily struggle to submit to God's will, in a battle with his own egotism. He needed to recognize that he could only do things by letting God handle his life.

God can work miracles of change for every one of us, if we enter this year expecting and actively seeking such changes.

A second argument against procrastination is that to postpone is to attempt to give God something we have no power to give: tomorrow. Tomorrow is not within the grasp of any human being. "Now"—today—is the only part of this mystery called time that is ours to give.

In our text James says, "you do not even know what will happen tomorrow. What is your life? You are a mist that appears for a little while and then vanishes" (James 4:14). Human life is so fragile. In a moment, all the promises and commitments we have postponed, suddenly can be broken forever. These mortal lives are far too vulnerable a foundation upon which to stake our responsibilities to God. Believing there will always be tomorrow to fulfill our commitments is a glass crutch that can instantly be shattered. Indeed, because of the very delicacy and brevity of life, procrastination is one excuse God cannot possibly accept. No wonder Paul wrote:

> *The hour has already come for you to wake up from your slumber, because our salvation is nearer now than when we first believed. The night is nearly over; the day is almost here.* (Rom. 13:11–12)

> *Now is the time of God's favor, now is the day of salvation.* (2 Cor. 6:2)

Last night, many of us saw that great film *Fiddler on The Roof.* Upon the marriage of the daughter, the song "Sunrise, Sunset" was sung. Most of us know the message of that song—how quickly the years roar swiftly by, and children become all grown up overnight. One thrust came to my heart: "Whatever I want to do with and for my children, to demonstrate my love, I'd better plan to do now." To postpone easily could mean I will never be able to do it. Because of the very nature of time, the Bible urges us to do the important things today. Today is the day to show our husband or wife how much we love them. Today is the time to make a response to the love Jesus lavishes upon us. Tomorrow is a gift we can give no one. Leaving important issues on that elusive cloud of "someday" could cause us the deepest of heartaches, as it does in the popular song "The Cat's in the Cradle," where the father's busyness prevents him from having time for his son until the little boy is grown and too busy himself. There will always be "planes to catch and bills to pay," but there will not always be those moments to be with loved ones.

A third more subtle reason for God's impatience with procrastination is that he understands how such a response is a polite way of saying, "*No!*" I consciously attempt never to answer requests of my children with "someday we will go there or do that or buy that." Already they know such a response usually means no.

When the Bible speaks of time, it uses two different words. One refers to time measured by the clock or the calendar. A second word for time is in our text today, *kairos,* referring to time as opportunity—a moment of critical decision—a crossroad on which one changes the direction of a life. Jesus usually viewed time in this second dimension. He knew he didn't have much earthly time. When he called his disciples, we read how they immediately left their tax table or fishing nets, anything and everything that had previously been foremost in their lives, and they came and followed him. I am convinced Jesus is making similar demands of immediacy today. These are critical times in which we live. Discipleship should have the highest priority in our hearts and minds. I would like to believe this worship hour could be a *kairos* for us.

I want us to make a practical response to this biblical teaching about procrastination. Obviously the first responsibility God lays on every human heart is to respond to the good news of Jesus Christ—to become a Christian and receive eternal life. In Acts it is recorded how Paul witnessed to King Agrippa. The king was interested, but postponed making a decision until a more convenient time. Nowhere in Scripture do we read that the "convenient time" ever came. I have deep compassion for those who one day will face God, lacking the robes of righteousness provided by faith in Jesus Christ. Tragically they will be lost, simply because they postponed making a commitment.

For those of us who know Christ, there are so many areas of challenge and hills to climb. When is your family going to make time for reading the Bible together, praying together, attending worship regularly, playing together? Perhaps the aches and human needs of the inner city, of the convalescent homes, or of world hunger are heavy on your heart. When are you going to take steps to become involved? Perhaps you are convinced to take the initiative about ending a feud with that friend or family member—to aggressively seek an end to the stalemate in your marriage or in relationships with your parents or children. When will you take the first step? What about that habit or behavior pattern or relationship which you know has to go, but like Augustine you are saying, "Give me chastity, but not yet!" God is convicting some of us about our lavish lifestyle in a world of need. What changes and subsequent sharing are we going to begin this year?

I want to close with a few moments of silence, to allow the Holy Spirit to speak to all of us on this issue individually. Hopefully we will go home today and lay out some goals for 1979 and the strategies involved in achieving those goals. Let us go to a time of silent prayer.

Questions for Study and Discussion:

1. What is on your to-do list that you've been putting off, in your daily life and in your spiritual walk? Have you ever finally gotten around to something and crossed it off your list? What was the result?

2. After spending time in reflection and prayer, what is the "now" you have to offer God? What strategies can you come up with to help you achieve those spiritual goals?

A DAY FULL OF SURPRISES

Matthew 25:34–46
May 1–2, 1999

Today, I want us to think about Judgment Day, a subject most would prefer to ignore— yet we ignore it at our peril. Jesus often talked about that time when we will stand before God and give an account of our lives on Earth. Note his agenda for that day in our Scripture is rather surprising. Usually we think of Judgment Day having to do with things we did and shouldn't have done, but Jesus also talks about "sins of omission," things we ought to have done and didn't do:

- the man with one talent, who buried his treasure in the ground, rather than investing it in God's work (Matt. 25:14–30)
- the rich man who failed to give to the needs of Lazarus, begging on his doorstep (Luke 16:19–31)
- the rich fool whose response to his increased wealth was to build bigger barns, rather than share (Luke 12:13–21)

There are some valuable lessons here for us to consider. First, Jesus defines sins of omission as ignoring people in need. Our text says:

I was hungry and you gave me nothing to eat, I was thirsty and you gave me nothing to drink, I was a stranger and you did not

invite me in, I needed clothes and you did not clothe me, I was sick
and in prison and you did not look after me. . . . Truly I tell you,
whatever you did not do for one of the least of these, you did not do
for me. (Matt. 25:42–43, 45)

Let me suggest that the needy are not only the economically poor. Every day we interface with people who are hungry, thirsty, and in various kinds of prisons, including psychological ones. Even among the so-called successful, we see addiction to the frantic pace and stress of working sixteen-hour days; people trading relationships for wealth, and paying an enormous price; and self-destructive behavior.

Jesus calls us to adopt a lifestyle that enables us to recognize and relate to the needs in the lives of those closest to us. The greatest need in the lives of most of our neighbors is not material. They need Jesus. Before they can know Jesus, they must experience his caring through us.

One of the surprises about Judgment Day will be for those who thought they knew Jesus, but who, lacking compassionate hearts, will hear him say: "I don't know you!" That's an alarming thought.

A second truth: Gratitude to Jesus is the motivation for reaching out to our neighbor. Once we understand that every blessing we enjoy is a gift of God's grace, gratitude becomes a dominating force in our lives, motivating us to take our Savior's love into our neighborhoods, our offices, and around the world. As one man commented to me as he was helping to load the container going to Russia, "I believe every individual, if motivated, can make a difference in the world. Just look at what a few of us can do. Imagine what our church family could do together, if we could just get the vision."

The warning in this text is that Judgment Day is not only about sins related to the Ten Commandments, but it's about all the little acts of caring we did, or failed to do, for our neighbor. Our Lord's biggest bombshell hit me when he said that to ignore our neighbor is to ignore *him*! When Mother Teresa was asked what motivated her to love and care for the sick, dying, and rejected of Calcutta, she declared that, in the face of a needy person, it was the face of Jesus she saw. May Jesus enable us to see his face, in the faces of our neighbors, whose wealth can mask their deepest needs.

A church family that shares our love, time, talent, and resources to meet our neighbor's need models God's answer for the selfishness and indifference rampant in our culture. I was amazed at the press describing those preparing for the potential mayhem related to the Y2K crisis. Some people are frantically gathering all kinds of survival goods and food along with guns to protect their treasures. What a parable of how some live, with self as their primary focus. A sense of community and belonging to each other is being lost. Why does it take a Colorado tragedy to wake people up to the fact we need each other? That we belong to each other?

I mentioned last week that we will be presenting in the days ahead what we call our Vision 2000, a vision of what our church family is accomplishing for Jesus Christ and what more we can do in the future. Our ministry here in our community extends to the inner city and stretches around the globe. I believe all of us will stand in awe, once we realize what Jesus has done and will do through us, as we continue to invest our resources to touch the world.

A third truth: There are consequences for those whose hearts are hardened and indifferent to human need. I'm fascinated by the excuse those in our story gave for not relating to human need: "If we had known it was you, Lord, we would have served you!"

As your leaders, we have a threefold responsibility:

- to introduce you to Jesus as Savior;
- to nurture you into maturity as disciples; and
- to deploy you into the world to meet the needs of people.

To grow as a Christian is like any other personal growth. I enjoy my one-year-old granddaughters. At this stage, they are totally preoccupied with themselves, and that's normal. Yet imagine an adult with a chronological age of twenty and a mental age of two, whining about *me* and *mine*, oblivious to the pain in their neighbor's lives. Jesus challenges us to grow up, so he can deploy us into the adventure of loving and being loved, sharing, getting involved, and creating caring communities in which people can experience the grace of Jesus Christ.

I need to highlight that this message makes sense only to one who knows Jesus as Savior. Otherwise, much of what we say about gratitude won't compute. Let me explain. Last summer, two guards in our nation's capitol building gave their lives to save others from the bullets of a crazed gunman. One of the assistants, whose life was saved by a guard putting his body in front a bullet meant for her, said, "I will live the rest of my life indebted to this man and make certain he didn't die in vain."

Jesus put his body in front of the bullet of God's judgment and eternal death that will fall upon those who reject or remain indifferent to his gift. Once we become a Christian, our primary motivation in life is to express our gratitude by making a difference in the world by caring for others. If our eyes are closed to this truth, it simply means we don't know Jesus, and he doesn't know us. That's what makes this Scripture of such eternal importance.

Jesus claims that Judgment Day will be full of surprises, because in heaven, the "head tunas" of this world will not lead the parade. Heroes in heaven will be the most surprised, because their only claim to fame is that they loved and cared for others out of deep gratitude to Jesus. As we think about the future of our church's ministry, I want our life together to be living proof that we do know him. To prove it, we are investing our time, resources, and money to make a difference. And that action makes our Savior smile!

A neighbor is simply anyone whose needs we can meet. Let's find one this week.

Jesus planned for us to celebrate communion on a regular basis, so we will never forget what he did for us. Let us think on these words of this hymn: "I gave my life for you, what have you given to me?"

Questions for Study and Discussion:

1. This sermon focuses on sins of "omission." When you consider the people you run across in your life, what might they be struggling with, either on or below the surface? What would they be surprised to know you struggle with?

2. What motivates you to meet others' needs—guilt and obligation, or gratitude? Have you ever experienced the gratitude toward God that motivates you to obey him?

OUR SEARCH FOR SATISFACTION

Ecclesiastes 2:1–11
June 15–16, 1991

Last summer, I was walking along the shore of Lake Tahoe, coveting boats. My eye fell on a beautiful ski boat with this name inscribed on its transom: *Mid-Life Crisis*. I assumed that the owner expected his high-powered boat to satisfy the restlessness deep inside his soul. Similar hunger pangs haunt the hearts of most of us, hunger for something beyond tedious routine which makes life seem totally predictable. I'm certain the ski-boat owner soon discovered that neither his boat—nor anything else he could buy, achieve, or experience—would fully satisfy his search for satisfaction.

Jesus Christ promises satisfaction to those who trust him. The problem with most Christians is that we verbalize that Jesus is enough to satisfy us, but our conversations indicate restlessness:

- Sue is getting another transfer.
- Bill and Jane are moving again to a bigger house.
- Don is going back to school for another degree.
- Sally will be okay once she is married.

Many of us are looking for something more than Jesus to meet our needs. If only I can get that job or degree; live in that neighborhood; take that special vacation; or find that special partner. Let's study our text, which points us to the true source of satisfaction—Jesus Christ himself.

First, our text warns us that, no matter how much of this world we are able to buy or experience, it will never be enough. Listen to a man who tried it all:

> *I said to myself, "Come now, I will test you with pleasure to find out what is good."... I tried cheering myself with wine. ... I amassed silver and gold for myself, and the treasure of kings and provinces. ... I denied myself nothing my eyes desired; I refused my heart no pleasure. ... Yet when I surveyed all that my hands had done and what I had toiled to achieve, everything was meaningless, a chasing after the wind.* (Eccl. 2:1, 3, 8, 10–11)

Similar restlessness and frustration is rampant. Without commitment to Jesus, frequently the possession of wealth is associated with an absence of satisfaction. Usually after horrible mistakes, broken hearts, and spiritual poverty, too many learn too late that the things of this world, in themselves, cannot satisfy. Using another translation of this same text, the writer says:

> *Anything I wanted, I would take. I denied myself no pleasure. I even found great pleasure in hard work. ... But as I looked at everything I worked so hard to accomplish, it was all so meaningless—like chasing the wind. There was nothing worthwhile anywhere.* (Eccl. 2:10–11, NLT)

In contrast, Jesus does give us satisfaction and meets our deepest needs. Jesus quiets restlessness and turmoil surging in our souls. Jesus gives us these promises:

> *I have come that [you] might have life, and have it to the full.* (John 10:10, emphasis added)

> *[M]y peace I give you. I do not give you as the world gives.* (John 14:27)

Now let me spend a few moments describing two ways our Lord provides the gift of satisfaction to those who trust him. First, in contrast to the person in our text who searched for satisfaction in things, Jesus points us in another direction:

> *Do not store up for yourselves treasures on earth, where moth and rust destroy, and where thieves break in and steal. But store up for yourselves treasures in heaven. . . . For where your treasure is, there your heart will be also.* (Matt. 6:19–21, NIV1984)

Our Lord exposes the values of indulgence and consumption as deficient to meet our needs.

As I think about the future of our church family, I want God to make us people who recognize that things and experiences of this world cannot meet our deepest needs—people whose central passion in life is Jesus himself—people who care for people more than we care for things, and people who will make this church a place of refuge, encouragement, and healing for those who have lost their own families and support systems. Together, we can make our individual lives and the life of our church a fulfillment of the mission of Jesus, which he described as follows:

> *[T]he Lord has anointed me to proclaim good news to the poor. He has sent me to bind up the brokenhearted, to proclaim*

freedom for the captives and freedom from the darkness for the prisoners . . . to comfort all who mourn. (Isa. 61:1–2)

May we avoid at all costs this diagnosis Jesus made of a church in the book of Revelation:

I know your deeds, that you are neither cold nor hot. . . . So, because you are lukewarm—neither hot nor cold—I am about to spit you out of my mouth. You say, "I am rich; I have acquired wealth and do not need a thing." But you do not realize that you are wretched, pitiful, poor, blind and naked. (Rev. 3:15–17)

By rejecting the "Me First" syndrome of our text, by joining Jesus in his mission of caring for others, we will find satisfaction! Listen to Isaiah the prophet:

[I]f you spend yourselves in behalf of the hungry, and satisfy the needs of the afflicted, then your light will rise in the darkness. . . . The LORD will guide you always; he will satisfy your needs in a sun-scorched land and will strengthen your frame. You will be like a well-watered garden, like a spring whose waters do not fail. (Isa. 58:10–11)

Will anything you buy or achieve in this world make this kind of promise?

A second way Jesus gives us satisfaction is by encouraging us to live in the present moment. The writer of our text sought to accumulate things so he would never have to worry about future security. In contrast Jesus says, "Therefore do not worry about tomorrow, for tomorrow will worry about itself. Each day has enough trouble of its own" (Matt. 6:34).

Too many Christians are failing to find satisfaction in the present because we are still looking to some future change, some new acquisition, some exotic experience, to bring us what Jesus alone can give. Here is a vital fact to remember about living the Christian life: If we are not finding satisfaction *today* by trusting Jesus, nothing can happen *tomorrow* that will give us this elusive treasure.

Jesus invites us to squeeze the nectar out of every present moment, to live in breathless expectation of what God can do with the circumstances confronting us today. Such a lifestyle brings inner satisfaction.

Last week I saw a billboard with these words: "Every moment lost with your children is gone forever!" I feel this wisdom of "treasuring the present moment" can be applied to every area of our lives. Too many of us fail to fully live today—and therefore miss the joy of events and relationships that give life meaning.

Let me read a poem by Robert J. Hastings, entitled *The Station:*

Tucked away in our subconscious is an idyllic vision. We see ourselves on a long trip that spans the continent. We are traveling by train. Out the windows we drink in the passing scene of cars on nearby highways, of children waving at a crossing, of cattle grazing on a distant hillside . . . of city skylines and village halls.

But uppermost in our minds is the final destination. On a certain day at a certain hour we will pull into the station. Bands will be playing and flags waving. Once we get there so many wonderful dreams will come true and the pieces of our lives will fit together like a completed jigsaw puzzle. How restlessly we pace the aisles, damning the minutes for loitering—waiting, waiting, waiting for the station.

"When we reach the station, that will be it!" we think. "When I'm 18." "When we buy a new Mercedes Benz!" "When we put the last kid through college." "When we have paid off the

mortgage!" "When I get a promotion." "When we reach the age of retirement, we shall live happily ever after!"

Sooner or later we must realize that there is no station, no one place to arrive at, once and for all. The true joy of life is the trip, the journey itself. The station is only a dream. It constantly outdistances us.

"Relish the moment" is a good motto, especially when coupled with Psalm 118:24 (KJV): "This is the day which the Lord hath made; we will rejoice and be glad in it." It isn't the burdens of today that drive men mad, but the regrets over yesterday, and the fears of tomorrow. Regret and fear are the twin Thieves which rob us of today.

So, stop pacing the aisles and counting the miles. Instead, climb more mountains, eat more ice cream, go barefoot more often, swim more rivers, watch more sunsets, laugh more, cry less. Life must be lived as we go along. The station will come soon enough.[21]

Today, if you are searching for satisfaction try this wisdom from Jesus:

- First, look at your calendars! How many hours a week do you devote to the business of Jesus . . . and how many hours to the business of accumulating? Write in some time devoted to meeting needs of people. Commit yourself to give part of yourself away every week, and Jesus says you will find satisfaction.

- Secondly, try trusting Jesus just for today . . . and squeeze the nectar of meaning out of every moment of everyday, so you will have no regrets about losing a life, while you were busy making a living!

Questions for Study and Discussion:

1. What have you spent the most time, money, and effort pursuing and accumulating? What satisfaction did it give you? Once you achieved it, did it solve all your problems and quench further desires?

2. Have you ever pursued something of God? Something different and eternal? If no, why not? If yes, what impact did it have on your other pursuits?

What's it like to work for Walt Gerber? Lace up your Adidas and start moving! It's a little like running the 440-hurdles, the steeplechase, and marathon all rolled into one! The team spirit spills over, however, and as the race progresses it's riddled with enthusiasm, joy, laughter, and a few tears. "Running the race" with this very human, type-A sort certainly has its moments . . . lots of them!

Bobbie Brunzell,
secretary

Dear Walt,

This is to let you know how much your two favorite front-office workers will miss you when you retire.
Among other things we will miss:

- *The slamming door*
- *The fast trips down the hall*
- *The conversations from the chairs next to our desk*
- *The out-of-control hilarity from your office during Tuesday morning staff meetings*

Cordially,
Phyllis Wood, receptionist,
Virginia Woodson, administrative assistant

Discovering Indescribable Joy

1 Thessalonians 5:16–18; John 15:9–11
February 5–6, 2000

What do you think is one of the most common words in the Bible? If "joy" was your choice, you would be right. Last week Scott [Dudley] reminded us that there are not many "happy" people in the Bible, but there are many who were filled with joy. Jesus promised his followers, "I have told you this so that my joy may be in you and that your joy may be complete" (John 15:11).

As we grow into the likeness of Jesus, we radiate his joy. If we are missing joy, something is wrong. Let me ask you, have you discovered our Lord's contagious, indescribable joy? Are you aware that exhibiting a joyful spirit is a strategic Christian responsibility?

I received some hysterical cards for my recent birthday, and shared them with staff. Our laughter attracted others in the office who came to check out what was going on. Joy is contagious! After being seated at a restaurant, the hostess said to me, "It's so good to see a smile on your face. Most people seem so stressed, cold, and sad. I try to give my customers a smile, but most of them ignore me."

How strange that in these so-called "good times" a kind of grimness has taken control of many faces and hearts. What does your face say about the impact knowing Jesus is having upon your life? Let's turn to our text, in the hope God will stoke some new fires of joy in our hearts.

> *Be joyful always; pray continually; give thanks in all circumstances, for this is God's will for you in Christ Jesus.* (1 Thess. 5:16–18, NIV1984)

First, discovering indescribable joy is related to giving thanks in all circumstances. To seek joy by giving thanks to God, even in stressful horrible situations, must seem like lunacy to a logical thinker. Suppose we had a loved one on that airliner that was lost last week? Would we thank God? Some friends lost their sixteen-year-old son last Thursday morning to leukemia, after having lost another nine-year-old son several years before to the same disease. But listen to their reaction:

> *We are thankful for the impact of our son's faith on the staff and patients in the hospital, where he spent so many months. We are thankful he won't have to live with a body that would never be able to sustain a normal life. Even death is a blessing.*

Listen carefully: It would be heresy to teach that thanking God for horrible happenings is a Christian act. But believers will trust God's goodness and *thank* him in advance for how he will use our pain, stress, loss, failure, illness for our good. This unique certainty of a Christian is our secret for experiencing indescribable joy!

Do you trust God enough to thank him in advance, even though right now you don't have the foggiest notion how anything good can emerge from your situation? This kind of trust is rooted in our absolute confidence that God is head over heels in love with us! He would no more harm us, than we could hurt our own children. Nothing that happens to us today or tomorrow will distort God's plans for our future here, and in eternity.

To sing praises of gratitude to God at the midnight hours of life's most difficult circumstances is a wonderful alternative to a grim look of stress on our faces. Do we realize we hurt God's reputation when we wear a grim face that might tell observers we feel God has forsaken us? That life's burdens are too heavy? That things couldn't get worse, and won't get better?

But you might ask at this point: "How can I be joyful all the time, with the burdens I carry, with the hurts and stresses God has allowed to enter my life, with all the unknowns my tomorrow might hold?" Like every dimension of living the Christian life, this kind of trust can't be developed in our own strength. Trusting God is a gift of grace that we can only pray to receive. I ask God every day to give me the gift of being able to trust him more.

Remember, God seldom explains in advance how he will bring good out of bad. He does ask us to trust him, even in the darkest times. As Hal Helms writes, "Faith grows in the shadows, but shrinks in the light . . . In the shadows practice praise."[22]

I like to think of Paul and Silas in the Philippian jail. They had been beaten and chained without cause. Yet at midnight, they were singing hymns of praise to God, so much so that the other prisoners wondered what these guys possessed that they were missing. The result was, the jailer and his family became Christians.

One of my greatest personal challenges in trusting God has to do with my children. Through the years the Lord has been absolutely faithful in caring for them and guiding their lives. Yet recently, an issue with one of them, who is a fully competent adult, has caused me much unnecessary stress. I have attempted to do my usual micromanaging of his future plans, by giving him my "suggestions" about certain decisions he has made. Rather than experiencing the joy of resting in God's provision and guidance for my son, I sweat bullets about his future. Then, as I was preparing this sermon, I said to myself, "I'm doing it again! Not only am I denying that I believe God is in control of my son's future, I'm assuming a responsibility God did not intend me to carry. This habit is driving me nuts." What's more, I'm communicating to my son, "I don't think you are competent to make good decisions!"

Now I'm back on track. I've put my son into God's care, and I am free to love him, rather than control him. Possibly some of you have experienced a similar struggle. This leads us to another truth in our text.

A second step in discovering indescribable joy is to pray continually. Joy is the fruit of prayer. Prayer provides the privilege of leveraging God's resources with our own. Prayer is putting our hand into God's hand, so we confront overwhelming challenges with the certainty God will make a way. Once I turned my son's future over to God in prayer, saying, "If you want him to practice his profession in this area, you will provide a place," prayer freed me to enjoy the process of waiting in faith. This is what the psalmist meant when he wrote:

> *He who dwells in the shelter of the Most High will rest in the shadow of the Almighty. I will say of the LORD, "He is my refuge and my fortress, my God, in whom I trust." . . . He will cover you with his feathers, and under his wings you will find refuge.* (Ps. 91:1–2, 4, NIV 1984)

Some time ago, my sister contracted cancer. During her long months of chemo, we prayed often. God was merciful and her life was spared. Just last month, she had a biopsy that could have indicated a return of cancer. While we waited for the results of the biopsy, both of us felt a sense of inner peace and joy as we turned the outcome over to God in prayer. We knew that whatever the answer, God is our refuge. God is in control, his plans for us are good. He died for us! Happily, the biopsy revealed my sister is free from cancer, although we were free to accept any answer as part of God's long-term plans for her good.

The serendipity of praying about everything and worrying about nothing is to discover an inner joy, that is the special gift of Jesus to his followers.

If it were in my power to give you a gift this weekend, I would pray God would enable you to trust his love so much that no matter what storm is raging in your life right now, or will rage tomorrow, you would experience his indescribable joy because you trust this promise: "He who did not spare his own Son, but gave him up for us all—how will he not also, along with him, graciously give us all things?" (Rom. 8:32).

Would you like to discover this joy? Then stop believing the myth that joy can be experienced only by the absence of pain and the fulfillment of all your desires. Trust God enough to turn your need over to him in prayer, and thank him in advance for how he will weave all the complex broken ends into His perfect pattern.

If you are like me, you need to be reminded of these truths almost daily, sometimes hourly. That's one reason we come to worship and hear sermons on subjects we have heard before. Frederick Buechner makes this beautiful statement about joy in the life of a Christian:

> *I believe . . . that all of us have not only the right to be joyful, no matter what, but also a kind of sacred commission to be [joyful] . . . in the sense of being able to bless even the sad times of our own lives. . . . It's all good. There is nothing to worry about. That is the gladdest and most final of all secrets which I suspect the whole human family, since the world began has glimpsed always in its holiest dreams.*[23]

This week, let's celebrate the light Jesus brings to us, even when there is much darkness. Next week, if I asked you, "What is your face saying to a watching world about the impact Jesus is having upon your life?", I trust our smiles would tell it all.

Questions for Study and Discussion:

1. Do you consider yourself a joyful person? Do others consider you a joyful person? Why or why not?

2. Which of the steps to joy do you practice already—giving thanks, trusting, or prayer? What circumstances in your life do you find it difficult to thank God for? What can you do in that situation?

Does God Give Personal Guidance to Believers?

James 1:5; Psalm 32:8
January 20–21, 1996

L ast fall, one of our staff was struggling with a big decision and commented to me, "Walt, I wish I could just sit down with God, look him in the eye, and ask, 'What do you want me to do?'" All of us have moments when we want to just hear God's directing voice or receive some definite sign regarding a relationship, a business decision, a career choice, an expenditure. Our text offers help.

First, the text affirms that God does give specific guidance on many issues.

> *If any of you lacks wisdom, you should ask God, who gives generously to all without finding fault, and it will be given to you.* (James 1:5)

It's true. God does give believers personal guidance and he uses many sources—the Bible, friends, circumstances, our prayer life. I have found that most often God uses the Bible for giving me directives regarding moral decisions, money, relationships with husband, wife, children—priorities for the "game of life," as we learned last week in pastor Jay's sermon. The psalmist uses 176 verses in Psalm 119, thanking God for the guidance his laws offer, and summarizes by saying, "Thy word is a lamp unto my feet, and a light unto my path" (Ps. 119:105, KJV).

Henry Drummond once said, "There is a will of God for me, which is a particular will, different from the will he has for anyone else . . . a private will . . . a will which no one else knows about."[24] The psalmist articulates this truth when he says, "I will instruct you and teach you in the way you should go; I will counsel you with my loving eye on you" (Ps. 32:8).

The struggle in seeking divine guidance, for most people, seems not to be in finding it but in obeying it once we know what it is. For me, the difficulty in discerning God's will often rests in my outstanding ability to rationalize when it comes to interpreting and applying God's guidance. Let's be honest, most of the time we know exactly what the Bible says on a certain issue. But we like to play around the edges. We easily come up with fifty reasons why our situation is the exception for this divine directive. We keep on seeking advice from others, until we find something or someone that agrees with what we really want to do.

Sometimes people talk to me about searching for God's will on a certain decision, and immediately they begin telling me what they have learned from their friends, family, or therapist—advice which sometimes contradicts what they already know to be God's will on the subject.

I believe friends, family, and even circumstances are good sources for guidance, but their advice must always be tested by what the Bible says. Personally I must be careful in this area because I don't like to offend people by rejecting their advice after I asked for it. What's more, sometimes advice from secular sources is much more attractive. It's advice that feeds my feelings, rather than God's truth. The secular world will always tell us to take the easy way, to do what everybody else is doing, to do what feels good, and will scoff at self-denial and submission to God's laws as guilt-ridden demons from the past.

One safeguard against rationalization that works for me is to be daily in the Bible, where God has a habit of hitting me between the eyes with a verse speaking directly to my particular struggle. The Bible won't let me dodge or change the truth. I'm convicted! A verse can also highlight the fallacy of other advice I might have received.

You know the cliché: "Let your conscience be your guide." I believe we need to qualify that statement. Our conscience is only a good guide if we submit it to God's Word, rather than to feelings and our tendency to rationalize. My conscience, independent of God's Word, can lead me in a hundred different wrong directions.

I have found that asking counsel from Christian friends, who I know will be honest with me can help me find my blind spots in rationalizing. I love it when friends will listen to me, point out fallacies in my argument, and pray for me. This fact is one more reason we urge everyone to be in some support group.

Another weapon against rationalizing is to be in prayer, so our wills can be softened into submission to God's authority, no matter how intense the temptation, how complex the problem confronting us. As followers of Jesus, we acknowledge an authority higher than our own will and desire. This fact makes us a different breed of humanity.

Henry David Thoreau once said, *"If a man does not keep pace with his companions, perhaps it is because he hears a different [drumbeat]. Let him step to the music he hears, however measured or far away."*[25] It's in prayer we find the stillness to hear the drumbeat of God above the roar of stress, confusion, and lust that temptation can thrust upon us. God does give directives.

This leads to a second question in our text: How do we recognize and apply divine guidance to our personal situation? Lloyd Ogilvie offers help, when he quotes F. B. Meyer in describing an incident in crossing the Irish Channel on a dark, starless night.

I stood on the deck by the captain and asked him, "How do you find Holyhead Harbor on so dark a night as this?" He said, "You see those three lights? Those three lights must line up behind each other as one, and when we see them so united, we know the exact position of the harbor's mouth."[26]

Then Ogilvie spells out this lesson: When we want to know God's will, there are three important keys to keep in mind:

- the Word of God;
- our feelings on the issue; and
- the trend of our circumstances.

Finally, here are some questions that can be very helpful in checking the legitimacy of God's guidance on a particular issue:

1. Is what I want to do consistent with the Ten Commandments?

2. If I do it, will it glorify Jesus and enable me to grow as his disciple?

3. Has prolonged prayer and thought produced an inner feeling of "rightness" about it?

4. Is it an expression of authentic love, and will it bring ultimate good in the lives of the people involved?

5. Are circumstances indicating that what I want to do is feasible or will pursuing what I believe is God's will impact negatively my family and other commitments?

6. Will my expenditures still allow tithing plus generous giving of my money for the Lord's work and the needs of others?

Sometimes only in retrospect can we see how submitting to God's Word, rather than our own feelings, has protected us from terrible decisions. Let me offer this warning: submitting to God's Word over feelings is not a popular philosophy in our current culture. The theme today is "do what feels good," and let the devil take tomorrow. The problem with that philosophy is that tomorrow comes, and we must still face the consequences of our choices.

This leads us to our third truth: Our text qualifies finding God's guidance, by affirming we must rely on our faith, rather than feelings and desires. James warns:

> *But let him ask in faith, with no doubting, for the one who doubts is like a wave of the sea that is driven and tossed by the wind. For that person must not suppose he will receive anything from the Lord; he is a double-minded man, unstable in all his ways.* (James 1:6–8, ESV)

We will not receive God's guidance if we are doubleminded. To be doubleminded can mean several things. First, it can refer to our habit of saying, "I want God's will on this issue," while at the same time we want something else so badly we say to ourselves, "I only have one life to live, and I have a right to be happy . . . so if it isn't God's will I'm going to do it anyway. Other people are doing it, getting away with it, and they seem happy, so why am I so concerned about God's will?" Or we might say, "My circumstances make me unique, and it's only logical that God is making an exception in my case."

Doublemindedness can also refer to our refusal to believe God really is involved in our crises, causing us to say to ourselves, "I don't really believe God knows or cares about my needs. He won't answer my prayers for guidance."

And doublemindedness can refer to a common fear that, if we seek God's will, His response will be the opposite of what we really want. His will might ruin our pleasure, take away our joy, or make us so miserable we will wish we hadn't asked for His guidance.

To conquer double-mindedness is to reaffirm our commitment as disciples, that our lives are not our own—we have been bought with a price—we belong to Jesus. Jesus said, "Whoever wants to be my disciple must deny themselves and take up their cross and follow me" (Matt. 16:24). A cross implies dying to self, to desires that make us doubleminded. Sometimes it's only the Holy Spirit within us that can provide the supernatural power we need to say "no" to feelings and "yes" to the will of God, particularly in those times when we are in pain, or stressed to the breaking point, or tempted to the brink of giving in to what we know is wrong.

I want to affirm that God's will for us is always rooted in his love. He withholds nothing from us that is ultimately for our good. His will is always best. Sometimes we have to wait patiently for it, and struggle through long periods of silence, but in the end his will always works all things together for our good. God knows more than we do; he sees the big picture. In days of instant gratification, email, and quick responses, waiting upon God for his guidance can seem agonizingly slow. But the Bible assures us he is never late.

So the answer to the question, "Does God give personal guidance to believers?" . . . is *yes!* However, to find his guidance involves a choice of trusting his promises revealed in the Bible, and giving priority to his authority over our feelings, friends, circumstances, and desires. The choice is up to us!

Questions for Study and Discussion:

1. Do you have a situation where you have been wishing for discernment? Whom or what have you consulted so far? What do you wish they would say? What would the Bible say, if it speaks to that issue?

2. Who in your life do you trust to speak truth to you, whether or not it's something you want to hear? Have you ever had someone give you advice which you rejected, only to realize later that it might have been good counsel?

LIVING IN THE PRESENT

Matthew 6:25–34; Mark 10:14–16;
Philippians 4:4–7, 10–13
September 23, 1984

Some of the best advice Jesus offers his followers are these words:

Do not worry about tomorrow, for tomorrow will worry about itself. Each day has enough trouble of its own. (Matt. 6:34)

Can you imagine what would happen if we could suddenly obey these words and break free from our worries about tomorrow or yesterday? One fact is certain: The present moment is the only time any of us actually possess. Last Sunday's celebration[27] provided the opportunity for me to live fully in the present moment. As each event unfolded, I decided to savor every minute—not worry about anything, and just let it happen! My wife and I will consider that special day one of the happiest of our lives. What's exciting is that Jesus suggests we can choose to live fully in the present every day, not waiting for special occasions.

Every day is special—a gift from God that can be used for his glory. I'm certain such wisdom is not new for any of us. What's amazing is how few really claim these words of Jesus, even though we might have them memorized. Our lifestyle exposes what's going on in our hearts. Consider how many of our waking hours are spent all stressed up about fear of tomorrow, or we pour our efforts and talents into the task of filling our barns for the future! Such behavior exacts a terrible toll in our lives. How many people do you know who have had their eyes so fixed on tomorrow that they postpone many treasures—vacations, hobbies, leisure moments with friends and children, and above all, the adventure of seeking first kingdom business—as a priority in their lives? How many people do you know who postponed living too long and died before they had time to taste of their dreams?

Even more tragic, Dr. David Elkind suggests in *The Hurried Child* that we are teaching our children to be like us. We train them to live so much in the future they miss childhood and become victims of stress at a young age, stress regarding college and their future vocation.

In a nutshell, living anxiously in the future, rather than savoring the present, is robbing us of the abundant life our Lord promises those who follow him. Spencer Johnson, in his delightful book *The Precious Present*, claims that the ability to enjoy fully the present moment is a gift, a gift all of us once possessed as children, but gradually lost as we became adults. It's no coincidence Jesus said we must become little children again if we would enter the kingdom. Dr. Johnson gives a clue why Jesus used the illustration of a child: young children are happy because they know how to enjoy the present moment fully, refusing to allow worries about tomorrow to interrupt their pleasure. Trusting their all-powerful parents to take care of things, they don't have to worry about tomorrow. Jesus wishes that gift of kingdom life for us—that we would so fully trust our Heavenly Father for tomorrow, we could totally enjoy today.

Our text offers some practical help for rediscovering our ability to enjoy the present and be delivered from the torment of worrying about the future. Jesus tells us to consider the lilies of the field and the birds, noting how God provides for their needs. Neither is able to gather provisions into barns of tomorrow, yet daily their needs are met. Isn't it logical, asks our Lord, if God cares for the flowers and the birds, that he will also care for us, his own children? What's more, since we have no control over the length of our time on Earth, why are we consumed with providing for tomorrow's food and shelter, to the neglect of our eternal souls? Therefore, Jesus commands, "Do not be anxious"!

Like following all of God's commandments, learning to live in the present is a discipline and a process, involving failure and new beginnings. Every Christian can adopt the discipline of choosing to be fulfilled now, rather than postponing finding joy to "when" or "if" something happens. Jesus invites us to savor the now, good or bad, knowing his hand is in it. Learning to live in the present is to taste eternity before we arrive in heaven. Eternity is existence without past or future, a sort of timeless present. If we seek first kingdom business today, we will find joy, and God will take care of all of tomorrow's needs.

A second nugget of wisdom from Jesus about learning to live in the present is his suggestion we focus our energy upon trusting God for today's needs once we give up worrying about tomorrow. He says, "Let the day's own trouble be sufficient for the day." Paul caught the same wisdom in our text from the Philippian letter:

> Rejoice in the Lord always. I will say it again: Rejoice! Let your gentleness be evident to all. The Lord is near. Do not be anxious about anything, but in every situation, by prayer and petition, with thanksgiving, present your requests to God. And the peace of God, which transcends all understanding, will guard your hearts and your minds in Christ Jesus. (Phil. 4:4–7)

I give a little plaque to patients in the hospital which reads: "Lord, help me to remember nothing is going to happen to me today, that you and I can't handle together." Believing our Heavenly Father is with us in the present, no matter what's going on, frees us from panic, murmuring, or complaining. Trusting God in the present literally enables us to rejoice constantly and be relieved of anxiety.

Last August I met a man at Mt. Hermon[28] who had lost a leg. Sitting down with him, I listened to his story. He had been injured in a motorcycle accident ten years ago. Three years in a hospital and sixty-nine operations later, he found himself hopelessly in debt, disfigured, and unable to perform his former job. He added how, shortly before coming to family camp, he learned he had terminal cancer and had just been fired. I asked how he managed to sustain such a sense of joy, much less sanity and faith in God. His answer incorporated the wisdom from these words in our text:

I have learned to be content, no matter what's going on! I learned to enjoy each month in the hospital and find meaning in each day, rather than live for that time when I would leave the hospital. I am now busy enjoying every day God allows me to live. I refuse to be bitter about the past or worry about the future. God has all eternity to restore to me what my accident took away.

A woman attended that same camp who had a special-needs daughter and six other handicapped women for whom she was caring. I noted her joy and talked with her. She told me at the time of the birth of her daughter, she decided she would open her home to other children with handicaps, whose parents could not provide for them. For thirty years, she has taken care of these handicapped women, loving and caring for them. Her secret for finding joy is to live one day at a time, enjoying the adventure of watching God meet every need. Joy from that group of ladies radiated throughout the camp. We watched them care for each other, enjoy every little happening throughout the day, and make the most of the present. I know many of us, at the end of seven days at camp, felt perhaps we were the ones handicapped when it came to living.

To trust God for the present opens the door for us to make a ministry out of everything: drying dishes, fighting it out in the board meeting, hitting the books, facing financial challenges, waiting through the long hours of illness. Every moment can be filled with meaning, if we perform our ordinary tasks as ministry for Jesus! In this sense, Paul commands us to rejoice always.

Well, what about us? If we commit ourselves to seek first the kingdom and his righteousness, we must take that risky step of trusting God for our tomorrow. I believe, if we will set godly priorities today, God will honor our commitment and take care of our tomorrows. I have never found God to break a promise. Why don't we take him at his word, and begin today to live in the precious present? Give our worries about the future to him! At Mt. Hermon, this sign hangs in one of the meeting rooms: "Today is the tomorrow you worried about yesterday!"

Questions for Study and Discussion:

1. What evidence is here in your current lifestyle that you do not yet trust God for tomorrow?

2. If you decided to seek kingdom business first, what immediate changes in priorities would you have to make (time invested in providing for tomorrow's food and clothing versus God's call to ministry today)?

When I think about growing up with Walt as my dad and what it was like to be his son, the word "lucky" comes to mind. You may be thinking, "Awwwwww," but allow me to explain.

It never failed, any time I complained about anything, my dad was quick to tell me I was "lucky." I learned to hate that phrase, though now see that it is so true. I am indeed lucky. I was lucky to be adopted at birth and raised by Walt and Metta as my dad and mom. I was lucky to learn at a young age about the love and grace of God. I was lucky to live in a home filled with brothers and sisters, friends, and pets. And I have been lucky that my children have been raised to know their grandparents.

In my dad, I watched the constant dependence on God, rather than self, get him through the struggles of life and work. There was no facade of competence; in fact, we saw the battle first-hand of fear, frustration, patience, anger, and inadequacy. He wasn't perfect at it, but daily dependence on God allowed him to keep going.

John Gerber, son

Don't Be So Negative!

Matthew 6:22–23;
Philippians 4:8–13
May 27–28, 1989

If there's one area in my character I want to change, it would be my tendency to be negative and to question the motives of people. To see the dark side of an issue and ignore the upside potential of what God can do. I observe that upbeat people stress strengths, not weaknesses when talking about other people, attributing to them the best of motives. Upbeat people never spout doom and gloom when confronting tough situations, but hold to their trust that with God, nothing is impossible. Remember our theme verse for this year?

Trust in the Lord with all your heart and lean not on your own understanding. (Prov. 3:5)

Today we are not talking about "positive thinking." We are talking about trusting God enough to make positive responses to situations that otherwise would be overwhelming. In this context, let's study our text and look for some answers out of our bondage to negativism.

First, *negativism is conquered by renewing our trust that God really is involved in our lives.* There comes a time when every Christian must decide:

- if God is a God of the impossible or he isn't;
- if God answers prayer or he doesn't; and
- if God is personally involved in what happens to us or he isn't.

Our conclusion determines our perspective of life and people. Listen to Jesus:

> *The eye is the lamp of the body. If your eyes are healthy, your whole body will be full of light; but if your eyes are unhealthy, your whole body will be full of darkness. If then the light within you is dark-ness, how great is that darkness!* (Matt. 6:22–23)

Jesus warns that if we do not confront life armed with trust in God, we are going to live in darkness.

Two weeks ago, my neighbor shared in worship her choices when confronted with the reality of being a single parent, saying she could choose cheers or tears, faith or bitterness.

Recently I received a beautiful letter and a rose of answered prayer, describing the faithfulness of God to one in our church family. Having lost her husband in divorce and her father to death within one year, having gone through what she terms "hell," she writes, "Why was God continuing to test me? How could there be a God who would allow me to experience such suffering? Was there a God at all . . . ?" Then in bold type she declared:

> *The answer is Yes, Yes, Yes, there is a living God! I still at times do not feel his presence in prayer. I even doubt his presence on occasion in church. But he is ever present in my life. He is in my friends who have helped me through this ordeal.*

Then she concludes, "Yes, life is difficult. My path has been a crooked one. But the good news is that I know God has a purpose for me!"

Every Christian lives potentially in two worlds: a world of trusting God, or a world of carrying our load all alone. Trusting God prevents us from being eaten alive by negativism.

We then come to a second truth in our text: *Negativism is a habitual pattern of thinking which the Holy Spirit can change.* Our text outlines thought patterns of trust for the Christian:

> *Finally, brothers, whatever is true, whatever is noble, whatever is right, whatever is pure, whatever is lovely, whatever is admirable, if there is any excellence, if there is anything worthy of praise, think about these things.* (Phil. 4:8–9)

Negativism is a habitual pattern of thought, causing us to:

- see people or situations as a continual parade of insurmountable problems, divorced from God's arena of activity; and
- to hold the mistaken belief any solution to these problems rests solely on our shoulders.

In contrast, our text challenges us:

- to take control of our negative thought patterns; and
- to think about what is true, just, and pure regarding God's potential involvement in our needs.

With God, nothing is hopeless, nothing is impossible. He has solutions we haven't even considered.

Finally, let's go to the question: "If we want to break free from this trap, how do we do it?" *Negativism is a habitual pattern of choice that can be changed by spiritual discipline.*

Changing any habit requires new learning and spiritual discipline. Personally, I'm working on monitoring my thoughts and reactions to situations and people—a process proving very embarrassing. It's incredible how much negativism I find in my thoughts and conversations! As a kind of spiritual discipline, I'm asking questions, before I blurt out with my usual responses. "Regarding this problem or this person, am I responding in trust or am I acting like it all depends on me? Do I believe God is involved or not?"

Last month I learned that a lifetime friend was diagnosed as having pancreatic cancer. She is my age and would leave a husband and family. I called her after church last Sunday and asked how it was going. More specifically I asked, "Trudy, you and I have been preparing since third grade for this event of dying. Is your Christian faith working for you as you walk through the valley of the shadow?"

Immediately she responded, "The support of my family and church are helpful. The chemotherapy is making my hair fall out, but it might buy me a little time. My faith in God is the rock I lean on. I choose to trust him now, even when I can't understand or see, and it's working!" No negativism or bitterness, only unshakable faith in God. Trust is winning this battle. She has disciplined her thoughts to boldly trust God, even when facing the ultimate challenge of death.

When the bottom drops out of our lives, our response to deep pain will hinge largely on whether or not we believe God's power reaches us in the depths. Sometimes trusting God means nothing more than the discipline of just "showing up," of taking one step after another through our painful valley of darkness—not expecting God to give easy logical answers. Most of the time trusting God brings no ecstasy, no feeling we want to praise or give thanks—just the discipline of hanging on, enduring one moment to the next, confident our Heavenly Father is going to come through in the end. Sometimes it's only as we look back on these tough places that we realize we weren't alone in our struggle.

I find the most helpful act of spiritual discipline that develops my trust in God is to saturate my mind with promises of Scripture. As we close, I want the Holy Spirit to do some therapy on troubled hearts and troubled relationships right now. Let me share promises of Scripture that make us aware of how close God really is to our need:

> *Let your gentleness be evident to all. The Lord is near. Do not be anxious about anything, but in everything by prayer and petition, with thanksgiving, present your requests to God. And the peace of God, which transcends all understanding, will guard your hearts and your minds in Christ Jesus.* (Phil. 4:5–7)

> *My help comes from the LORD, the Maker of heaven and earth. He will not let your foot slip—he who watches over you will not slumber. . . . The LORD will keep you from all harm; he will watch over your life.* (Ps. 121:2–3, 7)

> *Whoever dwells in the shelter of the Most High will rest in the shadow of the Almighty. I will say of the LORD, "HE IS MY REFUGE AND MY FORTRESS, MY GOD, IN WHOM I TRUST." . . . He will cover you with his feathers, and under his wings you will find refuge. . . . You will not fear the terror of night, nor the arrow that flies by day. . . . "Because he loves me," says the LORD, "I will rescue him; I will protect him, because he acknowledges my name. He will call on me, and I will answer him; I will be with him in trouble, I will deliver him and honor him. With long life I will satisfy him and show him my salvation."* (Ps. 91:1–2, 4–5, 14–16)

I close with a question: "Will negativism or trust in God be your response to tough times and difficult people?"

Your choice will determine what life companions fill your soul: hope or despair; joy or bitterness; security or fear. May God enable us to choose trust. May God make us upbeat people in the midst of a society that has lost its ability to smile. May our optimism be a magnet drawing people to faith in our Savior, the Lord Jesus Christ.

Questions for Study and Discussion:

1. If someone asked you, "Does God answer prayer? Is he person-ally involved in our lives?" how would you answer? Does your approach to life reflect trust in God or negativity?

2. Try monitoring your thoughts for a day or for a week. When you encounter a negative thought, try asking the questions Walt posed: "Regarding this problem or this person, am I responding in trust or am I acting like it all depends on me? Do I believe God is involved or not?" Counter negative thoughts with "saturation" in Scripture, whether it be reading one of the verses Walt sug-gested or finding another of your own.

TIME TO FALL IN LOVE AGAIN

Ephesians 6:19–20; James 4:1–3
November 6–7, 1993

Two weeks ago, Libby Vincent mentioned in her sermon a story from *Newsweek* about an Afro-American brother and sister who, while watching the beating of truck driver Reginald Denny during the Los Angeles riots, couldn't just sit there and watch it happen. Because they were Christians, the love of Jesus drove them out of the comfort and safety of their living room into the streets, to provide Mr. Denny the protection and care that ultimately saved his life. When Libby told that story, I asked myself: "Where is my passion? What would drive me out of my comfort zone?"

We claim the goal of this church family is to help people become more like Jesus. To become like Jesus implies that his love increasingly captures our hearts, changing our focus from self to others. Many of us feel spiritual stagnation in our Christian life. Our comfort zones have become a kind of prison. Why? Could it be that we are so infected with the rampant viruses of suburbia . . . achieving, consuming, controlling, acquiring . . . that our journey to become like Jesus has taken a detour? That our first love for our Lord has grown cold? When our love for Jesus cools, our concern for others is diminished and we fall increasingly into bondage to self.

In the book of Revelation, God addresses the church of Ephesus, saying: "I hold this against you: You have forsaken the love you had at first" (Rev. 2:4). If our love for Jesus has cooled, how do we stoke the fire? I'm convinced that one secret for falling in love again with Jesus is to grow in our understanding and practice of prayer. Prayer is the door through which we must walk to maintain intimacy with Jesus in a busy, distraction-filled world.

Consider the importance of prayer to Paul the apostle. Although chained to Roman guards twenty-four hours a day, his prayer life fills him with infectious joy, indomitable trust in God and a deep desire that his guards come to know Jesus as Savior.

Our prayers expose our priorities. What we say to God reveals what's really important to us. Paul writes, "Pray also for me, that whenever I speak, words may be given me so that I will fearlessly make known the mystery of the gospel" (Eph. 6:19). At this point, Paul is under house arrest, chained to several shifts of Roman soldiers around the clock, awaiting trial and possible execution. Yet, he isn't whining in his prayers. He doesn't say, "Lord, after my faithfulness to you . . . why did this happen to me? Get me out of this mess, so I can get on with my life. Help me, if you love me!"

His focus is not on his own pain. He is not asking for a return to his comfort zone. Convinced that knowing Jesus is the only thing that really counts in life, a passion burns in his heart, for the hardened guards to which he was chained to become Christians. Calling the gospel a mystery, he prays for clarity and courage in sharing with them the good news of Jesus. And "mystery" means, if these guards are ever to be convinced to follow Jesus, it will require supernatural power from God, power activated by prayer!

Can you imagine what would happen if this same passion for people trying to make it in today's world without Jesus began to grip our hearts? Maybe it's time to stop reducing Jesus to little more than a divine source for keeping us in our comfort zones, and to stop being so preoccupied with our own needs and pain that we become blind or indifferent to the growing needs of our neighbors.

A beginning step to break preoccupation with self is to look at the content of our prayers. Paul's prayers, even in time of deep personal need, were focused on others. I found it embarrassing when I did an inventory of my prayer life. Most of my prayers are focused on my needs and unfulfilled dreams, my problems and fears.

It's a no-brainer to understand why our love for Jesus and for others grows cold. Our culture has taught us to promote self, to push our own agendas, to arrive at the top of the heap with enough money, power, and material possessions to assure personal security. No wonder we can't hear Jesus calling us to deny ourselves, to give ourselves away, to discover the joy of becoming involved with others. No wonder we feel spiritually stagnant and dull, and wonder where we lost the joy and adventure in being a Christian.

How do we restore a lost passion to be like Jesus? How do we break with our preoccupation with self? By taking that first step: to analyze our prayers. What do our prayers reveal about what's really important to us?

Secondly, Paul believed God answers prayer. Paul asked his friends to pray for him because he believed prayer is always answered in the best way, not sometimes, but every time. But there is a condition, Jesus told us:

> *Until now you have not asked for anything in my name. Ask and you will receive, and your joy will be complete.* (John 16:24)

John goes on to write:

> *This is the confidence we have in approaching God: that if we ask anything according to his will, he hears us.* (1 John 5:14)

God answers prayer when we pray in the name or with the heart of Jesus. As we grow and become like Jesus, our prayer life should begin to resemble the heart of Jesus. When Jesus prayed in the garden he does so by saying, "Not my will but thine be done." Rather than using prayer exclusively to convince God to protect our comfort zones, our prayers should become a means for opening our lives, so God can use us as a blessing for others.

Consider James the apostle's warning in James 4: You want something, but don't get it. You do not have because you do not ask God. When you ask, you do not receive, because you ask with wrong motives, that you may spend what you get on your pleasures . . . your comfort zone (based on vv. 2–3).

Paul's prayer life models for us the adventure of becoming so caught up in our concern for others that our focus moves from self to others.

Every Saturday morning our men pray for others, for those who are in career transition, who are ill, who need Jesus. We receive letters telling us how God has responded to our prayers. Prayer works!

Lewis Grizzard, a syndicated columnist, last year was forced to undergo heart surgery. When he regained consciousness after surgery, the first thing he remembers was the hospital staff saying he was a miracle. He had survived a valve replacement, after everything that could go wrong did during his surgery. He writes, "To a man and woman, those doctors and nurses said, 'We exhausted all medical possibilities. We did everything we knew to do for you, and it probably wouldn't have been enough. What saved you was prayer.'" Can you believe that? Great men and women of science saying such a thing in 1993? One doctor explained, "Everywhere I went during your worst time, I ran into people who said they were praying for you. One woman said, 'I don't agree with anything he writes, but I'm still praying for him.'" Grizzard concludes by saying, "What I did to deserve any of that I don't know, but I do know I had spent a lot of that time in doubt. If the medical experts say prayer brought me back from certain death, who am I to doubt them?"[29]

Here is an instance where a group of Christians are so caught up in their love for Jesus that their prayers reach out to a columnist with whom they didn't even agree politically, but who needed healing help!

Prayer for personal needs is not wrong. Our text simply warns us not to become so focused on our own needs that we exclude concern for others. God is interested in the tiniest detail of our lives. He invites us to take every personal need to him in prayer.

Lieutenant Robert Wetzel tells of his experience as a prisoner in an Iraqi prison during the Gulf War. After several days without water he prayed, "God please give me some water." Within minutes, he writes, "a guard opened my cell and gave me the last drops of water from his pail. Then, after getting more water, he filled my cup a second time. . . . Some days later, as I shivered on the icy concrete floor while the nighttime desert temperature dropped to near zero, I prayed, 'God I'm so cold. I'm feeling pretty helpless. Can you give me a sign?' Minutes later the cell door opened and someone threw in a blanket. Finally, one night the prison was nearly leveled in an air raid. The terrified guards fled, leaving me and six other POWs locked in their cells. One more bomb would have reduced the prison to rubble. It never came and not a single POW was injured."[30]

God answers prayers for personal need, but personal need should not be the sole focus of our prayers.

Finally, prayer requires discipline and effort. People want to be thin, but won't exert the effort to go on a diet. Many want more spiritual vitality, but lack the discipline for developing a prayer life. Paul requests prayer while in prison because long years of a disciplined prayer life convinced him that if he needed supernatural help in times of crisis, he had better pray.

If we want to restore our passion for Jesus and for others, we must practice the discipline of prayer. We must make time to be intimate with Jesus in prayer. I often allude to the time I set aside for regular physical exercise. It requires discipline to keep my body fit. Developing a prayer life requires similar discipline. Let me suggest that you do some of the following:

- If you are a beginner or a doubter regarding prayer, begin setting a small amount of time aside to pray for one target of human need and watch what happens.

- Consider joining one of the prayer groups in our church where you can learn to pray.
- Ask God to give you a name or names of people who need Jesus. Imagine sitting next to a friend in church in the next few months, a person who came because you prayed!
- Pray for someone you know who is ill, out of work, having marital problems and tell them you are praying for them.

I want people in this community to view our church family as a group of people who care for others, people who believe God answers prayer—so much so that those who observe us might say, "I don't attend there, but if I had a need, I know they would pray for me and it would make a difference."

Prayer will lead us away from self and into involvement with others. When we take time to really pray, we begin to fall in love again with Jesus, and like an involuntary reaction, we begin to get involved with those who need us.

Questions for Study and Discussion:

1. Consider what you've prayed about in the past week. If an outsider looked at your prayers, what would they conclude were your priorities?

2. Who might God be calling you to pray for as a discipline? (It might be someone for whom you wouldn't ordinarily care, but who matters to God. It might be for an outcome of God's choosing, rather than your own.)

Jesus Heals Our Diseases
...But He Uses Us!

Matthew 8:1–27
November 3–4, 1990

As we continue our study in Matthew, remember he wrote this gospel believing that Jesus is God in the flesh. Today he reveals our Lord's deep compassion for people going through tough times. When we are really hurting and afraid and feel helpless, Jesus offers two helpful facts:

- God cares about what's happening to us.
- And, by faith and prayer, we can appropriate divine power that brings help and healing.

Here is a first great truth in our text: *Jesus does heal physical disease in response to personal faith and power.*

A leper comes to Jesus—a leper, the most despised and ostracized person in Jewish society. Leprosy was a living death, similar to the current AIDS epidemic. Yet the leper in our story is very aggressive in fighting back against his disease. Rather than crawl into a cave to await death, hope drives him to search for healing, even though medicine of the day would call him incurable. During his search, he finds Jesus.

Hearing about his miracles, he boldly approaches Jesus, although it was forbidden by law, under penalty of death, for him to come near anyone. His statement of faith is simple, as he asks for a miraculous healing of his leprosy: "Lord, if you will, you can make me clean" (Matt. 8:2, ESV).

Note that he doesn't make a demand. "Lord, *if you will*, you can make me clean." Faith in Jesus that brings healing seems to be a mixture of:

- humility that acknowledges we have no right to ask anything;
- submission to our Lord's will, though it might contain a higher purpose for us than physical healing; and
- a confidence that Jesus *can* heal, if that should be his will.

Note also that the leper did not ask Jesus to pray to God to heal him. His faith led him to view Jesus as God in the flesh, thus possessing personal authority and power to heal him of his dread, incurable disease.

Faith that leads to healing is rooted in this incredible confidence: Jesus loves us. We know it because the Bible says so, and because our personal experience proves it's true.

I'm impressed with how Jesus *always* responds to anyone who comes to him in need. There is no recorded incident in the New Testament where someone came to Jesus with a request for help, and it was denied. In our story, Jesus doesn't just pity this leper or withdraw from this dirty, infected piece of humanity. Jesus stretches out his hand and touches him, healing him instantly. Remember, because leprosy was thought to be contagious, this leper had not been touched since he first became ill!

Possessing faith that Jesus will heal us in response to our prayers is a force that heals. Surgeon Bernie Siegel has written two books, *Love, Medicine and Miracles* and *Peace, Love and Healing*. I recommend both these books to you, keeping in mind that, as Christians, our faith is not in faith itself, but in the person of Jesus Christ. In both books Dr. Seigel demonstrates the role played by the patient in participating in the healing process. He claims it's mandatory in healing that:

- a patient desires to get better;
- a patient believes he or she will get better, in spite of medical statistics and projections;
- a patient opens themselves to the love and support of other people who will participate with them in the healing process; and
- a patient believes in the power of faith to heal.

Faith in Jesus as a power to heal is not quackery or wishful thinking. Faith in Jesus opens the doors for us to experience miracles.

However, this first truth that Jesus heals might be expanded to say: Jesus heals physical diseases today . . . *often using the faith, prayers, and availability of Christians as his vehicle for healing.*

This year our theme is "Serving others with the love of Christ." When we love as Jesus loves, we open ourselves to become involved in our neighbor's pain—to reach out and touch those in need, as Jesus did while on Earth. We seek increasingly effective ways to go beyond warm and fuzzy feelings for people, to the point of making our neighbor's needs a priority in our own agendas, regardless of risk or cost.

As members of our church family, we have two responsibilities when it comes to appropriating the healing of Jesus for illness:

- We must be available for each other in times of weakness, which means we must know each other in advance of illness. This is the purpose of covenant groups and other sources of friendship within our church family.
- And, we must be vulnerable and seek help from each other, when illness strikes. No one should ever be sick alone.

My secretary is recovering from cancer surgery. I was amazed at how this church family stood with her during the diagnostic procedures, surgery,

234 | The Best is Yet to Come

and recuperation. Our prayers, phone calls, food, and touches of concern altogether became Christ's healing hand in Menlo Park this year. However, we could not have given to Jane had she not been open to accept the help of Jesus coming through us.

Come let Christ love you and heal you through us, when you are ill, in the same way the leper took aggressive action to seek healing for his disease.

The next character in our story illustrates a second truth how Jesus heals our diseases. A centurion comes to Jesus seeking healing for his slave. The leper represents the power of *personal faith* as a vehicle for healing. The centurion represents the power of faith to heal disease, expressed through *intercession* on behalf of another. The centurion was an outcast like the leper, a Gentile excluded for racial reasons. Yet the centurion was a special Gentile, in that he loved his slave. Slaves were considered beasts of burden and treated as such. Yet this tough Roman soldier cares so much for his slave, he comes to Jesus seeking a miracle. As a military officer, he is accustomed to giving orders, not asking favors. Yet his need creates in him a humility leading him to say to Jesus, "Lord, my servant is lying paralyzed at home, suffering terribly. . . . I am not worthy to have you come under my roof, but only say the word, and my servant will be healed" (Matt. 8:6, 8).

Jesus, filled with compassion, responds to this centurion's faith and concern for another human being. This drama reminds us that God loves us so much, it's okay to bring not only our own needs, but the needs of a stranger to him. This centurion was not a Jew—or, in modern terms, was not a member of Menlo Park Presbyterian Church. He didn't deserve any favor from Jesus, because he hadn't done anything to cultivate a relationship with him. However, he had a need, and believed Jesus could do something. That's all our Lord needed to respond to his request.

Note how the centurion respects Jesus' hesitancy as a Jew to enter a Gentile's house. Possessing such faith, he tells Jesus not to bother coming physically to his home to heal his sick friend. As a centurion, he understands power and authority. Realizing Jesus possesses authority to heal disease, he tells Jesus to simply *say the word*. Now that's faith!

Here is a beautiful picture of the power of prayer on behalf of someone who is in need. This paralyzed slave is healed by Jesus through the faith of the centurion. Nothing in the story indicates the slave has faith or even knows Jesus. Jesus gives us permission in this story to believe *for* others, without demanding they share our belief. Jesus doesn't ask the centurion, "Does your servant have faith to believe I can heal him?" Based on the centurion's faith alone, Jesus heals the sickness of the servant, saying, "'Go; let it be done for you as *you* have believed.' And the servant was healed at that very moment" (v. 13, ESV, emphasis added).

Here is a second truth about how Jesus heals: *The centurion shows us that when we pray for others, our faith frees God to accomplish miracles in the lives of people for whom we are led to pray.*

Our text closes with a drama at sea that offers a third truth about faith that leads to healing, faith that opens us to the help of Jesus in times of trouble. The disciples are confronted with a life-threatening storm, a situation so critical only Jesus can help. Impossible problems and frightening times can stimulate us to grow beyond viewing Jesus academically, to reaching out to him because we need his saving power and have no place else to go. When there seems to be no way out, that's exactly the moment Jesus acts.

The disciples are panicked. Waves are coming over the bow, threatening to swamp their little boat. Jesus proceeds to give them a very valuable lesson about how faith works: "Listen you guys, you are in serious trouble, and this is no time to talk about the logic of natural law. All of you are so bound to a mistaken belief that God is bound to follow his own natural laws. Isn't it logical that if God can make laws, he can break them? Happily, I possess power, with my Heavenly Father's blessing, to go beyond natural law and save your hides!"

For most of us raised in this culture, our faith in natural law is greater than our faith in God's ability to do miracles. Yet, if we believe in our Lord's resurrection from the dead in order to find salvation and eternal life, why is it so difficult to trust Jesus for other personal needs?

Here is some good news to take home. Jesus doesn't withdraw from his disciples because they were afraid in the midst of the storm, and their faith began to crumble. Jesus did a miracle anyway. You and I can approach Jesus with our "little faith" in times of crisis, and he will respond. Our faith doesn't have to be perfect for it to work. This gift is called grace.

Our Lord's miracle at sea blows the whistle on the notion that somehow the more faith, the more help we will receive from Jesus. These stories teach us Jesus will help us:

- in times of personal illness;
- when those we love are in need; and
- when we are in the midst of life's frightening storms.

Jesus hears our cry! He wants to help. We respond with what faith we have, even when it's tiny faith, and with astonishing eagerness Jesus responds to us. Comfort one another with these words.

Questions for Study and Discussion:

1. Have you ever prayed for healing for yourself or another? Did you expect much? What happened? How did it impact your prayers for healing thereafter?

2. Do you know of anyone who was miraculously healed? What was your response?

What I loved about Walt was what everyone who sat in the pews loved about Walt: he could make you feel like he was speaking directly to you. Not ever in an accusing or reproachful way, but rather he welcomed, he invited, even if what he offered was correction! Having come from a church that was heavy on accusation and reproach, I'd never heard or understood God's message of grace until I heard Walt.

Not only did he make Jesus approachable, but Walt was approachable. I remember one incident, when Walt had been stricken with Bell's palsy for the second time. Now, Bell's palsy is about the worst affliction you can lay on a preacher—having had it myself, I know the embarrassment of having one half of your face sag from unresponsive nerves. You look like you had a stroke, your eating and drinking are impaired, and your speech is affected. You'd rather spend the entire time it takes to recover hiding under a rock, but there was Walt at the church. And such was his friendly, joking, approachable relationship with the staff that one of the youth interns—knowing it would make him laugh—went up to him and teased, "Why the long face, Walt?"

Christina Dudley

LIVING BEYOND THE
SURVIVAL MODE

John 15:1–8
May 13–14, 2000

Today I want us to revisit and think more deeply about a truth we discussed Easter weekend. Living the Christian life:

- is not about following rules for good behavior;
- is not about accepting a set of church doctrines;
- is not about being religious at all.

A Christian is a person who cultivates a passionate, personal, all-consuming relationship with Jesus Christ. Disciples in the New Testament were devoted to a *person*, not a cause. Paul the apostle wrote, "For I resolved to know nothing while I was with you except Jesus Christ and him crucified" (1 Cor. 2:2).

All other issues of morality and right doctrine are rooted in what Jesus terms remaining or "abiding" in him. He uses the metaphor of a branch connected to a vine. As a branch draws its life from the vine, we believers draw our life from Jesus. When the life of Jesus flows into us, we experience a change in lifestyle that I am calling "living beyond the survival mode." Let's consider what it means to "remain" in Jesus. Some translations use the term "abide," which I am using today.

First, to abide means we relate to Jesus as a branch relates to a vine. He says, "No branch can bear fruit by itself; it must remain (or abide) in the vine. . . . I am the vine, you are the branches. . . . If you do not remain in me, you are like a branch that is thrown away and withers" (John 15:4–6).

Last year we purchased a very beautiful Christmas tree. On the way home, I broke a branch that was essential for its symmetry. Being very creative, I taped the broken branch into position. In a short time, cut off from the life of the trunk, that branch died long before the rest of the tree. Seeking to salvage something from my attempt at creativity, I realized I was witnessing a perfect example of what Jesus is teaching in his metaphor of the vine and branches. When I allow myself to become disconnected from intimacy with my Lord, my life, my power, my joy all shrivel up.

Following Easter weekend, I went away to recharge my emotional batteries. For a week, I resolved to take a total break from thinking about church business. Unfortunately, at the same time I cut back on my discipline of prayer and reading the Bible, which are my lifelines to Jesus. In a very few days I found my thought patterns becoming increasingly focused on challenges and problems, divorced from the provision Jesus promised he would give. I began to sink under the load of worry and stress and began drowning in what seemed to be a whirlpool of impossible problems. Very quickly I realized I can't take a vacation from intimacy with Jesus, any more than I can take a vacation from breathing. I need his life flowing into me constantly, or I will dry up like that broken branch on my Christmas tree.

My point: abiding daily in Jesus is a necessity for believers, if we seek the abundant life he promises his followers. What's more, it's a tremendous privilege to know that Jesus, God in the flesh, seeks intimacy with us.

I was viewing some outtakes of the life of Bob Hope, reviewing his relationship with eleven presidents of the United States. Throughout his career, he often stayed overnight at the White House and experienced intimacy with presidents few other people have ever known. One First Lady remarked how they enjoyed inviting Bob over for a weekend, during which time they would kick off their shoes and relate as ordinary people talking about ordinary things. I thought that description of Bob Hope's relationship with presidents parallels our incredible opportunity to be intimate with Jesus.

I will never fully comprehend the privilege of knowing Jesus at a personal level. As the old hymn states, "He walks with me and talks with me and tells me I am his own." Through conversation with him in prayer, by learning his heart through reading Scripture, how incredible to know Jesus as a friend with whom we share our deepest secrets and most pressing needs.

How well do you know Jesus? Too many Christians trust Jesus just enough to get to heaven, but never experience the exhilaration of being transfused with his supernatural power, undergirded daily with his unconditional love. Jesus wants every believer to do more than survive in this world, clinging to this mindset of "If I can just get through this next meeting, this semester, this financial crisis, this relational difficulty, this business deal. If I can just make it until my next vacation! If I can just survive!"

Jesus offers us his life, like a vine gives life to a branch, connecting us with an inexhaustible, supply of resurrection power! Possessing this power enabled Paul the apostle to say, "Do not be anxious about anything" (Phil. 4:6). The Lord is at hand!

Abiding in Jesus enables us to pass the breaking point and not break, to be filled with expectancy in circumstances that would otherwise crush us. Paul described it this way:

We are hard pressed on every side, but not crushed; perplexed, but not in despair; persecuted, but not abandoned; struck down but not destroyed. . . . For we who are alive are always being given over to death for Jesus' sake, so that his life may be revealed in our mortal body. (2 Cor. 4:8, 11)

Do we fully realize this potential of the life of Jesus in us? Listen to what Scripture says:

> *I can do all this through him who gives me strength.* (Phil. 4:13)

> *"My grace is sufficient for you, for my power is made perfect in weakness." Therefore, I will boast all the more gladly about my weaknesses, so that Christ's power may rest on me.* (2 Cor. 12:9)

> *For this reason, I kneel before the Father. . . . I pray that out of his glorious riches he may strengthen you with power through his spirit in your inner being.* (Eph. 3:14, 16)

This is the power from the Vine that can be ours, power to cope, to overcome, to endure, and to win, if we choose to abide in Jesus.

So how does one *abide* in Jesus?

A second truth: abiding or remaining in Jesus is a discipline. "No branch can bear fruit by itself; it must remain in the vine. Neither can you bear fruit unless you remain in me" (John 15:4). To remain in the vine means, as believers, we must *do* something. Jesus uses the term "fruit," which is later defined elsewhere in Scripture as the fruit of the Spirit: "But the fruit of the Spirit is love, joy, peace, forbearance [patience], kindness, goodness, faithfulness, gentleness and self-control" (Gal. 5:22–23).

These qualities of life, the alternative to a lifestyle of merely surviving, come as the fruit of practicing the discipline of abiding in Jesus. We were created to live connected to, dependent upon, Jesus. However, I have concluded that, beginning with this preacher, we will never practice this discipline of abiding in Jesus until we come to a place where we can't take another step, where we can't cope without him.

Our Lord's primary agenda for every believer is not to make us happy, nor to make life easier. His agenda is to do whatever is necessary to bring us into such a personal vital relationship with himself that we begin to bear the fruit of his character, so much so that we become like Jesus. There is an old gospel song that articulates this truth:

Let the beauty of Jesus be seen in me,
all his love and compassion and purity.
Thou Spirit divine, all my nature refine,
Till the beauty of Jesus be seen in me.

This prayer is answered as the fruit of practicing the discipline of a lifestyle that focuses on Jesus, maintaining the flow of his life into *us*.

- We can choose the habit of frequent prayer, bringing our Lord into every situation, rather than carrying the load alone. I talk to Jesus all day long, as I would with any friend.
- We can choose regular attendance at worship and participation in a small group, coupled with daily Bible study.
- We can "prune" our schedules that are so filled with other things, so that Jesus and his agendas are top priority. One regret many of us will have in heaven is how we wasted so many hours of our lives being involved in stuff that had no eternal significance, while being too busy to enjoy Jesus and be involved in his agendas for our lives.

I have a regular meeting at Starbucks with a friend, where we are always discussing what new thing Jesus is doing in our lives, or in our church. We have discovered that people watch and listen to us and get the idea Jesus and his business is very important to us.

- What do your conversations and daily agendas say about the priority Jesus plays in your life?
- What would people guess is the thing closest to your heart, if they spent a few hours talking with you? Conversation, time, agendas, and our money all tend to follow our hearts.

Abiding in Jesus is a discipline, similar to what it takes to cultivate any relationship. Friendships, marriage, children—all *take time*. There are no shortcuts. However, when you love someone, discipline isn't a task, it's a joy. That's why, over and over again, I offer the same prescription for cultivating closeness to Jesus. We love him because he first loved us, and died for us, that we might be with him forever. What greater motive do we need for making him the focus of our lives, for pruning our schedules, so we have time to enjoy and serve him?

So, our challenge today: stay connected to the Vine. Prune our schedules so, while chasing important things, we won't regret we have omitted the most important thing in life, our relationship with Jesus and doing the kingdom work he calls us to do. I pray every one of us who takes the name "Christian" will be able to look back on our lives, not as survival stories, but as adventures in trusting our faithful Savior. I pray we will be so close to him that his beauty will be seen in us, and others will be drawn to his irresistible love.

Questions for Study and Discussion:

1. If you consider the most important relationships in your life, how do you keep them healthy? How would those practices translate to your relationship with Jesus?

2. When have you felt most attached to Jesus? When have you felt like you're withering away? What choices did you make to arrive in either place?

Time Out!

Ecclesiastes 3:1–8
November 25–26, 1989

O n this weekend preceding the busy Christmas season, it seems appropriate that we think today about time, about busy calendars and past Christmases lost in a flurry of activity. Our study in Romans has focused on bringing various areas of our lives under the control of Jesus Christ. I'm convinced that one of the most out-of-control areas of behavior in our church family is addiction to overloaded schedules and hyperactivity. I believe God invites us to take control of our calendars so we can celebrate Christmas for the holy day it is! If we could take control of our schedules next month, the habit might spread into the New Year and change our lives. With this in mind, let's learn from the wisdom of Scripture about time.

First, our text tells us that *God has given each of us enough time to do everything he calls us to do.*

> *There is an appointed time for everything. And there is time for every event under heaven.* (Eccl. 3:1, NASB)

Overcommitted schedules are having a destructive impact upon our families, emotions, physical and spiritual health. Bondage to schedules robs us of:

- time with family and friends;
- time for worship and introspection; and
- time with no agenda other than to enjoy life!

When we talk about time, we talk about life. Queen Elizabeth said with her dying breath, "All my possessions for a moment of time."

Time magazine describes how overcrowded schedules are impacting our society. People no longer enjoy doing *one* thing, because we are always doing several things at the same time:

- Commuters used to read newspapers on the train. Now we read while driving, when we're not closing another deal on the cellular phone.
- At health clubs people ride stationary bikes and peer over a stack of reports, memos, and spreadsheets.
- Families rarely sit together at the kitchen table, robbing them of intimacy.
- Hallmark makes cards to tuck under Cheerios in the morning that say, "Have a nice day at school," for parents who cannot be with children in the morning; or a card to put under the pillow at night that reads, "I wish I were there to tuck you in."

An elder was describing time-based competition. Businesses are seeking to compress the time from inception of an idea to delivery of the product to market, because time is profit. This concept puts incredible stress on employees to meet stricter deadlines. One professor of psychology at Yale, commenting on crowded schedules, says, "We're at the breaking point as far as the family is concerned."

Pollster Louis Harris concludes that *time* has become the most precious commodity in our land. The amount of leisure time available to us has shrunk 37 percent since 1973. Many of us work 80+ hours per week. Vacations for many are nothing more than long weekends.

One reason given for a decrease in leisure time is our drive for more things, which leads to more bills, which means we must work longer hours to make ends meet. Then there are those who have enough money and don't need to work. Nevertheless, they are enslaved to schedules that rob them of being able to do what they really want to do.

Addiction to overcrowded schedules has spread like a virus to our children. Our children are scheduled to the point of the exclusion of leisure—programmed by parents into a lifestyle of super-achievement. Superachieving can become a disease from which we are forced to recover as adults. Children are being cheated out of childhood by schedules out of control. God says there must be time to be a child!

I'm beginning to realize that our church contributes to this problem. In a desire to meet people's needs, we have ministries going seven days and nights a week. Many feel guilty of slighting God if they don't sign up for everything. I want us to understand there is no spiritual virtue in being involved in this church to the neglect of family and other priorities to which God calls us. There is a time to be at church, and a time to be away from church.

Our text reminds us that God has given us enough time to do everything he wants us to do. When we crowd in extra things, our schedules spiral out of control. Remember, Jesus never allowed himself to be pressured into a crowded schedule. At critical moments of potential for ministry, he would grab his disciples and take off for the mountains, or go to the house of a friend and kick up his feet to relax. Jesus did not suffer from a harried schedule, even though his commission was to save the world!

Only a dramatic change will enable us to regain control of our lives in the area of time, a fact which leads us to a further truth: God has given us twenty-four hours every day. *It is our responsibility to decide how we will use those hours.*

God is not asking us to be overcommitted and overstressed, doing things we don't really want to do. We *choose* to live this way. Our personal schedules this December will be decided by choices we make now. It's not too late to take control of our calendars for next month, and clear them of everything except those events that we feel called of God to do.

Let me be specific. Two weeks ago, our staff was looking ahead at our church's Christmas schedule. We realized that we were asking our choir and musical staff to do an annual Christmas concert, special musical support for our Sunday before Christmas, and sing five services Christmas Eve. We asked, "What is this schedule doing to our own people—all in the name of Christmas?"

So we made a decision: We cancelled the Christmas concert, even though the musicians had already been booked, and rehearsals for the music had begun. Now our choir and musical staff will lead us through the Christmas season without feeling totally exhausted by the most wonderful holiday of our year. No one should be asked to give more than they have to give, in the name of Christmas.

My point? If we become serious about taking control of our Christmas schedule, we must make some choices and do some radical surgery *now*. Why not cancel some things if you are overbooked, so you can enjoy the things you choose to do? Tell people why you are canceling, and blame this sermon for your decision. How much is a stress-free Christmas season worth to you?

One reason the shepherds heard angels on the first Christmas is that they spent quiet nights *wondering—pondering—praying*. The three kings saw that Star of Bethlehem, because they made time to look at the heavens and to think about things beyond the stress and flurry of their immediate world. Christmas comes, inviting us to make time this year to wonder over and ponder the miracle of our Lord's birth and its impact upon the world and upon our personal lives.

This will be my sixteenth Christmas in Menlo Park. The first sermon I preached in this church was entitled, "Slow Me Down, Lord." It took a long time for me to obey this prayer. Dictated by my health, my family, and the inner voice of the Holy Spirit, I began to make choices that brought my calendar under control. I learned to delegate responsibility to an incredibly gifted team of colleagues. I take time away without feeling guilty, knowing that time away makes my ministry with you more effective. I seldom speak anywhere, but to this congregation. Our church has grown to four services and a seven-day-a-week ministry. Yet I feel less stress than I felt six years ago. Our church is not led by one charismatic overstressed leader.

This year I have every intention of enjoying Christmas. Planning for December I have said "no" to much, so I can say "yes" with enthusiasm to things I feel God wants me to do, and things I want to do. I tell you this story not to sound arrogant, but to encourage you to take similar aggressive steps in schedule control during this Advent season.

Listen to the words of John Wesley: "Though I am always in haste, I am never in a hurry because I never undertake more work than I can go through with calmness of spirit."[31]

You may have seen the words Erma Bombeck wrote, near the end of her life, where she thinks about what she would have done differently if she had her life to live over again. Being Erma Bombeck, she thinks she should've lit the rose-shaped candle she had, before it melted in storage, and let the family roll down the car windows, even though her hair was done just-so. But she also has more serious thoughts. About how she would have "talked less and listened more." About how she would have those friends over to dinner, even if the house was a mess. Or, when one of her kids kissed her, she wouldn't have said, "Later—now go get washed up for dinner." Bombeck concludes, "Given another shot at life, I would seize every minute . . . look at it and really see it . . . live it . . . and never give it back."[32]

Our December schedules can be planned so that God can give us a truly merry Christmas. Minutes to seize and really look at and live and never give back—the choice is up to us. There is an appointed time for everything. And there is a time for every event under heaven.

Questions for Study and Discussion:

1. If you're feeling overscheduled and overstressed, where might God be calling you to cut some things from the calendar?

2. In which area of your life would you choose to spend more time, if you had more time? How can you reduce quantity of commitments in order to increase the quality of them?

God is Listening . . .
Talk to Him!

1 John 5:13–15
February 15–16, 1992

Today I want us to consider a common cause of misery in the life of Christians, best expressed in the words of that classic hymn: "O what peace we often forfeit . . . O what needless pain we bear . . . all because we do not carry everything to God in prayer."

In January, *Newsweek* featured an article entitled "Talking to God," discussing the revival of prayer in America. According to a recent survey, 78 percent of Americans pray once a week, and 57 percent pray once a day. The article claimed even atheists pray, wagering that if there is a God who hears them, it's a good bet. Couples use prayer as a bond to hold their marriage together. Prayer as meditation is being used to help cure cancer. People seem to have a growing hunger for a personal experience with God.

However, prayer as discussed in *Newsweek* is a generic term, "talking to God as we choose to perceive him." Today I want us to think about what Jesus taught concerning prayer. Jesus said that for the believer, prayer is a potential power that can help us cope victoriously with life. If prayer holds that potential, let's study our text.

A first truth we learn about prayer is that Christians have confidence in approaching God! Our text says:

> *This is the confidence we have in approaching God: that if we ask anything according to his will, he hears us.* (1 John 5:14)

This is an incredible promise! Confidence before God is a key ingredient in Christian prayer. The Bible describes how the sacrifice of Jesus gives us confidence with God, saying:

> *[W]e have a great high priest . . . Jesus the Son of God . . . one who has been tempted in every way, just as we are—yet he did not sin. Let us then approach the throne of grace with confidence, so that we may receive mercy and find grace to help us in our time of need.* (Heb. 4:14–16)

In spite of our unworthiness, God is accessible to us because of the sacrifice of Jesus! This is the good news of Christianity. Think about average people on the street. Do they understand that the God who made and sustains this universe really cares about their personal needs and listens to their prayers? Jesus says he cares. He says, "If you believe, you will receive whatever you ask for in prayer" (Matt. 21:22). And:

> *Ask and it will be given to you . . . Which of you, if his son asks for bread, will give him a stone? Or if he asks for a fish, will give him a snake? If you, then . . . know how to give good gifts to your children, how much more will your Father in heaven give good gifts to those who ask him!* (Matt. 7:7, 9–11)

Here are the facts: God wants to be our friend, who journeys with us as we confront life's challenges. We make contact with his presence and power through prayer.

Last summer, while on vacation, I was awakened by my wife, who was in great pain. We were miles from our doctor and medical care. My immediate reaction was to pray, asking for divine help. What a comfort to know my Heavenly Father was there with us in crisis! To this day we don't know what was wrong with Metta, but whatever it was, God healed her. In the morning, she was fine.

Several weeks ago, Louie Evans led a healing service. I don't know all the results of that service, but I do know one story. A friend was facing quadruple bypass surgery for the second time. Doctors had given no hope surgery could be avoided. He was prayed for on that Sunday by elders. The next day he was at Stanford hospital being healed with angioplasty, *without invasive surgery*! My daughter was his nurse, and gave us the good news. This is only one story, but there are many throughout our church family of how God responds to prayer, in giving wisdom for tough decisions, comfort for heartaches, resources when our financial security is being shaken.

Let me ask you, what are you carrying today that should be turned over to God in prayer? Where are you hurting because you have not claimed these promises from Jesus about prayer? As a Christian, we can have *confidence* to approach our God in prayer.

A second truth in our text has to do with *conditions* God places upon responding to our prayers: "if we ask anything *according to his will*, he hears us" (v. 14, emphasis added).

Prayer does not give magical permission to use God to satisfy our shopping list of needs. God didn't send Jesus to take away our pain or to shield us from life's difficulties. When we pray according to the will of God, we are acting out our faith that God gives us what we *need*, not necessarily what we *want*.

Look at verse 15: "And if we know that [God] hears us—whatever we ask—we know that we have what we asked of him." In other words, once we pray about a need, our text says we have an immediate answer! The answer is that God has heard us, and we can trust him to respond in His own time and way to our requests. We pray asking for the will of God, thus allowing God to be God, rather than attempting to make him our servant.

Jesus promised that God is our Father who loves us. He will not send a scorpion, if we ask for a fish, nor will he send a stone, if we ask for bread. Our willingness to trust God with answers to our prayers, after we offer them, is the secret for finding victory in our prayer life. And such trust will determine whether tough times make us bitter or sweet. Whether they cause us to be miserable or hopeful.

Most of us know someone who claims they used to believe in God, attend church, follow the Christian life, but then a crisis came. They prayed, and God didn't respond. They couldn't handle the pain of God denying their request, so they trashed their faith.

Do you remember as a child asking your parents for something you desperately desired? Maybe too much candy? Or the use of the family car as a teenager? Do you remember your reaction? The rage, disappointment, and hurt you felt when your request was denied? As children, we lacked the ability to understand the love behind our parents' no, so we reacted angrily, saying, "You don't love me. You never give me what I want!" Only as we matured could we understand.

Someone gave me this poem:

> As children bring their broken toys with tears for us to mend, I brought my broken dreams to God, because He was my Friend.
>
> But then instead of leaving Him in peace to work alone, I hung around and tried to help with ways that were my own.
>
> At last I snatched them back and cried, "How can you be so slow?"
>
> "My child," He said, "What could I do? You never did let go."[33]

As our faith matures, we can reach a point where we trust God's responses to our prayers, particularly when his responses are not what we expected, desired, or felt we needed. God is loving, all-powerful, all-knowing, and he has promised to use his divine resources to accomplish his perfect plan for our lives. But his responses to our prayers will be according to *his* will, not our own.

A third truth about prayer implied in our text is the peace that can be ours, if once we trust God's wisdom and timing. Isaiah the prophet wrote, "You will keep in perfect peace those whose minds are steadfast, because they trust in you" (Isa. 26:3). And Jesus promised us, saying, "Peace I leave with you; my peace I give you" (John 14:27).

Remember that moment after the death of Jesus, when the disciples were huddled in fear in an upper room? Imagine what was going on in their minds. It seemed God had deceived them, regarding the identity of Jesus. Now it appeared all was lost. Then suddenly Jesus appeared, and his first words were "Peace be with you!"

How do we find peace, after taking a need to God in prayer? Recently, I rented the movie entitled *Bear*, a story about a young cub who loses its mother at an early age and must learn to survive in the wild on its own. Providentially it meets a giant male bear, who adopts the little guy, and teaches him survival techniques of catching fish and protecting himself from enemies. One day a leopard begins to stalk the little cub and finally corners him. Unable to run, the cub snarls and rears up like a vicious grizzly. Immediately the leopard slinks away in fear. At that point, the cub is feeling pretty good about himself. Then he turns around and sees his giant bodyguard—the male adult bear—reared up on his hind legs and threatening the leopard with great bodily damage if it attacks the cub. It wasn't the cub's strength that frightened away the enemy, but rather the strength of someone far bigger than he was, saving him in crisis—someone the cub didn't even know was there until the crisis had ended.

We can have *confidence* that our Heavenly Father is watching over us in our times of need. Someone far bigger and more powerful than we are is the means by which we find peace in our souls through prayer.

I trust God's Spirit will give you that priceless treasure of peace today, by convincing you God has heard you. He will take care of things. And that's all you need to know.

Questions for Study and Discussion:

1. The Bible tells us we can approach God with confidence in prayer. What is your own approach to prayer? Do you tend to rest in this confidence or come with a different attitude? Why?

2. Walt warns against turning God into a vending machine for our desires or a slave to our wishes. What are the consequences and dangers of such an attitude? How do you tend to respond, when God answers your prayers with a "no"?

Walt, a great mentor and friend, went through divorce as a young man. It nearly destroyed him. He thought it was the end of his ministry. But instead, that's where Jesus met him. In the brokenness of his own failure, Walt discovered the concreteness of God's everlasting love. And in fact, it was that experience of grace that really marked the beginning of his ministry.

George Hinman
Senior Pastor, University Presbyterian Church
Seattle, WA

Walt,

I led the divorce-recovery ministry for a few years. You came to speak several times. You shared with us how you suffered and how you survived. Your willingness to share was such a blessing to all of us in that room.

Doris Malmin

Walt,

I came to Menlo Park Presbyterian Church at the suggestion of a single mother. From the divorce-recovery group I began to grow and heal. Now, many years later, I have recovered from divorce and cherish all the efforts to support single mothers in this church. It is my safe haven and I have always felt welcomed.

Thais St. Clair

DIVORCE AND MARRIAGE

Matthew 5:27–32;
1 Corinthians 7:10–16; Luke 10:2–10
November 2, 1980

I feel it's time to talk about divorce and remarriage within the church—a subject that has been relegated to the realm of silence, resulting in myths and biases that create needless guilt, cause division within the body of Christ, and keep many from the nourishment of God's grace. Let me say two things by way of preparation:

- One sermon can do little more than scratch the surface. My goal is to stimulate you to further study, thus bringing it out of the closet.

- There is no universal position on divorce and remarriage among evangelicals. Some individuals and churches hold views that are carved in cement. If anyone violates their position, such a person is written off as ungodly, liberal, a destroyer of God's truth, and a humanist. Because of the burden of my heart, I am willing to take these risks.

A large percentage of this congregation has been divorced; many are remarried. Another group among us is unhappily married and is considering divorce. Christians are involved in divorce at an alarming and increasing rate. A recent secular study, done to determine the emotional struggles of students on Stanford's campus, claims that concern about parents getting divorced, or who are divorced, is the number-one problem. I have two goals in studying God's Word on divorce and remarriage. I believe the gospel possesses power to save marriages, so that divorce in our midst can be greatly reduced. God can do miracles in healing broken relationships! Secondly, Jesus Christ provides his church the grace to offer forgiveness and healing to those who have been divorced and remarried.

First, let me be clear about the position of Scripture regarding divorce. God hates divorce, as Malachi the prophet affirms (Mal. 2:16). From the beginning, God's plan is that a man and woman become one flesh when married—making divorce as unnatural, painful, and tragic as amputating part of our physical body.

Jesus chooses the illustration of bride and bridegroom to symbolize our unbreakable relationship with him. He warns, "What therefore God hath joined together, let not man put asunder" (Matt. 19:6; Mark 10:9, KJV). In God's original plan for creation, divorce was unthinkable. Nevertheless, sin invaded marriage, as it did all of creation. As early as Moses, we find him allowing a man to give his wife a certificate of divorce. Later, Jesus said that Moses' teaching was God's "second best," due to hardness in the human heart. Then he proceeded to give this teaching in our text.

> It has been said, "Anyone who divorces his wife must give her a certificate of divorce." But I tell you that anyone who divorces his wife, except for sexual immorality, makes her the victim of adultery, and anyone who marries a divorced woman commits adultery. (Matt. 5:31–32)

After the church was born, Paul the apostle gives continued teaching, expanding the grounds by which Christians can divorce; namely, for desertion by unbelieving mates. As I read countless interpretations of these texts by those who value the authority of Scripture, I'm convinced there is not now, nor ever has been, unity among evangelical Protestants about the "Christian" grounds for divorce. For example, one name you would all recognize states, "I have a hard time believing physical abuse of a wife, broken bones, and bruises are not a form of desertion."

My point is, when we sit down face to face with troubled couples, it's not too difficult to stretch Scripture, making it impossible to hold legalistic, inflexible interpretations of New Testament teachings about acceptable reasons for divorce and remarriage. However, let me tell you my conviction after twenty years in ministry, for you who are troubled in marriage. Finding a "Scriptural escape hatch" to validate your divorce is to *miss* the point. To divorce, for any reason, is a radical departure from God's plan, stark evidence of the invasion of sin and brokenness into human relationships, and a path that leads to pain. As Christians, we have been given divine power in the Spirit for conquering the impossible. Our weapons are the fruits of the Spirit—forgiveness, patience, love, joy, and kindness, by which we can heal brokenness in marriage. Seldom is there a situation that justifies the tragedy, the amputation of divorce. God urges us to seek his resurrection power to heal our marriage.

God's power works best in the graveyards of impossibility. Part of bringing glory to Christ is to allow him to heal what the world considers hopeless.

I give this truth, undergirded by all the love and trust I hope I have earned as one of your pastors for six years. I am not legalistic, nor anxious to put someone into an unbearable cage of legalism. I arrive at this teaching from experience in my own life and in my pastorate. Because God loves you, he would protect you from all the pain and tragedy associated with a Christian seeking divorce. I am not impressed with the experience of people who have sought divorce, against the teaching of Scripture, thinking they are finding release and a new life. Many discover, too late, that God was right. God opts to resurrect what is dead, rather than bury part of you in the divorce court. To water down God's Word is to rebel against God's plan for creation and inflict incredible pain upon the innocent and guilty.

After affirming this truth, we recognize that divorce does happen to Christians. There are cases when sin invades so totally and distorts a person's relationships and perspectives so completely, that to remain married is impossible. There are other cases where Christians openly rebel against God's plan. For those who have been divorced, and are single or remarried, and who have received no help from the Church except an embarrassing silence, a silence which indirectly labels you as a kind of "leper" in our midst, we acknowledge that Satan's arrows of guilt can limit our effectiveness in serving you in the name of Jesus Christ.

Let me state the problem. Some churches claim that previously married people cannot remarry. If such persons marry, they are not married in God's sight and are, therefore, living in sin. There are churches that forbid remarried people from teaching or holding office within the congregation, thus labeling divorce as a kind of partially forgivable sin. I always wonder why a congregation, seeking a totally holy environment, doesn't include gossips, the greedy, and adulterers on their list of those unqualified to lead. Where in Scripture do we find reason to exclude divorced people? One text is often used about choosing elders who are husbands of one wife, a text that throughout history has been exegeted to mean a prohibition against polygamous or mistress-type relationships, as often as it has been interpreted to refer to the divorced. God offers full grace, forgiveness, forgetfulness, and restoration to the previously married. In making such a statement, I am not tampering with God's Word, but with a legalistic tradition that has grown around the Word and must be challenged.

I repeat, God hates divorce. But he also hates murder, stealing, and covetousness. The church has accepted brokenness in all areas of human conduct and supplied grace to heal the "walking wounded in our midst." I cannot justify divorce and remarriage, but neither can I isolate it from God's full grace. It too must stand under the cleansing fountain of Christ's death at Calvary!

Let's go back to the woman taken in adultery as an example of grace and law. Jesus knew the Old Testament law in Leviticus 20:10, "If a man commits adultery with . . . the wife of his neighbor—both the adulterer and the adulteress are to be put to death."

Our Lord willfully ignored that law and injected grace into that situation, saying, "Let him who is without sin among you be the first to throw a stone at her" (John 8:7, ESV). He offered grace, because he knew his own death would meet the requirements of Old Testament law. That woman was not "let off," but was ransomed at the cost of the life of Jesus. Divorced and remarried people are forgiven, not acquitted, at the cost of Calvary. Once that forgiveness is received, there are no strings, no stigma. Any church that erects barriers Christ has torn down is deficient in understanding grace. Again, some might argue, "Won't this position encourage divorce?" Jesus didn't believe his grace toward the woman caught in adultery would encourage adultery. Someone has said, "It is good for us that God is more merciful with his children than his children are with each other."

One example of deficient grace practiced in some churches is refusing positions of church leadership to those who have been previously married. The argument is that these people need our spiritual support to thrive once more for their Lord—that they are still a part of the garden of God, but "in shadow." Nowhere in Scripture can I find any indication there is any sin only partially forgiven, leaving us in the "shadows" of usefulness to God.

For the sake of clarity, let's summarize where we have been:

- God hates divorce—it's against creation, and innately wrong.

- Christians should not seek divorce—rather they should seek divine resources available for forgiveness, patience, love, and endurance, that become the raw materials God uses to heal and resurrect dead and hopeless marriages.

- When unbearable happenings occur, causing separation, the Christian's first pathway should always be to seek reconciliation, praying for the miracle of God's healing. Only after strong evidence reconciliation is impossible, should dating and remarriage be considered a possibility.

- And finally, for those divorced and remarried, even against scriptural grounds: According to your repentance, you are forgiven. The slate is washed clean. You are free. Use your experience to help others escape the pain you have had to endure.

I trust these words will lead to wide discussion in our midst. Where you challenge the teaching, go back to Scripture and agonize over the texts.

If your marriage is in need of healing, I pray these truths will become power for resurrection and new beginnings. For those who worship with divorce part of your past, I trust you have been "bathed" in God's grace this morning. I might add, part of accepting grace is fulfilling obligations to the past, not leaving needy people in the wake of your new beginning.

And a final word to those who have not gone through divorce—be grateful, be humble, and always hold in your heart that Christian attitude, "There, but for the grace of God, go I." Try to understand the agony, frustration, and desperation that lead Christians to seek divorce, the feeling of abandonment even by God, when prayers for healing have not been answered. That kind of empathy provides an environment where the "walking wounded" who come here on Sunday morning can find the healing of Jesus Christ our Lord.

Questions for Study and Discussion:

1. How has divorce and remarriage impacted your life and relationships? What consequences have you seen that help you understand why God "hates divorce"? What attitudes toward it from other Christians have you experienced?

2. If you have considered divorce, would you say your motivation lies more with the heartbroken admission that no other road lies open, or rather that you seek "release and a new life"? Would your spouse and Christian friends agree with that assessment?

GIVING: A SPONTANEOUS RESPONSE TO LOVE

2 Corinthians 9:6–15; Luke 12:13–34
December 6, 1987

This morning I want to share some Christmas wisdom guaranteed to bring you joy: "It's more blessed to give than to receive."

As part of our preparation for Christmas, we are going to allow 2 Corinthians to teach us about giving. A first lesson from our text: "If we give little, we will get little." As Paul puts it, "Whoever sows sparingly will also reap sparingly, and whoever who sows generously will also reap generously" (2 Cor. 9:6). This paradox is one radical teaching of Christianity. We enrich ourselves by sharing, and we impoverish ourselves by hoarding. The Persian proverb was right: "What I kept, I lost. What I spent, I had. What I gave, I have."

Listen to Jesus on this subject:

Give, and it will be given to you; a good measure, pressed down, shaken together, running over, will be poured into your lap. For with the measure you use, it will be measured to you. (Luke 6:38)

Watch out! Be on your guard against all kinds of greed; life does not consist in an abundance of possessions. (Luke 12:15)

Sell your possessions and give to the poor. Provide purses for yourselves that will not wear out, a treasure in heaven that will never fail, where no thief comes near and no moth destroys. For where your treasure is, there your heart will be also. (Luke 12:33–34)

Most of us agree intellectually with our Lord's words, but our behavior doesn't follow our belief. For that reason, many Christians miss the joy God intended us to experience. Someone has written: "If we try to live by getting instead of giving, we are going against the grain. It is like trying to go against the law of gravity. . . . Giving is what we do best. . . . It is the action that was designed into us before our birth."[34]

Because we've never tried "living generously," we keep on hanging on to our bank account for dear life, no matter what it costs or how it stresses us out. But if we truly were designed for generosity, for giving, and not for getting, surrendering to that design means discovering "the soaring and swooping life of grace." Because what we receive is a factor of what we give. If we give little, we will receive little.

Now consider a second lesson in our text: God loves cheerful givers. He seeks nothing from reluctant donors. "Each of you should give what you have decided in your heart to give, not reluctantly or under compulsion, for God loves a cheerful giver" (2 Cor. 9:7).

One symptom of a person in love is an irresistible urge to give. In a story by Dan Clark, a real-estate agent gets this snazzy new car from his brother and drives it downtown for business. When he comes back to where he parked it, he finds this small, ragged-looking boy admiring the car. When the real estate agent tells the boy that his brother gave it to him, the boy responds, "I wish I could be a brother like that." Not "I wish I *had* a brother like that," but "I wish I could *be* a brother like that." Well, this melts the grown-up's heart, so he asks if the boy wants to go for a spin, and the boy answers, "I would, but can

I take my brother?" They end up driving to a rundown part of town, where:

> *The boy jumped out of the car, ran quickly up the steps, and in a short while returned, carrying a small boy with withered legs. He placed the crippled child in the front seat of the car and explained, "Harry is my brother. Someday I am going to buy him a car like this."[35]*

The three had a wonderful ride, and the crowded heart of the salesman was melted with a beautiful lesson of love prompting unselfish sharing.

As followers of the Greatest Giver in history, we see this story as an explanation of why we Christians are addicted to giving. We give because Jesus treats us as this boy treated his brother.

I feel warm inside when people during this season ask, "Walt, do you know a need where we can plug in? God has blessed us so richly and we just have to share."

If giving is one measure of our love for God, how are we doing? One of our pastors dug up some statistics about giving in our own church family:

- If all of us gave 5 percent of our income based on the median income of our area, our budget would be between 6 and 12 million dollars.
- Twenty percent of our people give 80 percent of the budget.
- It seems the more people earn, the less of a percentage they share.
- If our 2,800 giving units each gave the equal of 10 percent of a welfare check, which is $7,500 annually, we would come close to our annual budget of 3 million dollars.

So again, the second lesson from our text is that all giving should be spontaneous expressions of our love for our God, the Great Provider and Sustainer of everything we possess.

A third lesson about giving: *We can't outgive God!* Consider our text:

> *And God is able to bless you abundantly, so that in all things*
> *at all times, having all that you need, you will abound in every*
> *good work . . . . Now he who supplies seed to the sower and*
> *bread for food will also supply and increase your store of seed*
> *and will enlarge the harvest of your righteousness. You will be*
> *enriched in every way so that you can be generous on every occa-*
> *sion, and through us your generosity will result in thanksgiving*
> *to God.* (2 Cor. 9:8, 10–12)

Malachi the prophet put it this way:

> *Bring the full tithe into the storehouse, that there may be food in*
> *my house. And thereby put me to the test, says the LORD of hosts,*
> *if I will not open the windows of heaven for you and pour down*
> *for you a blessing until there is no more need. I will rebuke the*
> *devourer for you, so that it will not destroy the fruits of your soil.*
> (Mal. 3:10–11, ESV)

Many of us believe we cannot outgive God, and our belief is showing up in our behavior. I celebrate how people are putting God's kingdom's business as a top priority in their daily lives, taking Christ into their workplace and giving him lordship over their investments. In his poem "Keeping Christmas," Henry Van Dyke captures what happens to people who get involved in giving:

> *Are you willing to forget what you have done for other people,*
> *and to remember what other people have done for you; to ignore*
> *what the world owes you, and to think what you owe the world;*
> *to see that your fellowmen are just as real as you are, and try to*
> *look behind their faces to their hearts hungry for joy; to own that*
> *probably the only good reason for your existence is not what you*

*are going to get out of life, but what you are going to give to life;
to close your book of complaints against the management of the
universe and look around you for a place where you can sow a
few seeds of happiness—are you willing to do these things even
for a day?*

Then you can keep Christmas.

*Are you willing to stoop down and consider the needs and the
desires of little children; to remember the weakness and loneliness of people who are growing old; to stop asking how much
your friends love you, and ask yourself whether you love them
enough. . . .*

*To make a grave for your ugly thoughts and a garden for your
kindly feelings with the gate open—are you willing to do these
things even for a day?*

Then you can keep Christmas.

*Are you willing to believe that love is the strongest thing in the
world—stronger than hate, stronger than evil, stronger than
death—and that the blessed life which began in Bethlehem nineteen hundred years ago is the image and brightness of the Eternal
Love?*

Then you can keep Christmas.[36]

And if you can keep it for a day, why not always? But you can never keep
it alone. God planned for Christmas to come each year:

- so we can receive a fresh transfusion of his love; and
- so we can take a leap of faith and love him in return, by giving
  and giving and giving.

How long do we keep giving? As long as he continues to give to us,
knowing we can never outgive God.

In summary, our text tells us:

- Giving is an investment: To sow little is to reap little.
- All giving should be a spontaneous response to what our Lord has given to us.
- And: We can't outgive God.

Let me close with a true story that illustrates the message of our text:

A small orphan girl was hurt in a bombing raid, during the Vietnam War. Two American medics found her and realized a transfusion was necessary to save her life. Neither of them was her blood type, but several of the uninjured orphans did have her blood type. The medics asked if anyone would be willing to donate blood to save the young girl's life. Slowly, one hand went up, and a frightened little boy climbed up on the table.

During the transfusion, the medics noticed he grew very tense, even to the state of uncontrolled sobbing and panic. At this point a Vietnamese nurse arrived, and spoke to the little guy. After a moment, a huge look of relief spread over his face. The nurse told the medics, "He thought he was dying! He misunderstood, and thought you had asked him to give all his blood so the little girl could live."

But why would he be willing to do that? asked the medics. The Vietnamese nurse repeated the question to the little boy, who simply answered, "She's my friend."

Why do we give at Christmas? Because "God loved the world so much he gave his only Son" (John 3:16, ESV) and because "Greater love has no man than this, that someone lay down his life for his friends" (John 15:13).

I don't apologize for asking us to give. Jesus loved us enough to die for us. It's only natural we will want to respond by giving and giving and giving. We wanted to offer some help by giving various targets where you can share. How interesting that Jesus arranged it so:

[W]hatever you did for one of the least of these brothers of mine, you did for me. (Matt. 25:40, NIV1984)

When we share, feed the hungry, clothe the naked, love the poor—we are loving Jesus. And that's the meaning of Christmas!

Questions for Study and Discussion:

1. Do you give to the work of the church? If you give less than a tithe, what justifications do you offer for holding back? If you give a tithe and beyond, what compels you?

2. Have you ever experienced "a fresh transfusion of God's love" through your experience in giving? Have you ever given in faith and felt him catch you?

LIFE CAN BE MORE
THAN SURVIVAL

Joshua 3:7–13, 4:1–9, 21–24
May 29, 1988

Being Memorial Day weekend, it's appropriate we think together about the wonderful gift of memory. Last week I watched the one-hundredth-birthday celebration of Irving Berlin. Seeing clips of old movies and hearing songs that are ingrained in my memory, I found my heart warmed by the past. Memory acts like a family picture album, linking the past to the present, reminding us of those countless times when God intervened to help us in time of need, when he surprised us with blessings beyond our wildest dreams.

Memorial Day itself calls us to remember the gift of liberty and the fallen soldiers who paid the price for our freedom. Because this is a special weekend, today's text in Joshua is particularly appropriate, as it calls us to build stones of remembrance.

Moses has just passed the gauntlet of leadership to Joshua, who will lead the invasion of the Promised Land. Joshua's credentials as Israel's leader are established by God miraculously stopping the flow of the surging Jordan River long enough to allow the Hebrews to cross on dry land. One study suggests God might have used an earthquake upstream, causing the riverbanks to collapse, blocking the river long enough for the crossing. Whatever the cause, Joshua realized this "divine event" could become a catalyst to build faith among his troops, so he instructs the priests to pick up twelve stones as they pass through the river bed and to stack them into a monument on the other side. Our text says:

> *This is how you will know that the living God is among you and that he will certainly drive out before you the Canaanites.* (Josh. 3:10)

Conquering Canaan was a tough nut to crack for a group of ex-slaves. However, God gave them this promise, "I will be with you, and that's all you need to know!"

Crossing the Jordan River at flood stage showed Israel that God isn't limited by obstacles that we consider impossible. Many times, Israel would look back at this stack of stones and remember how God miraculously delivered them from merely surviving in the wilderness, and brought them to a life of joy and peace in the Promised Land. Let's take a moment and glean some lessons in this story about how our lives can become more than a struggle to survive.

First, it's important for Christians to build monuments of remembrance to God's activity in our past. Our text tells us,

> *In the future, when your children ask you, "What do those stones mean?" tell them that the flow of the Jordan was cut off before the ark of the covenant of the LORD. . . . These stones are to be a memorial to the people of Israel forever.* (Josh. 4:6–7)

It's vital we make time to collect stones of remembrance that celebrate those times God intervened to help us:

- in crisis with a child;
- in a financial emergency;

- in providing wisdom for an insurmountable problem; or
- in giving us strength to go on, when our own resources were not sufficient.

At my age, I find I have a large stack of stones representing God's faithfulness to me. Such memories act as a reservoir of strength from which I draw to face new challenges. Looking over my rock pile, I realize how God has helped me in every imaginable situation. Therefore, I can confront new challenges saying, "God and I have been here before. I don't have to panic. Together we're going to make it!"

Israel wandered in the wilderness for forty years because they didn't remember how God had delivered them from Egypt. Without that rock pile, they couldn't find the courage to face the new obstacles blocking their way to the Promised Land.

How many of us are living in a wilderness of merely surviving because we have short memories of what God did for us in the past? Or because we are carrying burdens God never intended us to carry alone? Or because we are beaten up by circumstances too complex for us, and yet are too proud to seek God's help?

Why do we act as if God has never done anything for us in the past? Do we realize our Heavenly Father wants us to do more than merely survive in this world? Taking time to stack stones of remembrance energizes our faith to trust our God—the same God who:

- stops rivers that appear to be overwhelming us;
- brings water out of rocks in our desert of hopelessness;
- raises the dead bones of our hopes and dreams; and
- conquers enemies and knocks down walls of impossibility.

Stones of remembrance carve into our consciousness that nothing is impossible for God. Dr. Bernie Siegel, in his book *Love, Medicine and Miracles*, says that about 15 percent of his cancer patients attack their illness with faith and hope. Those 15 percent are the ones who tend to survive.

Let's focus on what God can do about obstacles blocking our path to God's best. It required great courage for those priests to step into a raging river. However, God didn't stop the river's flow, until they took that first step of faith.

Specifically, if we want our lives to change from survival mode to coming fully alive, let's begin to build monuments of remembrance about what God has done and is doing for our families or our business. Let's remember how he is helping us through school. Let's remember how he is caring for our finances.

We Christians should be meeting together regularly to stack stones of remembrance and to tell stories and celebrate God's faithfulness.

Last week I heard our Sunday evening young adult group take time to celebrate what God has done for them. Wednesday, our staff looked back on this wonderful year and rejoiced in God's blessings. Such acts of remembering cure discontentment, complaining, fear, and anxiety, the emotional cancers that make life mere survival.

Let's look at a second lesson in our text: stacking stones of remembrance gives a witness to the world that what we are, what we have achieved, and what we possess, are all acts of God's grace. Remembering keeps us humble and grateful. As Joshua puts it, "that all the peoples of the earth might know that the hand of the LORD is powerful and so that you might always fear the LORD your God" (Josh. 4:24).

One of our businessmen recently addressed a group of his peers. He is a growing Christian who understands that his success in business, every deal he has ever put together, the family he enjoys—in short, everything he possesses—are all the result of God's grace. Such awareness only happens when we take time to stack stones of remembrance about how God has been involved in our journey. Giving God credit for our blessings protects us from being devoured by pride and self-sufficiency.

As a congregation, we are so blessed:

- We live in a land of liberty, purchased with the lifeblood of thousands of people.

- We live on a peninsula of green trees and safe neighborhoods.
- We know Jesus Christ.
- And, we enjoy a church family that is learning how to love and support one another.

I could spend an hour stacking stones of remembrance about God's gracious involvement in our lives! My point is, making time to build a monument of remembrance will protect us:

- from the sinful pride of taking personal credit for what God has freely given;
- from selfishness and indifference to the pain and needs of others, as if we were more deserving than they; and
- from a sense of independence from God, feeling "who needs him?"

Stones of remembrance keep life in the "promised land" from going to our head!

A final truth in our text: There are some things we should not remember. God did not ask Israel to build memorials to their hardships in Egypt, or to their trials while crossing the wilderness. Memorials focus on divine provision in the midst of human pain, not on the pain itself.

Some of us tend to collect stones of remembrance representing every pain, disappointment, tragedy, and heartache we have experienced. Then we visit those shrines so often we stay chronically miserable. All of us know persons we never dare ask "How are you?" knowing they will tell us the same story about their chronic misery, fixated on a memory of pain. Focusing on memorials of past hurt is *survival*; it isn't living.

Maybe it's time to bury some painful memories, and focus on what God did right in our past; on what he will do for us now, if we will trust him.

One scar I will bear all my life is the impact of my mom's worry about my dad's health. When I was four years old, Dad nearly died. That was 1941. Mom panicked, and spent the rest of her life expecting Dad to die. She literally became fixated on his death, so much so that she failed to find the security and joy trusting God could have given her. Ironically, Dad outlived Mom by four years. All her time focusing on that illness of the past she believed would reoccur could have been spent living, stacking stones to God's faithfulness.

What monument to the past do you need to stop visiting? What tapes need to be destroyed? This Memorial Day weekend is a great time to knock down memorials to things that should be forgotten, and to build new ones to the faithfulness of our Heavenly Father. Let's leave the wilderness of memories that paralyze us and cross the Jordan into a life of enjoying, trusting, praising, and celebrating life in the Promised Land of God's care and provision.

Questions for Study and Discussion:

1. Do you practice the discipline of remembering what God has done for you? What physical reminders do you have, or habitual behaviors?

2. Do you know those who visit monuments they should forget about? How has it impacted their lives? What monuments should you stop visiting, in order to experience a life remembering God's faithfulness?

Dear Walt,

You gave the sermon that moved me back into the embrace of God. You married my wife and me, and you baptized our children. Thank you for your faithful shepherding.

Bill Eberwein

Dear Walt,

In 1975, my first year of practice, I was struggling to keep food on the table. We were not yet members of the church, but you gave me an appointment. At our visit, you gave me a piece of paper with the following typed on it: "From the Desk of Walter Gerber—And the Lord is the one who goes ahead of you. He will be with you. He will not fail you or forsake you. Do not fear, or be dismayed." I have kept that piece of paper in the top drawer of my desk ever since, and indeed he has gone before. Thank you for being vulnerable, reminding us that we desperately need God's grace and to pray constantly. Thank you for the faith budget, the punctual session meetings, and allowing us to share in your sermon preparation.

Because of his love,
Drummond McCunn

GREATNESS IN THE SIGHT
OF MEN OR GOD?

Matthew 20:20–28
April 27–28, 1991

ast week Jerry[37] talked about the rich young ruler's craving for life beyond what he had found in his pursuit of wealth, power, and social status. Hunger in his soul for something more drove him to Jesus. Jesus told him to change his lifestyle—to stop accumulating things and start serving people. Because "Serving Others with the Love of Christ" is our pulpit theme for this year, it's appropriate we take a second look at a text we studied two weeks ago, as a sequel to our Lord's encounter with the rich young ruler. Today Jesus challenges us to seek greatness in God's sight—versus greatness in the eyes of the world—by adopting a lifestyle of servanthood.

Characters in our story seem to be caught up in the same distorted pursuit for greatness afflicting Silicon Valley. James and John had an ambitious mother who asked Jesus to allow her sons to sit at his right and left hand in his kingdom. Our drive for greatness is expressed in similar ways:

- We seek to be the best performer in the office or classroom, to be rated top gun, #1 by our peers.

- Or, we invest our lives acquiring symbols that society equates with greatness, such as large salaries, prestigious professions, or membership in the right social groups.

Nothing is wrong with doing the best we can do. Nothing is wrong with owning things. It's the motivation behind why we perform or why we seek to acquire things. Jesus reminds us that on Judgment Day, when God evaluates our personal worth, there are going to be big surprises, big reversals: "The first are going to be last, and the last first." The ten winners of last week's lottery won't suddenly be rich in God's sight. The Donald Trumps won't necessarily be big hitters in heaven.

God singles out for greatness those whom our society hardly notices, those who visit people in jail, give cups of cold water to strangers, feed the hungry, and care for the poor.

Servanthood is a tough call. How many of us really desire a life of servanthood—or encourage our children to pursue such behavior? How long since we praised our children for acts of self-giving? Yet we reward them for academic, athletic, or social achievement!

This poses the question raised in our text: How does God measure greatness? Who would be God's first draft choice in building his team for kingdom work? Our answers hold huge implications, if we would achieve greatness in God's sight.

Happily, our Lord is very patient with immature faith and distorted ideas of greatness. Rather than rip into his friends for their arrogant request, Jesus uses this occasion to teach them about qualities God values in people. He says, "whoever wants to become great among you must be your servant, and whoever wants to be first must be your slave—just as the Son of Man did not come to be served, but to serve, and to give his life as a ransom for many."

This is an astounding statement. The God of this universe came to us, not as a ruler to be served, but as a servant who washes the feet of his disciples. Oswald Chambers says Jesus was a failure by every standard but God's. Now Jesus tells us, "If you seek greatness in God's sight, be a servant. If you want to be #1, be a slave!" Jesus is describing a new breed of human being.

Before we react negatively to this call to servanthood, let me ask:

- Is Jesus really so divorced from reality, in recognizing the value of service to others versus *self*-seeking?

- Is someone who serves doomed to mediocrity, or even failure, in our culture?

You who are acquainted with the business world know that business is discovering that servanthood works!

- The employer who takes a personal interest in his employees builds a stronger company.

- The doctor who gives a personal touch to patients builds a better practice.

- And, the business that serves its customers is more successful.

Draeger's Market was featured in a national magazine as an example of how an independent market can compete with the big guys by giving outstanding service to its customers.

Currently a wave of patriotism is sweeping our country, and a military general is a new national hero. When General Norman Schwarzkopf was interviewed by *20/20*, I was impressed by this man's criteria for greatness:

- He had a Bible on his nightstand, which he reads every day.

- He is a committed husband and father.

- He can cry, and he says he's suspicious of men who cannot cry—interesting comment from a general.

- And, he claims he is not a hero in this war—his troops are his heroes![38] His role was to support and serve his troops.

General Schwarzkopf isn't hungry for money or power. He said, "You don't get rich in the military." And when asked if he would like to be a five-star general, he answered, "I feel totally unworthy to stand in the company of men who previously held this honor." When asked what he wants to do when he retires: "I want to go on serving others and my country in some capacity."[39] By biblical standards, Norman Schwarzkopf understands greatness.

For centuries, the Jews had dreamed of a Messiah, a conquering general, who would deliver them and create a mighty nation of Israel. And then Jesus came along, saying, "The Son of Man did not come to be served, but to serve."

Many of us have reached a point of insight where we want to invest our lives in something that will matter a hundred years from now. We have noticed in the obituary columns that, when a person's life is recounted, data of how they served, rather than what they accumulated, is almost always mentioned. The wisdom of Jesus about a life of self-giving makes sense. But how do we start?

Servanthood is not very complicated. Many people in our church family have already begun. What are they doing?

- Having tea with an elderly shut-in and sharing memories for a few minutes;
- taking a single parent and child into their family because they have nowhere else to go; or
- taking food to someone home from the hospital or suffering grief.

Lovie Lewis had some extra food and decided to put it into the trunk of her car, drive to East Palo Alto, and give the food away to hungry people. That one act sowed the seeds of the Bread of Life ministry, in which many of us are involved.

Serving others in little things with the love of Jesus can spread like a virus. One person can have tremendous impact for change. I want our church family to be known as a loving and caring people. By definition, "Christian love is compassionate concern for the well-being of others."

Let's suppose you wanted to respond to Jesus this week, and test the waters of servanthood. Where would you begin? Let me suggest you start at home, and make sure you are serving your family before you reach out any further. Then, as you look further, don't look for big things. Find one person or situation to which you can respond—and then do it! Let me suggest a prayer used by one elder that is guaranteed to open the door to servanthood: "Lord, bring into my life today situations and people to which you want me to respond."

God will answer that prayer. Make sure you are serious in your request and willing to pay the cost involved.

Lee Yih, at the Lausanne Congress in Manila, told about what happens when we take our Lord's call to servanthood seriously. He says we stop being frogs and become lethal lizards. Frogs sit on a lily pad and wait for their prey to come within reach of their quick tongues. Lizards don't sit around and wait; they go out in search of prey. Lee Yih challenges us to be lethal lizards, taking the aggressive step to search for people who need us, rather than merely sit around and wait for them to come to us.

Let me assure you, our church family can make a difference if we take seriously our Lord's challenge to invest our lives in people. Marvin Olasky wrote about social conditions in America in 1890, conditions worse than now: "Thousands of orphans roamed the streets. New York Police Commissioner Thomas Byrnes estimated that 40,000 prostitutes worked the city. Gambling, drunkenness, robbery, and murder were more common than now."[40]

This all changed when platoons of Christians took on the cause of reform under the titles of the Olivet Helping Hands Society, Union for Homeless and Friendless Girls, and the Salvation Army.[41] Our church family can make a difference in the lives of needy people.

This week ask God to show you an area of need or a person you can help—then *do something about it,* remembering these words of Jesus:

> *[W]hoever wants to become great among you must be your servant, and whoever wants to be first must be your slave—just as the Son of Man did not come to be served, but to serve, and to give his life as a ransom for many.* (Matt. 20:26–28)

Questions for Study and Discussion:

1. Where in your life are you striving for recognition and "greatness"? What criteria are you using? Does the news of Jesus' "upside-down kingdom" irritate or inspire you? Why, in either case?

2. When you read Walt's sermon, what opportunity for service came to mind, in your own family and in your circle of influence?

When All Else Fails, Read the Instructions

Psalm 1
September 25–26, 1999

Today I want to share with you a roadmap for making choices that will lead us safely through the landmines of a society addicted to self-destructive behavior. Daily, we are confronted with crossroads of decision: Do we draw the wisdom for making our moral choices from the secular world or from the Word of God? The philosophy of the secular world was illustrated by one Hollywood icon, quoted in *People* magazine, describing why he divorced his wife: "Life is too unbelievably short to waste one day in an unhappy marriage."[42] Notice he makes choices based on what he believes will make him happy, without considering the impact of his behavior upon his wife, children, or himself.

Christians believe choices cannot be divorced from biblical morality without grave consequences.

I met a couple while on vacation. Learning I was a minister, the husband happily told me that they were on their honeymoon. After living together twenty-five years and having five children, he said, "Coming out of the seventies, marriage to us was nothing more than a piece of paper." I asked him what changed his mind, and he replied, "After so many years it didn't seem right anymore, so we decided to make it legal."

I'm convinced that somewhere in every human heart, there is an innate sense of right and wrong. One can reject it or ignore it, but this inner voice—call it conscience—never goes away. We eventually heed it, or we crash into a wall.

Sometime ago I watched a house-wrecking crew tear down an old home across the street from our church. What took months to build came down in minutes—a parable of what so-called freedom to write our own rules can do to a life.

- A reputation that has taken years to build can be destroyed overnight by scandal.
- A marriage, as delicate as a spider web, can be destroyed in minutes.
- Character can be destroyed by a momentary compromise of integrity.

The breakdown of the family and public morality, the growing violence we hear about, are only glimmers of the tragic price our nation is paying for rejecting biblical morality as our authority for making moral choices.

Jesus Christ offers Christians the challenge of doing more than wringing our hands about these tragedies. He empowers us to live transformed lives in a society where many are looking for models that provide hope people can change for the better. We will consider the wisdom of Psalm 1 as our roadmap for growing into the likeness of Jesus.

A first step to a transformed life: avoid walking in the counsel of the wicked. "Blessed is the man who walks not in the counsel of the wicked" (Ps 1:1, ESV). The "counsel of the wicked" refers to those who urge us to "just do it." Do what brings pleasure today. Ignore divine laws. Eat, drink, and be merry.

I was listening to a psychiatrist being interviewed about widespread immorality. When asked, "What's your solution?" her response was, "Society itself is sick. Religion isn't the answer. One must swim against this sickness in society by carving out personal values of health."

Events in our country validate that a personal value system, not rooted in God's law, is no answer at all. Creating a personal value system, based upon our own desires, frees us to do almost anything, like the Hollywood personality who said, "Life is too short to waste one day in an unhappy marriage." Or like the teachers in Florida who were caught in compromising sexual activity, and claimed their private morals had nothing to with their leadership in the classroom.

The agenda of the ungodly is simple: "Since I only have one life to live, my primary goal is to do what makes *me* happy today. Anything or anyone getting in the way of my happiness is expendable."

Because we Christians view our lives through the perspective of eternity, because the Holy Spirit enables us to postpone gratification and put the needs of others ahead of our own, we can live transformed lives where self is not number one! The serendipity of this choice is that we discover joy and freedom.

So, a first piece of wisdom from the psalmist for living a responsible life: Don't walk in the counsel of the ungodly. It's always a bad deal! Remember, the evil one is a master of deception—the father of lies.

A second step toward a transformed life: Don't stand in the way of sinners. Walking in the counsel of the wicked impacts our thinking. Standing with sinners impacts our behavior.

Last summer I spent hours at a local coffeehouse where people debriefed their activities of the night before, including drugs, alcohol, and aberrant sexual behavior. Their mood was almost a celebration of freedom to engage in irresponsible behavior. Maybe it was my age, but I wanted to tell them, "Hey, you guys, look a little further down the road. Remember there are consequences."

Last week there was a documentary on the last days of Elvis Presley. Those closest to him described how his addiction to drugs and to self-indulgence destroyed him. What makes his story so tragic is that he denied he had a problem, resisting any help up to the very day of his untimely death.

To pursue a pattern of behavior that goes against the grain of our human nature as created by God, is a tough way to live, doomed to serious consequences—consequences like unhappiness, restlessness, discontentment, selfishness, insatiable greed, loneliness, and guilt. The facts of life dictate we reap what we sow. God's laws do not deprive us, but protect and enrich us.

The psalmist says, "Don't stand in the way of sinners." Don't do what the crowd does. For a Christian, Jesus—not culture—defines what is right and wrong.

A third step toward a transformed life: Don't sit in the seat of mockers! A mocker is a cynic. One elder was commenting on how "cool" it is to be a cynic in Silicon Valley, to be critical of everything, including Christians and the church.

Cynicism is a sad disease, often caused by rejecting the truth that God is in control of history and of our personal lives. Push God out of the picture, and all you have left is fate, or human potential to solve problems. How long has it been since you felt good after a newscast? Pessimism permeates the public mind of America, as we feed on bad news, fear, and tragedy. How awful it would be to approach the future, with no hope that our all-powerful, loving God is in control of history and of our personal lives, and that he will write that last chapter for the Christian, which is eternal life, joy, and peace.

Psalm 1 confronts us with a choice of which road we will travel in life: God's way, as found in the light of Jesus Christ, or the way of secular culture, which leads to death. The psalmist says:

[The righteous are] like a tree planted by streams of water that
yields its fruit in its season and its leaf does not wither. In all that

he does, he prospers. The wicked are not so, but are like chaff that the wind drives away. (vv. 1–4, ESV)

Chaff refers to what floats in the air when wheat is harvested and the straw removed. Those who reject God's authority are easily blown around by every new wind and fad. However, for Christians, these times offer us an incredible opportunity. People are hungry for truth, for moral guidelines, for power to make good choices. Many are concerned about violence and moral decay.

Following the volcanic eruption of Mount St. Helens, the intense heat and ash left nothing but a barren landscape. Philip Yancey describes the aftermath:

> *Then one day a park employee stumbled across a lush patch of wildflowers, ferns, and grasses. It took a few seconds for him to recognize that this patch of vegetation formed the shape of an elk that had been buried by the ash. From then on, naturalists looked for such patches in an aid for calculating the loss of wildlife.*

The decaying animal provided food for new life. In the same way, Yancey adds:

> *Long after society begins to decay, signs of its former life continue to assert themselves. Without knowing why, people cling to moral customs of the past, habits of the heart. These patches of moral green bring life to an otherwise barren landscape.*[43]

Our Christian faith is rooted in the hope that Jesus can transform people into his likeness. Believers can be agents of change and hope, bringing new life to our environment. As Dwight L. Moody said, "Of one hundred men, one will read the Bible; the other ninety-nine will read the

Christian."[44] Never underestimate the power of a minority, who have a vision to change the world.

Our executive staff went for a short retreat last week. One of the great gifts I received was to watch the Spirit of God convict us to seek transformation in our own lives, before we preach about it too much to all of you. The good news that gives me hope is that Jesus is more anxious to transform all of us, even more than we are to ask. And he will do it. Best of all, regardless of our past, he will launch us on a journey of conforming our will to his will. As the apostle Paul puts it, "Do not conform to the pattern of the world, but be transformed by the renewing of your mind" (Rom. 12:2).

Bob Buford tells about a crossroads, in which he had to decide what would be the central focus of his life—Jesus or self. Would he follow the guidelines of Jesus, or those of the secular world? One thing he discovered was that he couldn't do both. If God's Word has struck a chord in your heart today, where do you begin?

- Make a decision about who or what will be the authority upon which to base your choices.
- Confess to God those areas where self has won the battle. Repent and ask for the power to change directions.
- Begin to saturate your mind with God's will. As the text says, "and who meditates on [God's] law day and night."

An elder reads his Bible every morning before picking up the paper, so that his thoughts are directed to God's Word, before they are impacted by all the stuff of the secular world. I can't describe how often the Lord has used the Bible to give me insight about a decision or a rebuke and warning about a temptation I was facing.

Jesus will provide the power for us to be transformed into his likeness—if we want to be. He will use us individually to bring change to society. I invite you to join me in making that journey toward change and purity.

Questions for Study and Discussion:

1. What secular counsel are you most inundated with? Is it the news? Social media? What you see on television or hear on the radio? What discrepancies have you seen between the counsel of the world and the counsel of the Word?

2. Have you ever decided to follow God in an area of your life, despite the counsel of the world or direction of our culture? What happened? Did you feel cut off, or planted by streams of water? Why?

STEPPING-STONE OR
STUMBLING BLOCK?

1 Corinthians 8:1–3, 9–10
May 29, 1977

I n the June issue of the *Saturday Evening Post,* a gentleman is seeking to sell his guidebook for survival in what he believes to be the coming economic crash. Among the things he promises his readers is the know-how for overcoming our natural human tendency to be concerned for our neighbor, by replacing those emotions with the animal instinct for survival of "me and mine." Included is a step-by-step process for making your home a fortress against those who will be hungry and in need. The awful truth highlighted by such a book is the fact that loving our neighbor is easy when it is convenient and costs us little, but to love one another sacrificially when our welfare and rights are at stake requires a form of love beyond what we naturally possess. Today, our text describes just such a dimension of love.

Launching into his subject, Paul discusses a problem troubling the Corinthian Christians: whether or not to eat meat which had been offered to idols and then sold in the open marketplace. Some in the church said yes; and others, whose conscience was weak or who were recent converts from idol worship, said no.

Meat offered to idols is not a problem for us, but the principle involved is very contemporary: "How can we as Christians maintain our bonds of love, while coping with issues about which we find ourselves in radical disagreement?" Alienation feeds on the truth that it is much easier to love those who think like we do, than to love people with whom we disagree strongly. Potential hot spots for disagreement among Christians always exist, running the gamut from alcohol to the contemporary questions of abortion, capital punishment, holding stocks in companies doing business in South Africa, etc. One challenge our church family will soon face is how we are going to handle the growth God is giving to us. Whether we expand or decide to do nothing, not everyone is going to agree. Thus, the challenge raised by our text goes something like this: "Because we differ greatly in matters of conscience, can we still hope to maintain and even grow in our love for one another in times of crisis? If so, then how?"

Paul gives us a principle whereby we can go ahead and have a nose-to-nose confrontation on an issue and emerge from that debate knowing we are still brothers and sisters in Christ. Obviously, such a happening involves a miracle because our natural tendencies simply do not lean in this direction! First Corinthians 8:1 (NIV1984) states, "'knowledge puffs' up, but love builds up. If anyone imagines that he knows something, he does not yet know as he ought to know."

"Puffs up" implies that our knowledge about any subject can make us feel proud—and thus can become destructive to human relationships—unless our knowledge is combined with Christ's love. Paul states that during times of tension and controversy, expressing love is more important than simply stating what we know, establishing our position, and holding firm. He illustrates this principle in the question of meat offered to idols.

In verse 9, Paul claims that knowledge convinces us that idols don't exist, but Christ's love in us prohibits us from using that knowledge as a stumbling block to our brother or sister, who is so young in Christ that idols are still terribly real. A stumbling block is defined as "any cause of stumbling, perplexity or error; an obstacle or impediment to steady progress."

When we are struggling with someone in controversy, love leads us to ask not only, "Am I right?" but also, "What effect does my course of action, my winning, have upon my neighbor?" It is so easy to flaunt our freedom. It is natural for us to want to win—to use our knowledge in an unloving way. Traveling in Turkey, some of our group walked out when a lady began to do a belly dance, which is a native dance of that country. I remember my unkind attitude to those people. I felt they were very narrow and rude and accused them of having all kinds of sexual hangups. At that moment, I felt I was right, but I failed to remember the wisdom of Christ's love in our text. Paul said in Romans 14:13–14:

> [L]et us stop passing judgment on one another. Instead, make up your mind not to put any stumbling block or obstacle in the way of a brother or sister. I am convinced, being fully persuaded in the Lord Jesus, that nothing is unclean in itself. But if anyone regards something as unclean, then for that person it is unclean.

I had asked the first question: "Will this evening harm me?" and my answer was no. But I failed to ask the second question: "Will this evening offend my brothers and sisters who possess different values?" It is tough to accept and live out the fact that my freedom in Christ is limited by love, by my neighbor's conscience! Verse 15 states, "If your brother or sister is distressed because of what you eat, you are no longer acting in love. Do not by your eating destroy someone for whom Christ died."

The ways of Christian love are difficult; the cost of maintaining togetherness is high! This miracle of sensitivity and unselfishness to our neighbor's convictions is a dimension of love Christ brings to our relationships. Here is what makes a Christian unique. Loving one another in times of tension is more important than being right! A spirit of compromise, willingness to listen to the other person on the chance that they also might have some knowledge, is Christ's love in action. By way of postscript—a few days later, when we shared communion in the Garden of the Empty Tomb, our traveling group was reconciled through forgiveness, and we became one again.

Chapter 9 of 1 Corinthians highlights a second guiding principle of love that makes us a stepping-stone rather than a stumbling block for one another. Paul affirms in verses 1–3 that he is an apostle, one uniquely chosen by Jesus Christ to preach the gospel. As an apostle, he has certain rights. In verses 4–6 he lists his rights, which include his right to be paid for his services, the right to have a wife accompany him, and the right to refrain from doing any other work than that of ministry. However, in verse 15 he declares, in essence, "I have used none of these because the needs of people are more important to me than my rights." Today, our society is inundated by people seeking rights—unions, minorities, women, teachers, the handicapped. Obviously, some of these seekers are very justified in their quest, and some are exaggerated. Paul renounced his personal rights, so that he could become the slave of all for Christ's sake (v. 19). This is the revolution in values that Jesus brings to us. Jesus himself surrendered all his rights as God's Son, and came to us as a slave, so we could be made whole.

A challenge that will test and purify our love for one another is that incredible question: "Not only do I have the right, but is Christ asking me in this instance to forego my rights for his sake?" I am impressed at how many in our congregation are learning to be servants of one another in times of sickness, job crisis, or other need. To forego the rights of our comfort and convenience to meet human need is what our love is all about.

I was reminded last week, by a member of the pastor-seeking committee that called me to this pulpit three years ago, that when they first sat down, they were so far apart in feelings and beliefs that it appeared impossible they would ever vote unanimously for one candidate. Each Saturday morning when they came together, they submitted themselves, their knowledge, and their rights, to God in prayer, saying: "Not our will, but yours be done." I remember vividly, when I was struggling about whether or not to come to Menlo Park, the biggest single factor God used to help me make my decision was the incredible unity I perceived present in that committee. They had surrendered their rights and differences to Jesus Christ, and that act gave them power.

Last week we talked about how some of us are unhappy in marriage or in our jobs because our rights, our needs, are not being met. What a revelation of love's power, if we could forget about rights, and respond in love on the job, in our marriage, or to our personal circumstances, with the spirit of self-sacrifice.

Can you begin to feel the potential impact of these teachings about love upon human relationships? Think what would happen in our midst, if we would begin to balance our rights and what we know, with Christ's love and concern for the opinions and feelings of our brothers and sisters? If we could begin to love those people in advance, with whom we know we will disagree, and be determined, in Christ, not to let our disagreement break our relationship. If economic disaster did hit us, to use that time not merely to survive, but to serve one another and share in the name of Christ. These are some of the ways of love Christ has called us to follow, a lifestyle whereby we become a stepping-stone for our neighbor, rather than a stumbling block.

Questions for Study and Discussion:

1. Have you ever been involved in a controversy between Christians? What impact did it have on those individual relationships, or on the church as a whole?

2. Where do you find yourself in disagreement with your brothers and sisters in Christ? On what basis do you think you are "right"? What would it look like, for you to lay down your right to be "right," in order to preserve Christian love and unity?

Walt,

Thank you for being just a regular guy. Your sermons and views on life I will remember forever.

Steve Bingham

Dear Walt,

Thank you for your humility. I will never forget your willingness to share your faults. You are the most humble man I have ever heard speak. When you spoke, it gave me hope in my weaknesses to serve the Lord.

Gloria Choma

Dear Walt,

One of God's blessings for me has been the joy of having you as a pastor. I always found it interesting when you would be speaking to a packed church and you would explain that you had a fear of talking in front of people. I have the same fears. I know that God has called me to be a nurse, a mom, a wife, a teacher, and a friend, yet obeying God has been scary. I don't suffer from panic attacks; however, I do suffer from chronic depression and anxiety. So, when you have the courage to tell people about your panic attacks it makes me feel like it is okay for me to share my afflictions with other Christians who won't judge me but who will pray for me.

Margaret Boeddiker

THE POWER OF WEAKNESS

1 Corinthians 2:1–5; 2 Corinthians 12:1–10
March 28–29, 1992

Visiting Southern California recently, I was impressed with a newscast anchor woman named Bree Walker. She has been physically deformed since birth, having only one finger on each hand. When asked how she acquired such a "public job" which exposed her hands constantly, she mentioned her family and friends who helped her believe there was nothing she couldn't do if she really wanted to do it.

We admire that kind of courage and perseverance that uses weakness as a springboard to achievement—based on the philosophy: "If we try hard enough, and hold positive thoughts, we can overcome any weakness, knock down any barrier, and accomplish any goal!"

But what about those of us for whom trust in our "human potential" isn't enough?

Paul the apostle describes in our text, how, in spite of his intellect and his training as a Jewish religious leader—when it came to ministry at Corinth, he didn't have it! Therefore, he had to learn to lean on God's resources.

Let's study a text that tells us about finding God's help in those areas where we feel fear, inadequacy, and weakness. A first truth that leaps out of our text: Faith in God's power frees the Christian from fear of weakness—fear of failure. Listen to Paul's words:

> When I came to you, I did not come with eloquence or human wisdom as I proclaimed to you the testimony about God. . . . I came to you in weakness with great fear and trembling. (1 Cor. 2:1, 3)

There was a book entitled the *Imposter Syndrome* describing:

- how many company executives are filled with feelings of inadequacy;
- how they fear young "turks" climbing the company ladder and replacing them;
- how they fear that one day their weakness and incompetency will be exposed.

In contrast, listen to Paul explain his successful ministry in Corinth: "Do you remember when I first came to you preaching the good news of Jesus? I was scared to death. Your church would have never gotten off the ground, if God had not transfused my weakness with his supernatural power. So let's give God the glory for what's happening here!"

Could you imagine Lee Iacocca addressing his board at Chrysler? "Listen, people, there is no question—a power bigger than any talent I possess helped turn this company around. Maybe we ought to give some credit to God." That wasn't what happened. The CEO of Chrysler received an $81 million stock bonus and claims he feels he is worth it.

Humility, vulnerability, and brokenness just don't cut it in our culture. Most of us feel the need to project this message: "My life is totally under control, the product of my hard work. I deserve the rewards I've earned."

But shouldn't we as Christians understand the power of weakness? I have a deep conviction that none of us will be of much use to God until we experience brokenness and gain the insight of knowing we can't make it without God. Don't all of us have some area of personal inadequacy? A shadowy side we don't like to expose? An area in life where we couldn't make it without God?

Bree Walker with her crippled hands—and others with human weaknesses—believe they conquered these obstacles by sheer willpower and human encouragement. The rest of us need God. The wonderful news in our text assures us that divine help is available to transfuse weaknesses in the life of a Christian with supernatural power. Therefore, we don't have to fear weakness any longer. Praise God!

Let me state this truth, from a second perspective: In the life of a Christian—weakness is power! Our helplessness is the door through which the divine enters the human scene. There is a beautiful verse in Isaiah the prophet:

> [T]hose who hope in the LORD will renew their strength. They will soar on wings like eagles; they will run and not be weary, they shall walk and not be faint. (Isa. 40:31)

If this is true, why do we fear weakness? Why do we fear being out of control? Why do we hesitate to confess, "I can't make it any longer without God?"

It's at the point where we have nothing left but God that we discover his power.

If you have followed my ministry at Menlo for eighteen years, you know that Walt Gerber has very little to do with what's happened here. Very early, I knew my inadequacies and offered them to God with fear and trembling. Many of you have prayed for me through the years. Together we have asked God to give me, supernaturally, what I don't possess in my own skills bank. God responded and entered this ministry through my weakness, and I'm awed by what he has done!

To keep me from being too proud of my humility, God sends me occasional reminders of just how important I am in this church. At a recent new members class, I was introducing myself to the people telling them about my past ministry, my family, my dreams. I went on for about five minutes, thinking they would be terribly impressed with my story. At the end of my discourse, a hand went up and a person asked, "Who are you, anyway?" This person was joining the church, and didn't have the faintest idea who Walt Gerber was and probably didn't care. Other forces had brought him to Menlo. This reaffirmed the truth of our text:

> *My message and my preaching were not with wise and persuasive words, but with a demonstration of the Spirit's power, so that your faith might not rest on men's wisdom, but on God's power.* (1 Cor. 2:4–5)

Personal weakness in the life of a Christian is power!

Simone Weil wrote, "The extreme greatness of Christianity lies in the fact that it does not seek a supernatural remedy for [weakness], but a supernatural use for it."[45] From another angle, Augustine said, "God wants to give us something but cannot because our hands are full. There is nowhere for him to put it."[46]

The power of weakness is that:

- It empties our hands and puts our expectation on God alone; and
- It enables us to risk beyond the parameters of our personal strength and experience miracles firsthand!

Paul said it well: "But we have this treasure [of God's power] in jars of clay to show that this all-surpassing power is from God, and not from us" (2 Cor. 4:7).

Paul, although feeling totally overwhelmed by the task God called him to accomplish at Corinth, didn't run away. There is power in keeping on, in doing it in spite of our weaknesses.

Kirk Bunnell, a friend of our church family, has multiple sclerosis. Through the years he has fought this debilitating condition. He still teaches men's Bible Study Fellowship, although he is physically weak and his speech doesn't have full clarity. His apparent weakness is a door by which God touches men. His courage gives witness to God's power, that he enables believers to confront insurmountable odds—and win!

This text calls Christians to give our weaknesses to God, to refuse to allow our feelings of inadequacy to paralyze us. To boldly trust God in the face of overwhelming circumstances. To push ahead in confidence, after logic says, "bail out."

Many of us are using that power right now to stay sane during a long job search and unbearable financial stress. Or to stay committed in a marriage, when every secular voice is telling us to get out. Or to find strength to "show up" to daily routine tasks that often seem so meaningless. Or to venture into a situation that we know is doomed to failure, unless God intervenes!

Weakness is power in the life of a Christian.

While walking the Rubicon Trail at Lake Tahoe, I was impressed with beautiful flowers God had planted in places where few human eyes ever see. Each one was unique and brought a kind of heavenly beauty to that one spot where it was planted. It reminded me of a plaque I keep in my office, which reads: "Bloom where you are planted!"

This week, rather than lament over your weaknesses, give them to God and allow him to empower you to bloom where you are planted.

May this discovery Paul made regarding God's power become your personal treasure: "I am content with weakness—because when I am weak, then I am strong!"

Questions for Study and Discussion:

1. Which of your inadequacies or weaknesses cause you the most anxiety? What do you do to compensate?

2. Can you think of a time where God used your weakness to demonstrate his own strength and care for you? What would it look like to place another of your weaknesses in his hands?

CALL ME A SERVANT—DON'T TREAT ME LIKE ONE!

2 Corinthians 4:5–18
March 28, 1982

I mention again three words proving helpful to me in making many personal adjustments to reality: *Life is difficult!* Life as a Christian, particularly if we commit ourselves to serve others, is difficult. Today I want to discuss the expectations we have about adopting a life-style of serving others. Holding expectations that correlate with reality can be a first step in conquering difficulties when we encounter them. Awareness of pitfalls and risks involved in serving will help protect us when we begin this dangerous journey.

A first danger seems obvious but isn't. There is all the difference in the world between saying, "I am willing to serve others for the sake of Jesus," and actually being treated like a servant by those we seek to serve. Rather than responding to our self-giving love with gratitude, love, and compliments, it's shocking to receive abuse and suspicion from needy people. It's much easier to say, "I want to be a servant," than to respond gracefully when treated like one. Yet this is exactly our ministry. Listen to Paul speak to the Corinthians:

> *For we preach not ourselves but Christ Jesus the Lord; and ourselves your servants for Jesus' sake.* (2 Cor. 4:5, KJV)

Sometimes when we serve others, lives are changed, people are helped, and those served respond with love and gratitude. Much more often, those we seek to serve initially resent our help or quickly begin to take it for granted, becoming hostile when we cannot give more, blaming us when we cannot solve all of their problems, turning against us after they are healed, becoming angry because we know about their weaknesses and needs, or smoldering inside about their dependence upon us. Here, then, is the first warning of danger if we embark on the adventure of servanthood: when we seek to serve others, expect to be treated like a servant. If we are unable to find joy and reward in the act of serving others for Jesus' sake, we probably are not ready to begin the journey.

There is a second, more subtle danger in servanthood. Paul gives the clue when he writes, "Not that we are adequate in ourselves to consider anything as coming from ourselves, but our adequacy is from God" (2 Cor. 3:5, NASB).

Christian servants are absolutely human, clay-footed sinners, prone to weakness and failure, potentially able to disappoint and hurt the very people we seek to help. Yet our temptation is to forget who we are. Getting caught up in serving, we tend to confuse the power of God flowing through us to touch others with our own power. Sometimes our role as a servant goes to our head. We become proud of our humility, proud of our ability to help others. Serving becomes an ego trip! We begin to expect the Christian community to consider us "super saints" or "Mary martyrs" for hanging in there in tough relationships, for reaching out to needy people. Such expectations are like a time bomb. The moment we confuse Christ's power operating through us with our own power, we forget who we are—clay vessels which only hold divine power, vessels that can be broken or begin to leak, to our own disillusionment and to the disillusionment of others.

Jesus alone is to be worshipped and valued in the Christian community. Even when we are on our knees washing our neighbor's feet in servanthood, our own clay feet are showing. Keep a sane perspective of who you are when you serve. Never communicate that what you share with others is anything but the presence of Christ in you. None of us is superior to the people we serve. When we fail, when we become inconsistent, such behavior shouldn't surprise anyone. People's faith should always be rooted in Jesus, not in us. It is Jesus alone who is the same yesterday, today, and forever.

One great fear I have as a preacher is that some might forget my leadership role does not place me above the struggle with "becoming" that everyone else faces. I haven't made it. I'm still a sinner, too! In fact, all of us will remain forgiven sinners, continually covered with Christ's grace, in process of growth all of our lives. Our right to serve each other is not rooted in our own personal holiness, but in the adequacy of Christ's grace that qualifies us to serve in his name.

A third danger in serving others is the obvious fact that terrible things happen to servants. Committing ourselves to servanthood does not protect us from anything. Servants struggle with everyday problems. We become overstressed, frustrated, depressed, confused, sick, betrayed, forsaken. Yet Chuck Swindoll is right when he says, "It is in the crucible of suffering that the servant learns to release his way for God's way."[47] Listen to Paul the apostle's words:

> We are afflicted in every way, but not crushed; perplexed, but not driven to despair; persecuted, but not forsaken; struck down, but not destroyed. (2 Cor. 4:8–9, ESV)

Consider the meaning of the words Paul uses:

- "Affliction" refers to pressure and stress, that feeling of being harassed and oppressed.
- "Perplexed"—not knowing where or to whom to turn for help, at a loss of what to do.
- "Persecuted"—being intimidated, assaulted, attacked: "all who desire to live a godly life in Christ Jesus will be persecuted" (2 Tim. 3:12, ESV).

- "Rejection"—struck down, cast off, left out of people's social circles, considered a weirdo, a freak. Paul was imprisoned and beaten.

One thing that bothered King David, and which can get to all servants of Christ, is the old question: "Why do the righteous suffer and the evil prosper?" Why do I get hit with financial reverses, or problems with my children, or sickness, while people who seem to live godless lives go along unscathed? The only answer David could find was to wait for God's eternal measure of justice. In eternity, the scales will balance out. There is a beautiful verse in Hebrews:

For God is not unjust so as to overlook your work and the love that you have shown for his name in serving the saints, as you still do. (Heb. 6:10, ESV)

When we suffer, rather than compare ourselves with those whose lot in life seems better, we should focus on Jesus, who lost everything in his role as a servant. During our time of greatest testing, we know Jesus is with us, and that with his help we are going to make it!

There is a fourth danger in serving—the potential temptation of greed, a subtle, deadly desire in our heart to be "paid off" for service, particularly when others doing the same thing we are doing are being paid. A story in the Old Testament illustrates such danger. Elisha the prophet had a servant named Gehazi. Naaman, a Syrian general, had come to Elisha seeking healing for leprosy, which he miraculously received. Naaman offered Elisha gold and silver in payment for his healing, payment Elisha refused. But Elisha's servant Gehazi couldn't understand such foolishness and ran after Naaman, asking for payment in silver and clothes. Elisha confronted Gehazi about his greed, and the tragic story ended with Gehazi contracting the leprosy from which Naaman had been healed (2 Kings 5). God does reward his servants in a way and timing that is best. To try to grab that reward too early is to risk disaster. Whatever treasure we might capture by devious means, on the premise God "owes" us for our labor, will always turn to gravel in our hands.

Greed represents only one facet of a greater truth. Every servant has an "Achilles heel." Each of us needs to pray humbly for protection about our personal area of vulnerability, so that in our serving we don't become a victim of our own weaknesses.

Let me share a beautiful truth with you. Everything that presents a danger to us has first passed through the permissive hands of our loving Heavenly Father. What confronts us is no surprise to him. Every hardship we endure is designed to prepare us for serving others more effectively. *Everything.* Tough times empty our hands of our own resources, so we will be forced to use God's resources. Poet Martha Snell Nicholson says it well in her poem "Treasures," in which she describes this emptying process:

> *One by one He took them from me,*
> *All the things I valued most,*
> *Till I was empty-handed,*
> *Every glittering toy was lost.*
> *And I walked earth's highways, grieving,*
> *In my rags and poverty.*
> *Till I heard His voice inviting,*
> *"Lift your empty hands to Me!"*[48]

It is only then, when our resources are gone and our hands empty, that God can fill them with what Nicholson calls "His own transcendent riches," and in such abundance that the speaker can hold no more. When our resources have failed us, God can step in.

Things may not be logical and fair, but when God is directing our lives, they are right.

Last week we studied the teaching of Jesus about prayer. I challenge you this morning to pray for at least one place where you can serve, one person you could commit yourself to care for. As a church, we will do everything we can to help you find that person or spot for ministry. As you leave today, there is a peach-colored sheet with dozens of suggested places and people where you might be needed. Today we learned that there is a cost and there is a danger in servanthood. Nevertheless, serving others represents Christianity at its highest and best, a lifestyle producing the greatest source of adventure and lasting joy. I believe our ultimate goal in life should be to win those words of our Lord when we appear before him someday, "Well done, good and faithful servant."

Questions for Study and Discussion:

1. Where have you served in your life, and why? Were you treated well and appreciated, or did you find it unpleasant for various reasons?

2. Have you ever fallen into one of the servanthood pitfalls Walt mentions? Who might God be calling you to serve, without earthly reward?

WHEN COMMITMENT CONQUERS COMFORT[49]

Esther 4
February 12, 1989

Have you ever felt like the only person left in your classroom, office, or social circle who has integrity without compromise? Or who sticks by commitments, no matter what the cost? God's people have always been forced to deal with such feelings because we are called to live by a different set of values than those of the world.

Today I want to tell you about Esther, a godly woman who lived by her commitments.

In ancient Persia, there was a faithful Jewish captive named Mordecai, who had a cousin named Esther. By a series of providential events, Esther became queen of Persia. After a brief time, it was obvious why God had placed her in this position of power.

Mordecai uncovered a plot by a top man in government who had convinced the king to put all Jews to death. Immediately, Mordecai sent a message, asking Esther to persuade the king to stop this impending slaughter. But Esther resisted going to the king without being summoned because it was dangerous. Esther told Mordecai, "You don't understand protocol. If I go to the king, I might lose my head. Anyway, why should I get involved? I'm safe here in the palace."

Mordecai responded, "If the thought of losing your comfort and security is stopping you from helping people, forget it. You share their predicament. God made you queen, so you could fulfill his plan. If you keep silent, God will raise up someone else to do his work, and you will miss the *privilege* of being used to help many people. God in his providence placed you where you are for this task. Such an opportunity might only come once" (see Esther 4).

Mordecai's words convinced the queen, and she went to the king. Her mission was successful. The king saved the Jews and executed the villain who conceived the evil plot. As a result, the Jewish race was preserved from extinction, as was the lineage through which Jesus would enter the world. I doubt Esther ever knew the importance of her decision to allow her commitments to conquer her comfort.

Mordecai's response to Esther is a challenge for us. We live in times when opportunities to do things for God are tremendous, and pressures to compromise are equally great.

First, like Esther, we share a common predicament. We live in a society under siege from the forces of evil.

Even secular leaders are alarmed at the widespread impact evil is having upon all of us: drug abuse; immorality breaking up families; a new generation of scarred adults growing out of these broken relationships; conspicuous consumption creating a growing gap between the poor and the rich; growing numbers of homeless and hungry in the richest nation on Earth; a loss of integrity in political, economic, and religious leadership; news reports of degenerates kidnapping our children; and the growth of child pornography. All of us could add to this list of inroads of evil into our lives. I know there are no quick or cheap "fixes" for these challenges. However, the living God has not abandoned his world. Quite the contrary, he seeks to use Christians to bring his solutions for these impossible problems.

However, like Esther, it's so easy to ask: "Why should we, as Christians, become involved in these ugly problems?" Here are two reasons:

1. God has called us to be involved.

2. Like Esther, we are tempted to hide in our palaces of security, believing our protective walls will insulate us from the chaos outside.

Tragically, we tend to become exercised about evil only when it touches us personally. When drugs capture our children. When immorality invades our home. When greed and dishonesty disrupt our business and local government. When a drunk driver hurts someone we love.

A first truth from Esther's story warns us: Don't think that we can avoid the hurt and pain evil is bringing to our society, by hiding in our palaces of comfort. All of us share the same predicament. The buffer between our palaces and the jungle out there is very thin!

A second truth from Esther deals with the issue of privilege. Like Esther, Christians have the privilege of being used of God to break the hold of evil on society. You and I can make a difference! Every Christian has been strategically placed to do battle with evil. Look at us:

- students and teachers in our schools;
- businesspeople in the marketplace;
- parents and children in the home;
- club members in our social circles; and
- workers on the job.

Our task is to stand for what is right out in the trenches of a hostile world. Continued growth for our church does not mean building a cathedral to which people flock. Real growth happens when we, who are already part of this church, are willing to use our lives to make a difference in the part of the world we touch during the week. Until that happens, bringing in more people is meaningless. If we become preoccupied with our own comfort, God will raise up another church to do his work—and we will miss this glorious *privilege* of being used to defeat evil. Elizabeth Dole, speaking to government leaders, said:

> *God doesn't want worldly successes. He wants me. . . . Life is not just a few years to spend on self-indulgence and career advancement. It is a privilege, a responsibility, a stewardship to be lived according to a much higher calling.*[50]

On the day of the Super Bowl, it was announced that Stanley Wilson, running back of the Cincinnati Bengals, had been suspended for drug abuse. Can you imagine investing your life in a sport, and then on the day of the Super Bowl losing your big chance and letting down all your teammates? Stanley Wilson was made to play football. Because he allowed himself to be distracted by drugs, he lost his big chance.

God made Esther queen not for comfort, but for the privilege of being a divine instrument for healing a world in crisis. God forbid we become so distracted in seeking comfort that we forget a war is going on, and miss the privilege of being part of God's Super Bowl offensive against evil.

Finally, Mordecai spoke to Esther of the divine providence in her being queen to accomplish God's purposes. Like Esther, every Christian is providentially deployed by God for a unique work for the kingdom.

I want God to help us realize that every one of us who takes the name Christian has a significant ministry to accomplish. If we are Christians, following Jesus means who we are and what we possess are at God's disposal to use for his purposes.

Last week my wife was able to attend the National Prayer Breakfast in Washington, DC. While there, she heard Mr. Arthur Taylor, former president of CBS, give his testimony. He was fired from CBS because his conscience would not allow him to continue broadcasting programs so detrimental to the family. Although it was costly, Mr. Taylor believed his commitments to God's purposes on Earth were more important than his position, salary, and personal future in this world. That's the kind of commitment that wins the battle with evil. Such commitment always involves cost. Esther responded to her call, saying: "If I perish, I perish." Somehow, she felt life wouldn't be worth living, even in a palace, unless she were living it in obedience to her God.

Each of us has a unique assignment by God that demands commitment, an opportunity to make our lives count for something big. Your task may be:

- to hang tough in a class and not cheat, when many are choosing to opt for dishonesty;

- to hold to your integrity in business, when it's so tempting to compromise;

- to remain faithful to your commitments in marriage or single life, when so many believe God's rules for morality no longer apply; or

- to live courageously with your pain, saying with Job (13:15, KJV), "Though he slay me, yet will I trust in him."

I believe many of us at MPPC have grown spiritually to the point where we are no longer comfortable remaining insulated, isolated, and immune from today's problems. We want our lives to count for God, and we are willing to pay the price.

One of our realtors lost a potentially profitable listing by daring to be honest about a certain issue with a client. You have already heard one of our doctors tell you of the stand he is taking in the hospital where he works. None of these sacrifices are isolated incidents, but part of God's cosmic battle against evil.

Listen to these challenging words of Thomas à Kempis:

Jesus today has many who love his heavenly kingdom, but few who carry his cross. . . . Plenty of people he finds to share his banquet, few to share his fast. Everyone desires to take part in his rejoicing, but few are willing to suffer anything for his sake.[51]

I want our church family to be living evidence that there are still Esthers in the world, people who will put God's agenda ahead of our own pleasure.

I challenge you this week: Go find *one* issue where you feel God is calling you to take action against evil. As incredible as it may sound, God will use our commitments in little things and big things to change the world.

Questions for Study and Discussion:

1. What comforts and privileges do you enjoy, that reading this sermon made you realize you would have trouble giving up?

2. Where in your life might God be calling you to take action against evil? To speak up or refrain from participating or demonstrate another way?

To Walt—The Gift of Encouragement

Without you, Walt, the journey wouldn't have been so wonderful. I can't even count the times you said to me, "You are such a gift!" This is not an exclusive compliment. Encouraging words are a part of your daily vocabulary to all those surrounding you.

Leanne Benton

BEING CIVIL IN AN UNCIVIL WORLD

Matthew 12:33–37
April 19–20, 1997

Tiger Woods was interviewed immediately following his epic victory and was asked, "What was the highest moment you experienced throughout the entire tournament?" Rather than choosing one of his incredible achievements on the golf course, he chose the time spent with his dad the night before his last round as the most meaningful for him. He described how his dad offered words of love and encouragement, assuring him he could face the huge challenge of that last day, and *win*! His dad's words acted as a blessing for Tiger, energizing him to face that final round.

Think of the power of words, either to build up, to affirm, to instill courage, or to tear down, abuse, and discourage! Many observers of our culture are expressing increasing concern about the loss of civility in society:

- the abuse people inflict on each other with words; and
- the loss of awareness that we human beings are connected, all part of the same community.

USA Today reports: "It's becoming impossible to ignore the growing rudeness of American life. . . . An overwhelming majority of Americans, 89% in a *U.S. News & World* poll last April, think incivility is a serious problem. . . . That is what happens when people lose a sense of community."[52] These happenings describe a dangerous trend. When we become uncivil, we soon become uncivilized. These facts highlight why Jesus places such importance on words we use. Let's study our text.

First, Jesus says words are important because words come from deep inside, from that part of us he calls our hearts:

> *[O]ut of the abundance of the heart the mouth speaks. . . .*
> *I tell you, on the day of judgment people will give account*
> *for every careless word they speak, for by your words you will*
> *be acquitted, and by your words you will be condemned.*
> (Matt. 12:34, 36–37)

James amplifies this truth:

> *The tongue is a fire . . . staining the whole body . . . set on fire by*
> *hell. . . . [N]o human being can tame the tongue . . . a restless*
> *evil, full of deadly poison. . . . From the same mouth come bless-*
> *ing and cursing.* (James 3:6–8, 10)

Because words reveal the "real us," it gets serious to realize God doesn't buy our glib excuses. "I didn't mean what I said." "I was just upset." "My blood sugar was low." "That person pushed me over the edge."

The other day a biker unloaded an avalanche of words on me, for doing something she thought invaded her turf on the road. Such venom! And I was a perfect stranger, who didn't even know what I had done to offend her. Lack of civility is real.

As we seek to become contagious Christians in an uncivil world, a strategic step would be to seek God's help in bringing consistency between the love of Jesus we claim is in our hearts and the words we use. Blessing and cursing should not come out of the same mouth.

Listen to Paul describe in Romans 3 the destructive potential of words:

> *"Their throats are open graves;*
> *their tongues practice deceit."*
> *"The poison of vipers is on their lips."*
> *"Their mouths are full of cursing and bitterness."* (vv. 13–14)

When our verbal eruptions, blessing and cursing, coming out of the same mouth, we face a question: Which is the real us?

Today we use the term "verbal abuse" to describe one form of domestic violence against husbands, wives, and children, or to indicate words of harassment in the workplace. Children are scarred for life by cruel words from other children, or by critical words from a parent or teacher. Words come gushing out in a fit of rage or jealousy, or in slander that destroys a person's reputation or self-esteem.

I heard a story about a man coming to a rabbi to confess his habit of gossiping, asking what penance he could do for his sin. The rabbi told him to get a pillow filled with feathers, go up to a high mountain, and then open the pillow and let the feathers fly into the wind. "Is that all I have to do, to atone for my gossiping?" "One more thing," said the rabbi. "Then I want you to go and retrieve every feather, and put it back into the pillow." The rabbi's point was made. Gossip, slander, and destructive critical words are like feathers. They go and spread everywhere and, once spoken, cannot be retrieved. No wonder Jesus urges us to be careful in what we say.

Happily, Jesus can forgive and heal the wounds our words cause, even when we can't do anything to fix the damage we have created in another life. Yet let's heed this warning to be more thoughtful and careful in what we say and how we say it.

The psalmist wisely asked God to put a "guard" over his mouth. I marvel at how easily I verbalize an opinion about people—how they dress, raise their children, spend their money, how they look. James was certainly right to call the tongue "a fire . . . set ablaze by hell itself" (James 3:6, NLT). God takes our words very seriously.

This leads us to a second truth: Only the power of the Holy Spirit can change how we speak, because only the Spirit can change our hearts. Paul writes to the Ephesians:

> *Therefore, each of you must put off falsehood and speak truthfully to your neighbor, for we are all members of one body. . . . Do not let any unwholesome talk come out of your mouths, but only what is helpful for building others up according to their needs, that it may benefit those who listen. And do not grieve the Holy Spirit of God, with whom you were sealed for the day of redemption. Get rid of all bitterness, rage and anger, brawling and slander, along with every form of malice. Be kind and compassionate to one another, forgiving each other, just as in Christ God forgave you.* (Eph. 4:25, 29–32)

Most of us would agree with what Paul says in this text. Our problem is we can't do it. We can't always speak the truth, or use our words to impart grace, or stop gossiping. The good news is that, as believers, we have supernatural power to exhibit kindness, gentleness, goodness, self-control, and love. These are character qualities that the Holy Spirit implants in our character over a period of time, as we follow Jesus and apply his teachings to our lives. Qualities that make it possible for us to make loving responses to rudeness and anger we inevitably encounter in our uncivil society. Qualities that give witness that we belong to Jesus Christ.

To be civil doesn't mean we have to like people or agree with them. The Spirit of Jesus in us enables us to see people as God sees them, as part of his creation, part of our community, as people in process who have value because God values them.

If I could describe the change the Holy Spirit seeks to bring in how we speak, it would be:

- an increasing willingness to say "thank you" more often;
- seeing more good things in others, and telling them, more often; and
- eliminating the whining, criticizing, murmuring habits that make us, and those who have to listen us, so miserable.

Let me also offer some suggestions of how the Spirit might make some changes in how we speak. First, when we hear a rumor, don't pass it on; let it die. Again, our text says, "Get rid of all bitterness, rage and anger, brawling and slander, along with every form of malice." I spend hours correcting information. If someone approaches you with the latest tidbit, why not ask some questions:

- Why are you telling me this?
- Have you talked personally with the person involved?
- May I quote you?
- Does this need to be said?

Another suggestion: Let's monitor our words this week. Choose a few friends who will give us honest feedback on the impact of what we are saying, and how we are saying it. Are we complaining, criticizing, comparing, being negative, ungrateful? It's good to hear ourselves through the perspective of someone else we respect. It would be fantastic if this prayer of the psalmist was answered in our church family:

> Let the words of my mouth, and the meditation of my heart, be acceptable in thy sight, O LORD, my strength, and my redeemer. (Ps. 19:14, KJV)

Another suggestion: Recognize that no one changes behavior because of our critical, caustic, negative words. Suppose Tiger's father, the night before his last round, had spent the evening criticizing, pointing out his weaknesses during the tournament. Rather than a blessing that acted like wind beneath his wings, negative words would have been a weight and hindrance.

And another suggestion: When we are tempted to give our personal blessing to a wayward driver, or someone in the office or classroom or neighborhood who gets in our face, let's consciously delay our first verbal barrage and ask God to turn our frustration into some form of self-control. As our text reminds us: "Do not let any unwholesome talk come out of your mouths, but only what is helpful for building others up" (Eph. 4:29).

This week I challenge us to ask the Holy Spirit to sensitize us to the power of our words. Let's focus on words that build up, encourage, offer forgiveness, affirmation, and gratitude. Think of the potential impact of our congregation on those parts of the world we will touch this week, as we give the Lord Jesus control of our lips! Such a decision will make us a group of very contagious Christians.

Questions for Study and Discussion:

1. In reading through this sermon, where did the Holy Spirit convict you, in your recent use of words? After confessing these to God, is it possible to ask forgiveness of those you abused?

2. What practices can you put into place, to prevent complaining, criticizing, comparing, being negative, and being ungrateful?

Living without Fear

Various Scriptures
September 15–16, 2001
(following the events of 9/11)

God is our refuge and strength, an ever-present help in trouble. Therefore we will not fear, though the earth give way and the mountains fall into the heart of the sea. (Ps. 46:1–2)

Are these words really true for us? In times like these, is God our refuge?

Strengthen the feeble hands, steady the knees that give way; say to those with fearful hearts, "Be strong, do not fear, your God will come." (Isa. 35:3–4)

Is trusting God's promises sustaining us during this crisis, helping us cope with our fear and the other emotions storming inside our souls?

I was thinking about airbags and seatbelts this week. Thankfully, I have never had a serious accident, so in reality I have no assurance the ones in my car will work when I need them. In a similar vein, we have been reading Scripture for years, stating what we believe about God. Now I ask, in this time of need, are these promises working for us?

One profound result of this horrific week in my life is that I have new confidence I'm not spouting happy religious clichés about God's power and faithfulness. These promises are the only bedrock upon which we can stand, when we have to cope with events too horrible to imagine, when we confront this horrendous unveiling of evil, in a dimension most of us have never experienced in our lives.

I offer this truth; trusting God's love in the midst of this tragedy can enable us to live without debilitating fear, to face the uncertain tomorrows with new hope because we know "There is no fear in love. But perfect love drives out fear. . . . The one who fears is not made perfect in love" (1 John 4:18).

A first major weapon in conquering fear is to really believe God loves us, is watching over us, and is protecting us as a loving parent cares for a child. Jesus asked:

> *Are not two sparrows sold for a penny? Yet not one of them will fall to the ground outside your Father's care. And even the very hairs of your head are numbered. So don't be afraid; you are worth more than many sparrows.* (Matt. 10:29–31)

Jesus often spoke about fear because he knew we would struggle with it, and he wants to repattern our thinking so we can live free from bondage to fear. Fear is an affliction, not a sin. It's okay to say, "I'm really scared." Our Heavenly Father understands our fears. Rather than condemning us for inadequate faith, his desire is to calm our anguished hearts, dry our tears, and steady our shaking knees. Isaiah gave these words of encouragement to a frightened Israel at a time of crisis:

> *So do not fear, for I am with you; do not be dismayed, for I am your God. I will strengthen you and help you; I will uphold you with my righteous right hand. . . . I am the LORD your God, who takes hold of your right hand and says to you, Do not fear; I will help you.* (Isa. 41:10, 13)

When Joshua was leading the Jews in a time of great stress and uncertainty, he gave this message:

> *Have not I commanded you? Be strong and courageous. Do not be terrified, for the LORD your God will be with you wherever you go.* (Josh. 1:9)

These words provide power for us to cope, to hope, to go on, knowing we have a tomorrow. These promises are God's gift, but like any gift they must be received.

A second answer to conquering fear is that we have to believe these promises. We must trust. Trusting God gives us unquenchable optimism that nothing can defeat us, despite dangers, hardships, stress. To trust means we hold on to God when life's experiences would make it appear he is absent. We hold on to him during impossible times, when evil seems to have won the battle, when all the evidence seems to vote against his love, his power, his ability to control our destiny. When we trust, we don't demand clarity. Jesus modeled trust as he hung on the cross, saying, "into your hands I commit my spirit" (Luke 23:46). Job modeled trust when he said, "Though he slay me, yet will I trust in him" (Job 13:15, KJV). When we confront the worst that evil can throw at us and still say, "Into your hands I commit my life," that's trusting God.

Uncompromising trust is possible for the Christian because at the center of our faith is the cross, testifying that God can draw good out of the most heinous evil. That he can bring light out of the worst darkness. That he brings Easter mornings, after evil has done its worst on Good Fridays.

In the midst of tragic events that leave us bereft of understanding, trust does not demand explanations but turns to the One who promised, "I will never leave or forsake you." Like a child overwhelmed with pain, we simply rest in our Father's arms, confident he is in control, even though we don't understand.

I read a story recently about a family of trapeze artists who perform in a German circus under the name the Flying Rodleighs. Until I read about the Flying Rodleighs, I assumed, like everyone else, that the big star of the trapeze show is the guy flying through the air, letting go of the bar and doing somersaults in space, but the leader of the troupe says this:

> *The real star is Joe, my catcher. He has to be there for me with split-second precision and grab me out of the air as I come to him in the long jump. The secret is that the flyer does nothing and the catcher does everything. When I fly to Joe, I have simply to stretch out my arms and hands and wait for him to catch me and pull me safely over the apron behind the catch bar.*[53]

In fact, the flying guy goes on to say, if he tries to catch hold of Joe, that's the worst thing he could do. He might break the catcher's wrists, or his own, and that would be the end of the Flying Rodleighs.

What a perfect metaphor of what it means to trust God's promises. Remember, Jesus said at the worst possible moment, "Father, into your hands I commit my spirit." We are the beloved children of God. He is here to catch us, when we are hurting, confused, with pain, rage, and fear surging inside our hearts. Trust means we stretch out our arms, hands, and hearts, saying, "Lord I trust you. Catch me as I feel myself falling into despair and unbelief."

I can't describe the joy, when we are convinced life is in a free fall, and suddenly the hand of our Heavenly Father catches us, and we know for certain his love is real and his promises can be trusted. We know it's really true, what Isaiah claims: "You keep him in perfect peace whose mind is stayed on you, because he trusts in you" (Isa. 26:3, ESV).

I pray each of us will find this peace, this freedom from fear as we focus on our God who holds the uncertain future in his almighty hands—as we face tomorrow, undergirded by these foundational truths:

> *When I am afraid, I put my trust in you . . . In God I trust and am not afraid. What can mere mortals do to me?* (Ps. 56:3-4)

The LORD is my light and salvation—whom shall I fear? The LORD is the strength of my life—of whom shall I be afraid? . . . be strong and take heart. (Ps. 27:1, 14)

Therefore do not worry about tomorrow, for tomorrow will worry about itself. Each day has enough trouble of its own. (Matt. 6:34)

It's good to know anything that touches us has passed through the loving scrutiny of our Shepherd.

For the Spirit God gave us does not make us timid, but gives us power, love and self-discipline. (2 Tim. 1:7)

Strengthen the feeble hands, steady the knees that give way; say to those with fearful hearts, "Be strong, do not fear; your God will come . . . he will come to save you." (Isa. 35:3–4)

Questions for Study and Discussion:

1. Where were you on 9/11? What do you remember of the day? How did you cope with the fear, and what provided comfort?

2. In day-to-day life, where does fear most often strike you? What lessons offered in this sermon can you apply, to face down that affliction?

He had no website. No blog. No Twitter account. He never published a book or developed any technology, though he was known to love a fast sports car. He wasn't on LinkedIn, Facebook, Instagram, Pinterest, or Snapchat. On the web, this man barely registers. But Walt was a Silicon Valley titan—a titan of grace, the kind of man whose impact will live long after his passing, not through the technology he developed, but through the hearts he touched, the lives he shaped. Perhaps in this divisive time we can again remember the way he described his mission—and the mission of all of us who share a faith in Jesus: "I'd like the pulpit to be a fountain of Christ's accepting love. Because that's how I experienced it."

Stephanie Kirtland[54]

Walt Gerber was my boss, mentor, and friend for more than two decades. Our close working relationship, cherished vacations, and family gatherings were a source of great joy for our family.

Our boss/employee relationship was always one of trust and grace. I have never worked for anyone else who had the ability to intuit what I needed in order to complete my assignments. Also, I have never known anyone who was so quick to extend grace when I failed to meet expectations.

Walt's office door was invariably open to staff—and many times, unannounced, I would pay him a visit to ask a question. He was always quick to respond and offer advice on how to resolve problems. His managing style may have just seemed casual to many, but it was extremely effective.

Walt enjoyed previewing sermons with me, as it was my responsibility to plan worship services based on the content of these messages. Walt had a rule: He never wanted sermons to be more than twenty minutes because he felt brevity was important to comprehension and successful assimilation. Time after time, I would watch him edit full paragraphs out of his talks. I admitted that I would have a difficult time throwing away so much work. He said, "If it doesn't bring value and Jesus to people's lives, it's not worth saying."

Without being conscious of it, Walt was a bit of a showman, though he never acknowledged it. He used to say, "Worship should be many things, but it should never be boring!"

And it never was! I loved working with the man!

Doug Lawrence
Minister of Worship

NEW BEGINNINGS

John 8:1–11
November 6–7, 1999

This passage we deal with is one of the most precious and yet, historically, one of the most controversial in all of the New Testament. Because every time we preach on grace, we meet with two reactions. On the one hand, the broken sinner rejoices in the news. On the other, the one who has been hurt by the sinner, or those of us not really aware of our own depravity, usually are made somewhat angry because we don't feel people should be let off the hook.

We're not going to solve this problem today because the church has been dealing with it for two thousand years. My prayer for you is that you have joy today, rather than anger. I'm convinced something is radically wrong in the hearts of too many Christians. Specifically, we tend to believe in the grace of Jesus in theory, and yet, over and over again, we deny it in practice when applied to ourselves or applied to others. So today, I want us to hear again: a Christian is not someone who is good; a Christian is a person who has experienced the goodness of God. Only Jesus is good.

When will we understand that Jesus did not create the church as a refuge for the super-spiritual or the morally elite, to the exclusion of those who can't measure up? Jesus came to heal those of us who know we don't have it all together. Those who are still unable to throw away the false support systems of sin, and yet who come again this morning, thirsty for the living water of hope and forgiveness and new beginnings that Jesus is more than anxious to give us.

My deepest desire in leading our church family through all these years is that, every time we come together, I want us to have an opportunity to experience again the outrageous love of God and to grow in our knowledge of that love. Too often that love is eclipsed by the heresy of judgmentalism, legalism, coldness, formality, and all of the baggage many of us carry from our past.

We need to know that our view of God impacts how we view ourselves, how we view others, and how others view us; and thus, how others view God. That's why the Bible talks so often about knowing God as Jesus revealed him. Jesus gave us the electrifying news that God is a loving Father with arms open to the sinner, not a vindictive judge just anxious to zap us! In fact, the Bible says, "where sin increased, grace abounded all the more" (Rom. 5:20, ESV). That's God's heart.

Our drama today is a kind of fiber-optic camera, enabling us to look right into the heart of Jesus on matters of sin, guilt, punishment, and grace. As we look at Jesus together, we're going to see what God is like, and that's good news.

In the story, scribes and Pharisees drag this nameless woman to Jesus, after she has been caught in the very act of adultery. Accusers stand ready with rocks in hand to put her to death, according to the law of Moses. But in reality, the whole scene is a crock. Roman law prohibited Jews from putting anyone to death. What's more, it takes two to commit adultery, and where was the male partner in this scene? Jesus recognizes the situation for what it is, a potential trap set by the uptight religious leaders. If he condemns the woman, he denies his claim to be a friend of sinners. But if he pardons her, he can be accused of condoning adultery and breaking the law of Moses. That tension still exists in the church.

What does Jesus do? He refuses to pass judgment. He stoops and writes in the sand (we know not what) and then rises, saying, "If any one of you is without sin, let him be the first to throw a stone at her" (John 8:7, NIV1984). A dramatic moment—and the passage goes on to say that, with the eldest being the first, the crowd walks away. The "eldest" leaves first, we understand, because they'd lived the longest and had the most opportunity to sin. Then Jesus turns to the woman and asks, "Woman, where are they? Has no one condemned you?" God is speaking to her, because that's who we believe Jesus is, and he says to her, "neither do I condemn you. . . Go, and leave your life of sin" (vv. 10–11).

The reason this passage is so difficult is that it breaks with a lot of our formulas. The woman didn't walk the sawdust trail in repentance! Actually, she hasn't repented at all yet. Jesus gives her forgiveness—without a lot of the preconditions we put on it—and this causes the church all kinds of trouble. So I want us to allow this story, through the Holy Spirit, to give us a fresh chapter of the grace of God, because I believe, to some degree, every one of us needs it today.

First, Jesus reveals how truth must be coupled with grace, or we distort the character of God. There was truth in this scene, but grace was missing until Jesus injected it. Truth in this story: the woman was guilty. According to the letter of the law, she deserved death. Then Jesus came along and brought something new to the scene of judgment. He combined grace, compassion, and mercy with the truth of her guilt. Thank God!

In doing so, he was modeling God's heart, and it was new. Yet it *wasn't* new. The Jews should have read the Old Testament, where it says that God is slow to anger, abounding in unfailing love, and doesn't deal with us as our sins deserve (Ps. 103:8, 10). That's the part we can't quite get through our heads: God doesn't deal with us as our sins deserve. Particularly if we've been hurt—we want somebody to pay the price.

Jesus stands in sharp contrast to the religious leaders, who found sadistic pleasure in demanding this woman's punishment. By their attitude, they were telling lies about God. God is not a vindictive judge anxious to punish sinners; he's a Father with his arms open, wanting sinners to come back home and get healed. If we could only apply that to our own guilt! If we could only apply that truth to those who have hurt us. It's hard.

Dr. Ian Pitt-Watson of Fuller Seminary rightfully points out how this story was deleted in many early manuscripts. If you've ever read the gospel of John carefully, there's always a little note that this was not really the original spot for it. Do you know why? Because from the earliest years, the scribes considered this passage too dangerous. They never doubted its authenticity, but they believed the grace Jesus gave to this woman would be misunderstood and used as a license for immorality or whatever, and the church has been worried about that ever since.

Grace frightens us. I don't know why—the fear of punishment, which the Old Testament was loaded with, didn't do a very good job keeping people from sinning. So why are we so worried that grace is going to do something worse? That strange fear of grace persists, particularly when it comes to sexual sin. How long will it take for us to understand that God loves us as we are?

As Brennan Manning reminded us during our time at Mt. Hermon, God loves us as we are, not as we ought to be. And not as we ever *will* be, at least until, one day, we stand at the feet of Jesus. To be a Christian is to live in joy and freedom, knowing God's love is not based on our performance and that it doesn't go away, although, even as Christians, we can't stop sinning.

As Manning points out, Christians should be the most nonjudgmental of peoples! They get along well with sinners. They're aware of their lack of wholeness, their brokenness, the simple fact they don't have it all together. And while we do not excuse our sin, we are humbly aware that it is precisely what causes us to throw ourselves on the mercy of the Father. We do not pretend to be anything more than what we are: sinners saved by grace. That's the church. Always has been.

I find this drama of Jesus giving mercy the most accurate picture in the Bible of the heart of God. Although Jesus never ignores the seriousness of our sin, his goal is not to punish. His goal is restoration, mercy, and new beginnings. He doesn't want to reject you. He doesn't want to condemn you. He wants to save you. That's why he died.

As we grasp, through faith, our Lord's unbelievable, *outrageous* mercy and grace, purchased at the cost of his cross, what should that do? Give us license for sin?

No.

It should lead us to repentance, to finding forgiveness and courage to pick up the pieces of our lives again and again and again. Although we can't stop sinning, every time we do and we look at the cross, we get a new motivation to continue that journey and never quit, until one day we stand at his feet. God is never going to give up on you or me. Love and gratitude, I offer, are far better stimuli for living obedient lives than fear and threats and false pictures of the heart of God. That's the truth in this story.

A second lesson Jesus reveals is that offering grace without truth distorts the character of God. Truth without grace distorts it; grace without truth distorts it. The truth is, the woman is guilty, but the revolutionary truth Jesus is unveiling is that God's love is greater than her guilt—that God's love is not rooted in our performance, but in our need. When Jesus lets her off the hook, he isn't just having a *laissez-faire* attitude toward sin. He's revealing the incredible truth that God would rather die for us than live in heaven without us. That's truth and grace combined.

To be saved, to be Christian, to be born again, to be transformed, is to accept this truth: We will never be good enough to be part of God's forever family, no matter how hard we try or how many resolutions we make. The only way we'll be good enough is to accept the free gift of grace made possible by the cross of Jesus. That's gospel, and it's so clear a child can understand it. Through the centuries, we always want to add something of performance on our part to complete the equation.

Because of what this story reveals about the heart of our heavenly Father, I offer that this is the reason we Christians should be celebrating every time we come together. Joy should permeate our worship, our daily lives. Our faces should radiate the fact we have been forgiven, we've been lavished upon by God's love. Our Father loves us before we shape up and doesn't stop loving us when we fall; no matter how many times we sin, we can come back home and find forgiveness. That's not license for sin—that's love. That's God's love.

Accepting acceptance, allowing God to embrace us in our sin, is the step of faith that saves us. Brothers and sisters, that's why our worship and our coming together should be so filled with joy. Formal, cold, lifeless, boring worship is the antithesis of Christian worship.

I want to affirm again, though, for those who get concerned here—because *I'm* concerned—this truth is not saying sin doesn't matter to Jesus. Broken hearts and lives, caused by breaking God's laws, always matter to him. It hurts the victim and it hurts us. The fact that sin caused the cross of Jesus makes sin matter. The whole point is, grace came in Jesus, and it's greater than our sin. That's what we have to work like mad to get into our brains. Accepting this grace leads to rebirth and transformation.

Let me see if I can show you how this process of truth and grace and grace and truth works. Remember when Nathan the prophet accused David of adultery? David didn't deny it. He didn't make excuses. He simply said, "I have sinned against the LORD" (2 Sam. 12:13). According to the law, David should have been stoned. Nathan, God's prophet, responded with the truth: "God forgives you. He lets you off the hook, even though you're guilty." This unconditional love propelled David, and it propels us, on a journey from the truth of our brokenness, to the transforming power of the grace of Jesus.

This good news of grace was articulated by the poet Louisa Fletcher.
I wish that there were some wonderful place
In the Land of Beginning Again.
Where all our mistakes and all our heartaches
And all of our poor selfish grief
Could be dropped like a shabby old coat at the door
And never put on again.[55]

There *is* such a place, and that's the foot of the cross of Jesus. The cross of Jesus means everyone has a second chance—if we believe in the outrageous love of God, and if we're willing to accept it because we're aware of our need. I trust that those of us who come to worship feeling guilty, crummy about ourselves—not once, but maybe a little bit every week—those of us who can't keep our promises, those of us who can't stop sinning, will experience the comfort of letting God love us and hearing his words.

This is so shocking to some, but it's so true. God said, "I never expected you to be perfect in your own strength. I love you as much when you're trapped in some sin as I love you in those rare moments in which, for a short time, you obey me. Rest in my love. I'll never, never cast you out unless you want to be."

In *The Message*, Eugene Peterson gives this version of the great prayer David offered in repentance after he committed his sin with Bathsheba:

> *Generous in love—God, give grace! Huge in mercy—wipe out my bad record. Scrub away my guilt, soak out my sins in your laundry. I know how bad I've been; my sins are staring me down. You're the One I've violated, and you've seen it all. . . . What you're after is truth from the inside out. Enter me, then; conceive a new, true life. . . . Don't throw me out with the trash . . . put a fresh wind in my sails!* (Ps. 51:1–4, 6, 11–12, MSG)

I'm happy to give you the good news today. God doesn't throw anybody out with the trash, unless they want to be. He lets us know how much he treasures us, not when we are what we ought to be, but when we are what we are: sinners saved by grace alone, and we'll never be anything else.

I want to close with a story from Brennan Manning. It's a parable. It's not a Christian parable, but it contains a Christian truth.

A monk was being pursued by a ferocious tiger. He raced to the edge of the cliff, spotted a dangling rope, and grabbed it. He stared down and saw huge rocks five hundred feet below. He looked up and saw the tiger poised atop the cliff. Just then, two mice began to nibble at the rope. What to do? The monk saw a strawberry within reach, so he plucked and ate it, saying to himself, "That's the best strawberry I've ever eaten."[56]

If he had been preoccupied with the rocks below (the future) or the tiger above (the past), he would have missed the strawberry God was giving him in the present moment. The point for this morning is God doesn't want us to focus on the tigers of the past. They've been defanged, forgiven. Nor on the rocks of the future—he's in control. But only on the strawberry of grace he brought you here this morning to receive, as unbelievably good as it sounds. God offers all of us his grace if we will reach out in faith and take it and believe it's greater than our sin.

That grace leads to new beginnings, and that, my brothers and sisters, is what the gospel of good news is all about. I don't know what you brought with you today, but I believe worship should always be a healing time of casting away and beginning again, and maybe you need to do that this week. I know I do. Why don't we take just a few moments of prayer and let this grace soak in a little bit and leave here free and forgiven? Would you pray with me?

Lord, for some of us, it almost is too good to be true that you can forgive sinners like us, even though we fall into it again and again. For some of us, it doesn't seem fair, when people have hurt us so much, that they can get forgiven. Lord, you know all this stuff going on in our hearts. Help each one of us to focus on one thing: We're sinners saved by grace, and we're so glad your arms are open, ready to receive us this morning, the moment we're ready to come back. Thank you that you don't stop loving us. You never give up on us, no matter how far we stray. Lord, give us the joy of that truth, and may we carry it with us all week long. I pray in Christ's name. Amen.

Questions for Study and Discussion:

1. Which sin, in yourself or others, angers you the most? Where are you most likely to want to deny grace and replace it with the "heresy of judgmentalism, legalism, coldness, formality, and all of the baggage many of us carry"?

2. Did you resonate with any of the reasons Walt gives for why people fear grace? Where in your life is God asking you to accept his grace and begin again?

A Request to Readers

Walt preached two sermons during his tenure wherein artificial roses were given to the congregation—the first on December 21, 1986, "When It Hurts Too Much to Wait," and the second on December 4–5, 1993, "Disappointed with God?" Each rose represented a prayer request. Walt asked for those who received answers to their prayers to return them to the church. A wreath was placed in front of the church to hold the returned roses as a celebration and visual reminder of God's answered prayers.

To our knowledge, the last rose was returned to Walt in the spring of 2013. Peter Gerber, Walt's last grandson, attended Kirkhouse Preschool, and the rose was returned by Geri Boegner, affectionately known as Teacher Geri. For countless years, Teacher Geri attended church alone with her son and daughter, always longing for her husband Kurt to join them and know God's grace and love. Through the passing of Kurt's father, they began attending church together and officially became members in 2013. The rose had been nestled in her jewelry box for twenty years and was returned to Walt eleven years after his official retirement. A long-awaited answered prayer!

We have been unable to locate an audio or written copy of the first rose sermon from 1986. If any reader has a version, we would greatly appreciate adding it to the library. Additionally, we are also hoping to locate an audio copy of the second rose sermon from 1993. Please contact us at gerbersermons@gmail.com.

The Gerber Family

DISAPPOINTED WITH GOD?

Ephesians 3:13–21
December 4–5, 1993

Have you ever felt disappointed with God—really cheated, ignored—so much so you became fed up with the struggle of doing things the right way?

Have you ever wondered if being a Christian is really worth the price, particularly when those who don't follow Jesus seem to have it better?

One chapter in the life of Moses provides encouragement for those of us who identify with such feelings.

While in the wilderness, the Israelites ran out of water and came complaining to Moses. God told Moses to speak to a rock in the desert, and he would provide water. Although it's only implied in Numbers 20, Moses, at first, probably obeyed God and spoke to the rock. But nothing happened. Worn out by years of leading this murmuring, rebellious group of people, this delay from God was the last straw. Taking matters into his own hands, Moses proceeded to strike the rock—a public act of disobedience for which he was denied the privilege of leading Israel into the Promised Land.

A small blip in the screen of his faith—running out of hope in the home stretch, this great leader disobeyed, stumbled, and fell.

What happened to Moses is an important warning for us. Many Christians, particularly in the Christmas season, hit low points in their personal faith. Unrelieved burdens grow heavy, unanswered prayers raise havoc in our souls. We begin to question whether God is listening or cares, whether our years of faithfulness and trusting are worth it.

Bottom line: we become disappointed with God. At such times we are vulnerable. One reason I believe God planned the Christmas season is that he knew most of us would need a transfusion of hope at least once a year, particularly in the dead of winter.

Many believers in Ephesus, like some of us, had become disappointed with God. Paul's prayer in our text for his Ephesian friends can help those of us who might be entering this Christmas season faltering in faith.

Let's study Paul's prayer.

A first boost for our faith: "I pray that out of his glorious riches he may strengthen you with power through his Spirit in your inner being, so that Christ may dwell in your hearts through faith" (Eph. 3:16–17).

In verse 13, we find the Ephesian Christians being disappointed with God because they could not understand how Paul, their spiritual hero, had been allowed to sit in prison for his faith. So Paul urged them, "I ask you not to lose heart over what I am suffering for you."

When our faith falters, due to happenings that seem to contradict divine love, it's easy to ask, "Why keep trusting?" Most of us occasionally have such feelings. It's important that our feelings do not take control and lead us into irresponsible behavior.

Disappointment with God happens if we:

- become fixated on getting our own way, rather than desiring God's will; or
- if we seek to force our ideas of fairness, justice, and timing upon God.

It wasn't fair by human logic that God didn't bring water out of the rock for Moses, when he spoke to it. It wasn't fair by human logic that God didn't spring Paul out of jail, when his only offense was to preach the gospel.

Remember, Paul isn't the one complaining! He suffered unjustly throughout his whole ministry, and yet listen to his response to personal pain as recorded in 2 Corinthians: "We are hard pressed on every side, but not crushed; perplexed, but not in despair; persecuted, but not abandoned; struck down, but not destroyed. . . . Therefore we do not lose heart. . . . For our light and momentary troubles are achieving for us an eternal glory that far outweighs them all" (2 Cor. 4:8–9, 16–17).

Paul's concern was not for himself, but for the faltering faith of his Ephesian friends. He prays that God will give them the Holy Spirit to strengthen them in their inner being and that Christ would dwell in their hearts by faith. Paul isn't asking God to take the pain of his friends away but to change their perspective.

To have Jesus dwell in our hearts, to be strengthened in our inner being by the Holy Spirit, refers to the miracle of God taking control of:

- that part of us that feeds our feelings, our emotions, our responses to life;

- that part of us that becomes disappointed, because we force our ideas of fairness and love upon God; and

- that part of us that panics, believing God has lost control.

As Paul states in verse 20, it isn't that God is unable to fix pain in our lives, it means he has something bigger and better for us than fixing our problem—a plan that may be unveiled only in eternity. Our problem is that we don't trust God. We are shortsighted, earthbound. Eternity doesn't mean much to most of us. We would much prefer God give us a short-term fix for a few years here on Earth, rather than allow an unrelieved burden to hone our character for eternity.

It's tough to trust God when life doesn't happen as we expected. As I observe God at work in the lives of people going through tough times,

I notice his cure is seldom to take problems away. Rather, as Paul prays, God changes our response, our perspective.

- We no longer focus on what's been taken away but upon what's left.
- We persevere; we pass the breaking point without breaking.
- We choose to trust that God is in control so we radiate a joy and hope as Paul expresses: "struck down, but not destroyed . . . perplexed, but not in despair."

A second boost for our faith is found in the remainder of Paul's prayer in Ephesians 3: "And I pray that you, being rooted and established in love, may have power, together with all the Lord's holy people, to grasp how wide and long and high and deep is the love of Christ, and to know this love that surpasses knowledge—that you may be filled to the measure of all the fullness of God" (vv. 17–19).

When we feel our faith is faltering, being reminded that God's love is real in spite of the pain he has allowed to enter our lives, and that he is still in control, in spite of what's happening to us, gives us an extra push to hang tough and trust him.

Christmas reminds us that God's love is:

- deep enough to reach any heartache,
- high enough to solve any problem, and
- broad enough to embrace any situation bigger than we are.

This knowledge of the fullness of divine love is what Paul meant in Romans with this promise:

Who shall separate us from the love of Christ? Shall trouble or hardship or persecution or famine or nakedness or danger or sword? . . . No, in all these things we are more than conquerors through him who loved us. For I am convinced that neither death nor life . . . neither the present nor the future . . . nor anything else in all creation, will be able to separate us from the love of God that is in Christ Jesus our Lord. (Rom. 8:35, 37–39)

As we enter this Advent season, I want to challenge you to put your situation that is painful, that seems unfair and you don't understand, directly into God's hands. Dare to trust God's love, even if he takes you along paths you don't understand.

When he unveils what he has been doing with your life—behind the scenes with those desires and yearnings you thought he had totally ignored or denied—you will be filled with amazement and awe.

Remember Paul's words from 2 Corinthians: "For our light and momentary troubles are achieving for us an eternal glory that far outweighs them all."

May this good news about God's love keep us from making the same mistake Moses made—becoming so disappointed and impatient that our faith falters and, by irresponsible behavior, we suffer an irreparable loss.

Several years ago, we handed out rosebuds to be kept until God answered what we considered then to be impossible needs in our lives. On this wreath are hundreds of answers to prayer. Today we want to give each of you another rose. When God responds to that area causing you pain today, an area for which answers seem impossible, send me a letter along with your rose.

By the way, I'm still waiting on God for my previous two roses, but I will take a third with expectancy. As we pass them out to you, remember these words from the song "The Rose": When we go through winter in our lives—when things are tough and don't seem to get better—there's a seed under the snow that, come spring, Christ's love will turn into a rose.

May your rosebud symbolize that rose hidden beneath the bitter snow in your life right now that seems to you like a thorn. May God fill you with hope that it will one day blossom into a blessing beyond your wildest dreams and expectations.

Questions for Study and Discussion:

1. What places in your life caused you to feel disappointed with God? Were you ever tempted to take matters into your own hands, as Moses did? What happened?

2. Why do you think Paul is more concerned with his circumstances affecting the Ephesians, rather than his circumstances affecting himself? How can we reset our focus as he did?

HOPING WHEN IT'S HOPELESS

John 11:1–6, 11–27, 38–44
March 5–6, 1994

Many observers of American society sense a feeling of hopelessness sweeping over America—the feeling that we are in a declining civilization. Many feel our problems are too overwhelming, and our resources totally insufficient to meet the challenges before us. A Christian friend describes how he lives with a sense of chronic dread and unhappiness, without any hope of anything getting better, implying he feels God has lost control of the world he created.

Confronting such pessimism, it's important for us as Christians to radiate our hope that God has not abandoned the world. That things are never so bad that God can't work a miracle. And that, in the final chapter, good will win over evil; life will win over the forces of death.

Whenever I read the story of Lazarus, I'm reminded that we follow a Savior who is capable of doing the impossible when we least expect it. As we prepare for Easter this year, it seems appropriate for us to be reminded of our Christian hope as that story illustrates.

First, why do we need hope? We need hope because life tends to confront us with happenings that seem hopeless—burdens with which we can't cope, problems we can't solve.

What appears more hopeless than a man four days dead? And yet, as we see in today's passage, Jesus shows up at the places of death—after hope has turned to despair, when the improbable has seemingly become the impossible. It didn't occur to anyone around the tomb that day that Jesus could or would defeat the power of death. When we really hurt and feel overwhelmed, it isn't easy to expect a miracle. All normal, human responses to impossible situations were present outside the tomb that day.

- The disciples were the *pragmatists*. The worst had happened—their friend was dead—they simply wanted to go to the tomb and grieve. The disciples represent those who hold no expectations of God's intervention in tough times.

- Mary is angry with Jesus, feeling if he had come sooner, he could have saved her brother from dying. Mary represents the *disenchanted*—people who used to believe, but now feel God and religion have cheated them.

- Martha is the *faithful* one—not knowing for sure what to expect from Jesus, but believing, somehow, he has power to bring her brother back to life. Martha represents those who believe nothing is impossible with God.

Jesus gives her and us this promise, when overwhelming situations make us feel like we are dying or already dead:

> *I am the resurrection and the life. The one who believes in me will live, even though they die; and whoever lives by believing in me will never die.* (John 11:25–26)

To prove his power, Jesus gives a cry of command, and dead Lazarus walks out of the tomb.

Remember, before promises about resurrection and hope can hold meaning, we must be in situations that make us feel helpless, hopeless, lifeless—so much so that nothing less than resurrection will meet our need.

Here is a fact of the Christian life: Awful things can happen to Christians. Equally frustrating, when we are caught in these miry bogs of helplessness, Jesus does not always respond to our cries for help with methods and timing we feel appropriate. Mary, Martha, and Lazarus were our Lord's closest friends. When Lazarus became sick, his sisters sent a message to Jesus: "Lord, the one you love is sick" (John 11:3). Assuming friends don't desert friends in time of need, they expected him to come immediately. Imagine their shock and hurt when Jesus intentionally delayed two days, during which time Lazarus died!

Let's imagine our response to similar moments when life throws us a curve. We go to Jesus asking for help. Nothing happens. In fact, things grow worse. Our reaction might be, "If this is how Jesus treats those he loves, who needs this kind of love?" When awful things happen, and we cry for help, God's response can seem slow, grossly inadequate, or even cruel.

Too often in ministry I am confronted with terrible happenings—babies dying, cancer striking, accidents occurring, homes breaking apart, dreams and hopes going unfulfilled. I have never discovered an answer to the heart-rending question "*Why?*" I do know clichés won't work. I do know Jesus is with us, even when we don't feel his presence. I do know one day he will give the shout of command and lift the curtain on his truth: "in all things God works for the good of those who love him, who have been called according to his purpose" (Rom. 8:28).

Think about your responses to happenings that are making you feel hopeless.

- Like the disciples, do you stoically accept reality with bitter resignation, rejecting all hope and expectation that the living God will intervene to help you?

- Like Mary, are you so hurt and disillusioned because God did not prevent or solve your problems, that you feel he doesn't care?

- Or, like Martha, do you trust the Lord so much, that even when confronted by painful situations, you are filled with hope that nothing is impossible for an all-powerful God who loves you?

I believe we need a transfusion of hope this Easter, because life does confront us with situations that are beyond our personal ability to cope.

Having stated *why* we need hope, the second truth in this text is that we Christians are called to trust God so much, we will expect the impossible. As followers of Jesus, we should radiate a calmness, optimism, and peace in the midst of trouble, giving witness to our confidence that God is in control of what's happening in the world and in our personal lives. Trusting God in dark times is the Christian alternative to the stress, panic, and despair so widespread today.

We Christians follow a Savior who can do anything—even raise the dead! Not appropriating that power through faith is to live defeated, limited, unfulfilled lives. Jesus performed this miracle with Lazarus to demonstrate his power to do the impossible—fix the unfixable. The Bible is full of illustrations of God doing miracles for people who trusted him.

- Abraham and Sarah gave birth to a son at age ninety-nine and ninety, respectively. After laughing when the angel told them about this miracle, the angel responded, "Is anything too hard for God?"

- Daniel was thrown into a lion's den and was miraculously spared when God closed the mouths of the lions.

- Ezekiel visited the valley of dry bones and asked God, "Can these bones live?" God said the word, and those bones rattled—the dead came to life.

Listen to what Jesus says about the impossible:

> *[W]ith God all things are possible.* (Matt. 19:26)
>
> *Nothing will be impossible for you.* (Matt. 17:20)
>
> *Everything is possible for him who believes.* (Mark 9:23)

The Bible is telling us that once we are Christians, we shouldn't feel hopeless or in despair about anything! Hard times provide the opportunity for us to know Jesus in his glory. Glory is a strange word, best defined as what happens when we discover who Jesus really is—God in the flesh. Glory is when we discover his power to surprise us with miracles to meet our needs.

Consider the text. Jesus says, "This sickness will not end in death. No, it is for God's glory, so that God's Son may be glorified through it." (John 11:4). Jesus will be glorified in your life when you allow him to use his power to change your impossible situation, or to change your response to it.

A final truth—what happens when we start really trusting God? Once we trust God for the impossible, deserts of hopelessness in our lives begin to blossom with new hope! This is the miracle I wish for you this Easter season.

Our Lord has an agenda for our lives, bigger than merely satisfying our earthbound wish list. Not every prayer is answered in the way we planned, but every prayer is answered. Jesus says in our text:

> *Your brother will rise again. . . . I am the resurrection and the life. The one who believes in me will live, even though they die; and whoever lives by believing in me will never die. Do you believe this?* (John 11:23, 25–26)

Although miracles do not always come to solve our deepest longings or take away our pain, this story gives us permission to go ahead and expect a miracle. God sometimes chooses to give us divine surprises.

Occasionally my wife and I take time for study in Rancho Mirage. I'm always impressed with the miracle that has happened in that desert area in the last twenty-five years. When I was in high school, I went hunting jack rabbits in the outskirts of Palm Springs. Then some visionaries like Walter Annenberg came to that town. These people didn't see a lifeless desert but what a desert could become—beautiful golf courses, miles of exquisite landscaping and green grass in a climate where the temperatures exceed 120 degrees in the summer! You see, these visionaries knew of a resource under the sand most people didn't believe existed—more water than anyone could imagine, enough to fill hundreds of artificial lakes and sustain thousands of residents in plush landscaped surroundings!

Listen to the Bible describe what God can do in your life:

> *The desert and the parched land will be glad; the wilderness will rejoice and blossom. Like the crocus, it will burst into bloom; it will rejoice greatly and shout for joy. . . . Strengthen the feeble hands, steady the knees that give way. Say to those with fearful hearts, "Be strong, do not fear; your God will come . . . he will come to save you." (Isa. 35:1–4)*

The miracle in Rancho Mirage is nothing compared to what God is prepared to do with the impossible deserts in our lives. As we trust God, he will either change our situation, or change our response to it—either way, it's a miracle—God will come to save us.

I have a deepening conviction that I don't want to reach the end of my life and be filled with dismay over many things that could have happened had I trusted God more. As we approach Easter, I pray we will begin to understand how insane it is to ever worry about anything! I give you this challenge: trust God this week in your area of greatest need and see what happens.

Questions for Study and Discussion:

1. When you face hard times in life, do you consider yourself among the pragmatists, the disenchanted, or the faithful? Why? What reasons or experiences have made you respond that way?

2. Do you believe that, with God, all things are possible? What miracles have you seen, where either the situation, or your heart about it, was changed? What miracle might he be asking you to trust him with now?

LIFE WITH OUR DAD

Dad was a character from day one—when, as a young child, he kicked his grandma in the shins and was never invited back to Ohio to visit again.

The stories are endless . . .

Christmastime

Dad was a fanatic about Christmas and decorating the house. He loved to celebrate the season. One year, he decided to be like the Grinch and put the whole Christmas tree in the fireplace, going halfway up the chimney. Minutes later, as fire was streaming out of the top of the chimney and smoke billowing into the living room, he realized that probably was not the best idea.

The Hawaiian Luau, or Waste Not, Want Not

On a family vacation in Hawaii, the budget would not allow for our family to attend a luau in the traditional way, so we snuck in to watch the dancing and fire show. The lure of the roasted pig was too much for Walt, however. When the lights were out and it was very dark, he snuck over to the buffet table to try to snatch a morsel. One morsel turned into several mouthfuls of that delicious roasted pig. Suddenly, the show ended, the lights went on, and he realized he had been eating out of the bin where the bussing station scraped all of the leftovers from each plate.

Katie's Dog House

Dad had an interesting relationship with his pets. We're not sure who was funniest—Walt or the dogs. But one incident with Katie, our Boston Terrier, sums it all up. Katie had done something wrong and Dad found out about it. The deep roar of his voice sent her into hiding. She managed to escape to the backyard, into her igloo doghouse, with Dad in pursuit, hollering, "Come here, Katie!"

First he stood yelling at the front of that igloo for her to get out of the dog house. She would have no part of it. After a few knocks on the side and shakes of the house, she still held her ground. The next thing we saw was Dad picking up the entire igloo and trying to shake her out of it. Katie tumbled out of the igloo opening twice, and twice she proceeded to jump back up inside while Walt was still holding the doghouse in the air. Eventually, he ended up taking the roof off the doghouse to get her out, but by then his anger and frustration had given way to amusement. He picked Katie up in his arms of love, and she licked his face all over. The hilarity led to compassion, and to this day no one even remembers what Katie did wrong—we only remember the laughter.

Model Rockets

When we were all children living at home, the family decided to take on a hobby of building model rockets. We went to the hobby store and bought the little kits. Family and friends would sit around constructing, painting, and creating their masterpieces.

One rainy evening, after a return from the hobby store with multiple bags of supplies, we were all busy building and enjoying a pleasant winter fire in the fireplace. "Where is the bag of supplies?" someone asked.

Instantly, Dad's hands went on his head, accompanied by a shriek of, "Oh, no! Everyone, step back!"

He realized that bag of trash he'd just thrown in the fire was no bag of trash—it was the bag of supplies! And those little rocket engines and batteries were about to ignite, providing us with Fourth of July in December!

Fortunately the damage was limited to some screaming, a few burns on the carpet, and a smoke-filled living room.

Time for an Oil Change

Dad loved cars. He bought, did minor mechanical repairs, and cosmetically fixed up over two hundred cars. And he was always eager to help friends with car maintenance.

When Dan Chun, one of the newer pastors on staff, purchased a new Toyota, it soon came due for its first oil change.

"Dan, bring it over to our house," Dad suggested. "We can change the oil ourselves." After some scuffling under the car, Dad drained the oil, changed the filter, and announced, "Job complete!"

Dan started up the engine, ready to pull it off the blocks. Putting the car in reverse, he gave it a little gas, but nothing happened. The car didn't move. "Walt," said Dan, rolling down the window, "I think something is wrong."

That was putting it mildly.

It turned out Dad had drained the transmission fluid instead of the oil and had filled the motor oil up to double capacity! Fortunately, after a quick trip to the auto parts store, all was remedied. Dan decided thereafter that it would be best to do any future car maintenance at the dealership.

A Word from Walt's Dad

In the 1970s, Walt received the following letter from his father:

Son, raising you was sometimes:

Educational

Mother and I saw every teacher you had through the eighth grade, telling them we were cooperating with them at home, trying to calm you down and keep you in line, but you still kept your class laughing and in stitches, most of the time out of control!

Improvisational

At the age of 2 1/2 years, I found you walking along the edge of the garage roof. You had climbed a rose trellis to get there, and were just trying to keep above us hounds, who had to put you in a harness to keep you from running away.

Inspirational

When you went to high school, I told you that you were on your own, that I was through visiting your teachers making excuses for you. I told you to go out for track because I knew you were able to run and too lightweight for football.

So—you applied yourself and won a track scholarship to Occidental College. From there you went on to Princeton Theological Seminary and graduated from San Francisco Theological Seminary. As a minister, God has richly blessed you, and you have been able to encourage many parents with problems of raising and training children.

Perspirational

With your hopped-up '41 Ford, you came home and told me you'd been stopped by a traffic officer, doing over 120 miles per hour, and that he'd only booked you for 75 miles per hour because you were on an open highway and it was after 2 a.m., with little or no traffic coming home from Palm Springs. I told you I had kept you from breaking your neck up to this point, and it was your neck to protect from here on out. I'm sure you've had a guardian angel on duty twenty-four hours a day doing just that!

Sensational

Love from a dad that has always loved you and had faith that you would turn out all right, with the Captain upstairs charting your life as he has mine for nearly eighty years.

Love always,
Dad

ACKNOWLEDGMENTS

A project of this magnitude involves contributions from many. One might think it a simple task to compile this collection of sermons, but in reality it is an incredible gift that we have the collection at all.

Sally Young attended MPPC for years and kept almost every printed copy of the sermons handed out to the congregation each week from 1977 to 2001. When Sally moved from her home, her daughter Susan MacLeod found the sermon notebooks and was kind enough to deliver them to Walt and Metta's home. The sermon notebooks stayed in a closet, mostly untouched and unread, except for an occasional question here and there. Walt even wanted to recycle the notebooks at one point, but Metta kept them. Upon Walt's passing, the notebooks became gold and the catalyst for this project. As former congregants heard of his passing, among them Terry Keith, they sent Metta additional sermons to fill in some of the missing weeks.

The first Thanksgiving after Walt's passing, our family gathered to celebrate the holiday and to share many thoughts and memories of him. We dearly missed his unbridled laughter and fervent prayers. We had collected a total of 487 written sermons, of the approximately 625 preached, so we divided the written sermons among all family members, with instructions to return their "favorites" by the New Year. The sermons were then narrowed down to two hundred. Several months later, God brought Christina Dudley into the project; Christina is the wife of Scott Dudley, who served with Walt at MPPC for six years. Christina sat in the pews while Walt preached, and experienced the teachings firsthand. Her literary talent and personal connection made all the difference in editing and assembling this work. The final process involved prayerfully and thoughtfully choosing the fifty sermons printed in this book.

The majority of Walt's sermons were recorded on cassette. Dave Swartz rescued the cassette library from the bottom of a storage basement in the next town over from MPPC. He delivered them to us and helped with their conversion to digital files.

Dennis Cailles is the gentle, quiet giant behind the copy center at MPPC. We called him often for last-minute requests, and he always came through.

We are extremely grateful to the Deep River Books publishing staff, and especially to Carl Simmons and Tamara Barnet for their editing skills.

Thank you to a dear family friend, Preston Butcher, who gave us the spark and encouragement to begin and finish this project.

Our hearts are filled with gratitude for everyone who contributed in making this book a reality, no matter how big or small their contribution, as this was an expansive team effort.

Sincerely,
The Gerber Family

APPENDIX 1

Sermons
by Scripture Order

APPENDIX 2

Sermons by Topic

Topic	Sermon Title	Page
Christmas	Someone Is Watching Over You	79
	Time Out!	245
	Giving: A Spontaneous Response to Love	265
Combatting evil	When Commitment Conquers Comfort	313
Confession	A Love Bigger Than Our Secrets	165
Discernment	Does God Give Personal Guidance to Believers?	207
Easter	If I Should Wake Before I Die	33
	Death Is Swallowed Up in Victory	71
	Hoping When It's Hopeless	351
Fear	Living without Fear	327
Forgiveness	Cultivating the Ability to Forget	65

ENDNOTES

Sermon 4: "House of Saints or Hospital for Sinners?"

1. If you listen to this sermon online at http://www.waltgerber.com/?s=house+of+saints, you can hear the poem "Listen, Christian" quoted verbatim. It has been paraphrased here for copyright protection purposes.

Sermon 5: "When You've Totally Blown It"

2. Brennan Manning, *The Ragamuffin Gospel* (Colorado Springs: Multnomah, 2005), 30.

3. Quoted in Brennan Manning, *Abba's Child* (Colorado Springs: NavPress, 2002), 27.

4. Manning, *Ragamuffin Gospel*, 22.

5. Quoted in Ibid., 25.

Sermon 6: "What to Do When You Feel Anxious"

6. E. Stanley Jones, *The Word Became Flesh* (Nashville: Abingdon Press, 1963), eBook, n.p.

Sermon 7: "Surviving in the Wilderness"

7. Margery Williams, *The Velveteen Rabbit* (New York: Doubleday, 1922), 5–7.

Sermon 9: "Death Is Swallowed Up in Victory"

8. A version of this story appears in Peter Marshall, *John Doe, Disciple* (New York: McGraw-Hill, 1969), 212–213. Quoted with the permission of The McGraw-Hill Companies, Incorporated.

Sermon 10: "Someone Is Watching over You"

9. Malcolm Muggeridge, *Conversion: The Spiritual Journey of the Twentieth Century Pilgrim* (Eugene, OR: Wipf and Stock, 1988), 88–90.

Sermon 12: "When Jesus Deals with Immorality"

10. Quoted in Erwin W. Lutzer, *Hitler's Cross, How the Cross Was Used to Promote the Nazi Agenda* (Chicago: Moody, 2016), eBook, n.p.

11. Ibid.

Sermon 15: "When You Feel Overstressed"

12. The poem has been given various attributions over the years, from American humorist Don Herold, to an eighty-five-year-old named Nadine Stair, to Walt's "monk." Because we could not ultimately source it, we've abridged Walt's quotation from it. To hear the poem in its entirety, listen online at http://www.waltgerber.com/?s=when+you+feel+overstressed.

Sermon 17: "The Barnabas Touch"

13. James Baker III, "The Remarks to the National Prayer Breakfast," February 1, 1990, Washington Hilton Hotel, Washington, DC, https://ufdc.ufl.edu/AA00062787/00074/65j.

14. Ralph Waldo Emerson, *The Prose Works of Ralph Waldo Emerson* (Los Angeles: HardPress, 2017), 461.

Sermon 19: "God's Answer for Chronic Fatigue"

15. Thornton Wilder, *Our Town*, http://content.caboces.org/_AMMS_AVAILABLE/331/14/ourTown.pdf, 65.

16. Harold Kushner, *When All You've Ever Wanted Isn't Enough* (New York: Pocket Books, 1986), 142.

Sermon 20: "Why Do Bad Things Happen to Good People"

17. Interview with Pastor Al Meredith, senior pastor, Wedgewood Baptist Church (Fort Worth, TX), "Larry King Live," *CNN*, September 16, 1999.

18. Charles R. Swindoll, "Quotable Quote," GoodReads, https://www.goodreads.com/quotes/267482-the-longer-i-live-the-more-i-realize-the-impact.

19. Unknown, "The Blessing of Unanswered Prayers," Beliefnet, https://www.beliefnet.com/prayers/protestant/gratitude/the-blessing-of-unanswered-prayers.aspx.

Sermon 21: "Prayer Transforms Merely Existing into Living"

20. Dr. Robert Boyd Munger came on staff as an associate after retirir Seminary. He had been pastor of First Presbyterian Church of Berk emphasis was prayer and Walt often said Bob taught him how to pray. He was a treasure, and author of the bestseller *My Heart, Christ's Home.*

Sermon 27: "Our Search for Satisfaction"

21. Robert Hastings, *The Station* (Golden Valley, MN: TRISTAN Publishing, 2003), n.p. Reprinted with the permission of TRISTAN Publishing, Incorporated, www.tristanpublishing.com.

Sermon 28: "Discovering Indescribable Joy"

22. Hal M. Helms, *Echoes of Eternity: Listening to the Father, Vol. 1* (Brewster, MA: Paraclete Press, 2011), eBook, January 26.

23. Frederick Buechner, *Telling Secrets* (New York: Harper One, 1991), 102–103.

Sermon 29: "Does God Give Personal Guidance to Believers?"

24. Henry Drummond, *The Ideal Life* (New Kensington, PA: Whitaker House, 2014), eBook, n.p.

25. "Henry David Thoreau Quotes," BrainyQuote, https://www.brainyquote.com/quotes/henry_david_thoreau_141463.

26. Quoted in by L. B. E. Cowman, *Springs in the Valley* (Grand Rapids, MI: Zondervan, 1968), eBook, n.p.

Sermon 30: "Living in the Present"

27. On September 16, 1984, MPPC held a celebration to mark the first decade of Walt's ministry there. In addition to a barbecue, churchwide picnic, and slide show, the congregation gave Walt and Metta five albums filled with cards, photos, and messages, expressing gratitude for ways Walt had touched their lives.

28. Mount Hermon (www.mounthermon.org), outside Santa Cruz, California, was the site for many of MPPC's family camps and retreats.

Sermon 32: "Time to Fall in Love Again"

29. Lewis Grizzard, "For the Record, It's Nice to Be with You Again . . . It's Just Nice to Be," *Northwest Florida Daily News,* May 12, 1993, https://newspaperarchive.com/northwest-florida-daily-news-may-12-1993-p-4.

30. "Lieutenant Robert Wetzel," Sermon Illustrator, http://www.sermonillustrator.org/illustrator/sermon2b/lieutenant_robert_wetzel.htm.

Sermon 35: "Time Out!"

31. Quoted in Gordon MacDonald, *Restoring Your Spiritual Passion* (Nashville: Oliver-Nelson Books, 1986), 35.

32. Erma Bombeck, *Eat Less Cottage Cheese and More Ice Cream: Thoughts on Life from Erma Bombeck* (Kansas City, MO: Andrews McMeel Publishing, 2003), n.p.

Sermon 36: "God is Listening...Talk to Him!"

33. Robert J. Burdette, "Broken Dreams," quoted at https://jesusthoughts.wordpress.com/2013/04/23/broken-dreams.

Sermon 38: "Giving: A Spontaneous Response to Love"

34. Eugene Peterson, *Run with the Horses: The Quest for Life at Its Best*, second edition, (Downers Grove, IL: IVP, 2009), 41.

35. Dan Clark, "A Brother Like That," in *Chicken Soup for the Soul: 20th Anniversary Edition* (Cos Cob, CT: Chicken Soup for the Soul Publishing, 2013), 48.

36. Henry van Dyke, "Keeping Christmas," American Literature, https://americanliterature.com/author/henry-van-dyke/short-story/keeping-christmas.

Sermon 40: "Greatness in the Sight of Men or God?"

37. Rev. Jerry Lambert, associate pastor at MPPC, who also held many different positions during his time at the church.

38. "Barbara Walters Interviews General Norman Schwarzkopf (1991) (part 2)," YouTube video, 14:54, posted Dec. 28, 2012, https://www.youtube.com/watch?v=ohNUIVHRWWo.

39. Ibid.

40. Quoted in Cal Thomas, "Some Modern Churches Showing Irrelevance," *New Philadelphia Times Reporter*, March 10, 1991, https://newspaperarchive.com/new-philadelphia-times-reporter-mar-10-1991-p-4.

41. Ibid.

Sermon 41: "When All Else Fails, Read the Instructions"

42. Quoted in Tom Gliatto, "Dreams Die Hard," *People,* July 13, 1998, https://people.com/archive/cover-story-dreams-die-hard-vol-49-no-27.

43. Philip Yancey, *Where Is God When It Hurts?/What's So Amazing about Grace?* (Grand Rapids, MI, 2009), ePub edition, 537.

44. Dwight L. Moody, "Quotable Quote," GoodReads, https://www.goodreads.com/quotes/172011-out-of-100-men-one-will-read-the-bible-the.

Sermon 43: "The Power of Weakness"

45. Simone Weil, *Waiting on God* (Abingdon-on-Thames: Routledge & K. Paul, 1979), 97.

46. Simone Weil, *Gravity and Grace* (London: Psychology Press, 2002), 81.

Sermon 44: "Call Me a Servant – Don't Treat Me Like One"

47. Chuck Swindoll, *Improving Your Serve* (Nashville: W Publishing Group, 1981), 141.

48. Martha Snell Nicholson, "Treasures," in *Treasures: Devotional Poems* (Pensacola, FL: Abeka, reprint, 1992), 1. For copyright purposes, this poem is abridged here. To hear it in its entirety, as Walt originally preached it, listen online at http://www.waltgerber.com/?s=call+me+a+servant.

Sermon 45: "When Commitment Conquers Comfort"

49. Much of this sermon is based on Elizabeth Dole, "Testimony of Elizabeth Dole before the National Prayer Breakfast," February 5, 1987, http://favoriteforwards.tripod.com/testimony_of_elizabeth_dole.htm.

50. Ibid.

51. Quoted in Carolyn Nystrom, *Thomas à Kempis: Imitating Jesus* (Downers Grove, IL: InterVarsity Press, 2002), 18.

Sermon 46: "Being Civil in an Uncivil World"

52. John Marks, "The American Uncivil Wars," *US News and World Report*, April 22, 1996, 67–68.

Sermon 47: "Living Without Fear"

53. Henri Nouwen, *Our Great Gift* (New York: HarperCollins, 1994), 66–67.

Story insert from Stephanie Kirtland, page 332

54. Stephanie Kirtland, "Guest Opinion: A Remembrance of Walt Gerber, a 'Titan of Grace' Whose Impact Lives On," *The Almanac*, April 21, 2016, https://www.almanacnews.com/news/2016/04/21/guest-opinion-a-remembrance-of-walt-gerber-a-titan-of-grace-whose-impact-lives-on.

Sermon 48: "New Beginnings"

55. Louisa Fletcher, "The Land of Beginning Again," The Writer's Almanac with Garrison Keillor, May 10, 2013, https://writersalmanac.publicradio.org/index.php%3Fdate=2013%252F05%252F10.html.

56. Quoted in the *NIV Ragamuffin Bible* (Grand Rapids, MI: Zondervan, 2013), eBook, Matthew 18:1–5.